# Producing Management Knowledge

At last here is a text for students undertaking research which shows them how different research methods work in practice. It is of vital importance not only to students but also to those who have to guide them through the quagmire of research practice. All contributors draw on case studies and explore how specific research approaches are developed and applied.

This text, authored by experts with many years' experience of conducting research in organizations, offers students important insights into research methods and demonstrates how different research approaches can be applied in a variety of organizational settings.

*Producing Management Knowledge* provides detailed accounts of processes of research and assists the student reader in choosing and applying the methods they have studied to real organizations. This text is essential reading for anyone considering a research project and for all those who have to supervise students undertaking research.

**Jan Löwstedt** is Professor in Business Administration at Mälardalen University and former Director of the Research Centre for People and Organization at the Stockholm School of Economics.

**Torbjörn Stjernberg** is Professor in Organization Theory at the School of Business, Economics and Law at Göteborg University.

# Producing Management Knowledge

## Research as practice

Edited by Jan Löwstedt
and Torbjörn Stjernberg

LONDON AND NEW YORK

First published 2006
by Routledge
2 Park Square, Milton Park, Abingdon, Oxon OX14 4RN

Simultaneously published in the USA and Canada
by Routledge
270 Madison Ave, New York, NY 10016

*Routledge is an imprint of the Taylor & Francis Group, an informa business*

© 2006 Jan Löwstedt and Torbjörn Stjernberg for editorial selection and material;
individual contributors, their own contribution

Typeset in Sabon by
Keystroke, Jacaranda Lodge, Wolverhampton
Printed and bound in Great Britain by
MPG Books Ltd, Bodmin

*British Library Cataloguing in Publication Data*
A catalogue record for this book is available from the British Library

*Library of Congress Cataloging in Publication Data*
Producing management knowledge : research as practice / edited by Jan Lowstedt
and Torbjorn Stjernberg.
p. cm.
Includes bibliographical references and index.
ISBN 0–415–38438–9 (hard cover) – ISBN 0–415–38439–7 (soft cover)
1. Management–Research. 2. Knowledge management. I. Löwstedt, Jan.
II. Stjernberg, Torbjörn, 1946–
HD30.4.P75 2006
658.4′038–dc22
2006011815


ISBN10: 0–415–38438–9 (hbk)
ISBN10: 0–415–38439–7 (pbk)

ISBN13: 978–0–415–38438–4 (hbk)
ISBN13: 978–0–415–38439–1 (pbk)

# Contents

*List of figures*                                                      xi
*List of tables*                                                       xiii
*Notes on contributors*                                                xiv
*Acknowledgements*                                                     xviii

**Introduction**                                                       1
JAN LÖWSTEDT AND TORBJÖRN STJERNBERG

*The researcher as producer of knowledge 2*
*Approaches to knowledge production 2*
*From data to theory 3*
*Co-producing management 4*
*Concluding management knowledge 5*

1   **Knowledge production in management: a messy practice**          6
JAN LÖWSTEDT AND TORBJÖRN STJERNBERG

*Management as a field of research 6*
*Management research as a messy practice 7*
*Knowledge production as interaction in social systems 9*
*Management research as a glocal practice 10*
*Management research is situated in time and space 12*
*Ethics of the knowledge production process 14*
*The product of research . . . 16*
*The duality of a messy practice 17*

**PART I**
**The researcher as producer of knowledge**                            21

2   **On issue-driven research**                                       23
MICHAEL EARL

*Introduction 23*
*Strategic information systems planning 24*

*The chief knowledge officer 27*
*E-commerce and IT 28*
*Strategies for knowledge management 29*
*A theory of triangulation? 31*
*Reflections and beyond 35*

3   **Writing as reflexive knowledge production and as self-production**   38
    DAVID SIMS

    *Writing for knowledge production 40*
    *Writing for self-production 41*
    *Reflexive knowledge production 43*
    *Of millstones, bastards and velveteen rabbits 45*
    *Conclusion 48*

**PART II**
**Approaches to knowledge production**   51

4   **Making sense of stockbrokers' performance: reflections about**
    **the phenomenographic approach**   53
    JESPER BLOMBERG

    *The epistemological journey 53*
    *A growing unrest 54*
    *The phenomenographic approach 55*
    *Studying the life-worlds of stockbrokers 57*
    *The empirical study 57*
    *Ideal types vs phenomenographic conceptions 58*
    *Faithful but not simply induced 61*
    *The benefits of phenomenography 62*
    *Phenomenography as a method 66*
    *Conclusion 67*

5   **Studying everyday life: an ethnomethodological and**
    **discourse analytic approach**   72
    PERNILLA BOLANDER

    *Introduction 72*
    *In search of authenticity in the interview society 72*
    *Studying reality-constituting practices in everyday life 74*
    *Analytic bracketing 76*
    *Discourse analysis 78*
    *Identifying interpretative repertoires 79*

*Analyzing how versions are constructed and made to
   appear factual 80*
*How does selection take place in organizations? 81*
*Conclusion 89*

6   Inside the school: an ethnographic approach to school
    management                                                     93
    ULRIKA TILLBERG

    *The study in brief and the choice of method 95*
    *Characteristics of an ethnographic approach 96*
    *Inside the three schools 98*
    *Lessons learned 102*

7   Tracing consultants' problem-solving processes:
    a simulation approach                                         106
    ANDREAS WERR

    *The problem – are methods used in management
       consulting? 106*
    *Studying problem-solving processes 107*
    *Designing the simulation 108*
    *Analyzing the data 113*
    *So – do methods influence consultants' work? 121*
    *Reflections on the research practice 124*

PART III
From data to theory                                              129

8   Interviews as a source of knowledge                          131
    TORBJÖRN STJERNBERG

    *The interview as a relationship 132*
    *Studying attitudes in an aggregate of individuals 133*
    *Studying individuals as separate cases 135*
    *The questions 140*
    *The analysis before, during and after the interview 142*
    *Conclusion 145*

9   Listening to executives: content analysis of life stories    148
    BARBRO ANELL

    *The study 148*
    *Content analysis history 150*

*Categories and coding 152*
*Preparing for analysis 153*
*Analysis: co-occurrences 154*
*Drawing conclusions 155*
*Interpretation 156*
*Conclusions 156*

10  **Building theory about small firms: a grounded theory
    approach**                                                    158
    TOMAS BRYTTING

    *Small firms – a field to explore 159*
    *Ontological and epistemological assumptions 159*
    *The grounded theory approach 161*
    *How data was collected 163*
    *How data was coded 164*
    *How data was analyzed 166*
    *Moving from A- to B-level categories 167*
    *Moving from B- to C-level categories 171*
    *Some thoughts on small firm organizing 173*
    *Some epistemological comments on the method 173*

11  **The making of a metaphor: developing a theoretical
    framework**                                                   178
    THOMAS DURAND

    *Introduction 178*
    *The making of a metaphor 180*
    *Introducing learning and 'competence leaves' into the
        model 185*
    *Conclusion 193*

PART IV
**Co-producing management**                                       197

12  **Researching organization design: comparative vs collaborative
    approaches**                                                  199
    HARVEY KOLODNY AND A.B. (RAMI) SHANI

    *Organization design as a research topic 199*
    *Organization design: an examination of two studies 201*
    *Some research components of organization design 208*
    *Organization members' involvement 213*

*Discussion 214*
*Conclusion 218*

13 The changing practice of action research                                221
PETER DOCHERTY, ANDERS LJUNG AND
TORBJÖRN STJERNBERG

*An offer to pursue 'action research' in Skandia*
*    Insurance Co. 221*
*Action research as studies of interventions in change*
*    processes 226*
*Action research in the twenty-first century 229*
*Discussion and conclusion 233*


PART V
Concluding management knowledge                                           237

14 The power of contrasts: comparative research for
   overcoming ethnocentric myopia                                        239
BENGT STYMNE AND JAN LÖWSTEDT

*We all design our little villages 239*
*Ethnocentric trappings produce research results 240*
*Principles of comparative management research 241*
*Comparative studies in management research 242*
*Three approaches to international comparative research 243*
*Industrial Democracy in Europe: an international*
*    comparative large sample study 245*
*Micro-electronics in the service sector (MESS): an international*
*    comparative case study 248*
*ORGNOVATION: an international comparative process*
*    study 252*
*Conclusion 258*

15 The innovative research enterprise                                     261
BENGT STYMNE

*Organization of the research enterprise 263*
*Methods: linking the inquiry system and the universe 263*
*Generating empirical data 264*
*Interpretation of data 268*
*Theory construction 269*
*Writing 270*

*Organizing the research enterprise  270*
*Perspective: how we look upon the universe of*
    *management practice  271*
*Criteria of relevance  272*
*Habits of communication  272*
*Suppliers of problems  273*
*Hoisting the sails of research enterprise  273*

Index                                                                275

# Figures

2.1   The three stages in the study of strategic
      information systems planning (SISP)                    27
2.2   The three stages in the chief knowledge officer
      (CKO) study                                            28
2.3   The three stages in the e-commerce and IT study        29
2.4   The three stages in the retrospective study            31
4.1   My epistemological journey, Part 1                     54
4.2   My epistemological journey, Parts 1 and 2              62
4.3   The development of two opposing types of
      conceptions of stockbroking                            66
4.4   My epistemological journey, Parts 1–3                  67
7.1   A brief summary of the surveying authority providing
      the input for the simulations                          111
7.2   Cluster analysis of the different consultants'
      approaches based on the relative time spent on
      different information categories                       117
7.3   The three basic dimensions summarizing differences
      in the consultants' reflections                        123
8.1   The chain of data transformation                       143
10.1  Relations between A-level categories from Case One     168
10.2  Cause map from two case studies of small, growing firms  170
10.3  A schematic representation of the different analytical
      steps from an actual organizational process to
      C-level categories                                     172
10.4  Some principle differences between inductive and
      deductive research                                     174
11.1  Sequence of stages from data and information to
      knowledge and expertise                                186
11.2  The dynamics of competence                             187
11.3  Competences leaves                                     190

13.1   The main phases and activities of the action
       research team in the Skandia project                     223
14.1   The funnel model of organizational design                253
15.1   Management research as a system for creating
       knowledge by sequences of innovations                    262

# Tables

| | | |
|---|---|---|
| 2.1 | Triangulation for issue-driven research | 32 |
| 4.1 | A rough interpretation of the resemblance between the individual brokers' conceptions and the four typified stories, on a scale of 1 (almost none) to 5 (very close) | 64 |
| 7.1 | Ranking of information categories according to proportion of time spent on gathering information for respective category | 118 |
| 7.2 | Summary of consultants' reflections on the client | 122 |
| 11.1 | Competence | 183 |
| 11.2 | Competence (degree of) | 183 |
| 11.3 | Parallel learning processes and stages | 186 |
| 12.1 | A comparison of two approaches to organization design analysis | 202 |
| 12.2 | Researching organization design through comparative and collaborative analyses | 210 |
| 13.1 | Three ways for researchers to work together with practitioners | 231 |

# Contributors

**Barbro Anell** graduated from the Stockholm School of Economics from which she holds a doctoral degree. She has been working at a number of universities and private research organizations. She has recently retired from a position as Professor of Administration at Umeå Business School, Umeå University. Her research has concerned change on several levels from the single firm, especially disbandment and turnaround management, to industry and society. She has also been interested in projects and project management and regional development questions. She is now a senior researcher at CRT, Denmark.

**Jesper Blomberg** is an assistant professor at the Stockholm School of Economics, where he also earned his PhD. His current research interests focus on the functions and organizational effects of organizing activities in different types of projects and of applying different types of project management tools, as well as organizational analysis of actors in the financial sector. Blomberg has written several books and articles covering both project organizing and organizational finance. Blomberg also gives courses and seminars on project organizing, organizational analysis and organizational finance for both graduate students and in executive education.

**Pernilla Bolander** is an assistant professor at the Centre for People and Organization, Stockholm School of Economics. Her research interests focus on assessment of competence, diversity in organizations and qualitative methods. She received her PhD from SSE in 2002. Her dissertation was awarded with a three-year scholarship for post-doctoral research by the Handelsbanken Research Foundation.

**Tomas Brytting** is an associate professor at the Stockholm School of Economics. His doctoral thesis was entitled 'Organizing in the small growing firm – a grounded theory approach'. Since 1990, he has been working within the field of business ethics, as a researcher, writer, lecturer and consultant.

**Peter Docherty** is a professor in the Department of Labour Studies and Work Organization at the National Institute for Working Life, Stockholm. His research is mainly in the fields of learning at the individual, group, organization and network levels and in the organization and management of sustainable organizations.

**Thomas Durand** is Professor of Business Strategy at Ecole Centrale Paris, where he founded the Technology and Management master programme and heads the Strategy and Technology Research unit (www.ecp.fr). He works in the field of strategic management and the management of technology and innovation. He has published extensively in the field over the last 20 years. Thomas Durand is President of CM International, a management consulting firm based in Paris (www.cm-intl.com). Formerly President of AIMS (association internationale de management stratégique), he sits on the Board of Euram (European Academy of Management) and chaired the Knowledge and Innovation interest group at the SMS (Strategic Management Society).

**Michael Earl** is Professor of Information Management at the University of Oxford and Dean of Templeton College, Oxford. Previously, he was Professor of Information Management at the London Business School, during which time he also served as Deputy Dean and Acting Dean. He has been a visiting professor at the Stockholm School of Economics and regularly visits the school to engage in research-related activities. Michael Earl works at the intersection of information systems and strategic management and has focused on the information system strategy process, the roles of 'C' class officers and knowledge management. He has been a frequent contributor to journals, such as the *Harvard Business Review* and *Sloan Management Review*, and has published several books.

**Harvey Kolodny**, BEng, MBA, DBA, is Professor Emeritus with the Rotman School of Management and the Department of Mechanical and Industrial Engineering at the University of Toronto. His fields of interest are organization design and change, innovative workplace practices – particularly those based on socio-technical systems design – and the management of technology. He has recently published research on the design of technology transfer organizations and continuous improvement organizations. He has co-authored books on the organizational and innovation aspects of advanced manufacturing technology, on the quality of working life and on matrix organizations. His current research is on the development of a change process model and on the integration of change management and project management.

**Anders Ljung** is a partner in the Scandinavian management consulting firm Cepro AB. He also teaches at several business schools in Europe in the area of strategy and organizational design. He is frequently asked to offer advice to the top management of several large knowledge-intensive firms. His doctorate at the Stockholm School of Economics in 1992 was based on an action research project with a focus on corporate stakeholder strategies and corporate social responsibility.

**Jan Löwstedt** is Professor in Business Administration at Mälardalen University. He has a PhD from the Stockholm School of Economics and during 1990–91 was visiting research fellow at Templeton College, Oxford University. He was Director of the Research Centre for People and Organization (PMO) at the Stockholm School of Economics, 1997–2005. During 2000 to 2004 he was Professor of Business Administration at Blekinge Institute of Technology. He has been a member of the editorial board of *Human Relations* and is now serving on the editorial board of *Nordiske Organisasjonsstudier*. Jan Löwstedt has published books and articles on organizational change, technology and organization, and managerial and organizational cognition. Current research interests (projects) are Mergers@Work, Schools in Transition, and knowledge production in organizations.

**A. B. (Rami) Shani** is Professor of Organizational Behavior and Change at California Polytechnic University, USA and a visiting research professor at the FENIX Research Programme, Stockholm School of Economics, Sweden. His most recent published research work, articles and books have focused on creating sustainable work systems, creating the learning organization and action research methodologies in the pursuit of actionable knowledge creation.

**David Sims** is Professor of Organizational Behaviour, Cass Business School, City University, London, Associate Dean and Director of the Centre for Leadership, Learning and Change. He has an academic background in operational research and organizational behaviour, and completed his PhD at Bath University. His research interests are in the relationship between managerial living, leading, thinking, learning and storying. He has applied these interests to topics as diverse as why people get angry in organizations, motivation of middle managers, how people love their organizations into life, agenda shaping, problem construction, consulting skills and mergers.

**Torbjörn Stjernberg** is Professor in Organization Theory at the School of Business, Economics and Law at Göteborg University. His doctorate at the Stockholm School of Economics in 1977 was based on an action research project, where he focused on the relation between organizational changes and the changes of the individual organizational members' quality of life. These are still key words among his research interests today, with a focus on work life in project organizations. His research interests also concern the viability and diffusion of organizational innovations, processes in organizational networks, knowledge development and knowledge transfer in and between complex projects, methods and tools in organizational changes, and new forms of organization on the labour market.

**Bengt Stymne** is Professor of Organization Theory at the Stockholm School of Economics and Research Director at the FENIX Research Programme. He was a co-founder and Managing Director of SIAR (Scandinavian Institutes of Administrative Research), has been Managing Director of EFI (the Economic Research Institute) at the Stockholm School of Economics and is one of the founders of SSES (the Stockholm School of Entrepreneurship). He has published books and articles on organization design and strategy, on organizational values, on industrial democracy and on IT and management.

**Ulrika Tillberg** has a PhD from the Stockholm School of Economics. She has an acting role as project manager, programme director and lecturer at the Stockholm School of Economics, Executive Education programme. Her thesis work on leadership and cooperation in schools is used as reading material in different school management programmes in Sweden, and she is also a co-writer of management and organization books and articles. Her current research interest lies within the field of ideal leadership models and everyday leadership processes.

**Andreas Werr** is an associate professor at the Stockholm School of Economics, where he also earned his PhD with a dissertation focusing on the functions of methodologies in the work of management consultants. His current research interests focus on the rhetoric of management consulting, the procurement, use and consequences of management consultants in client organizations, and the management of consulting companies, specifically the management of knowledge and knowledge processes. Andreas Werr's work has been reported in several award-winning conference papers and published in journals such as the *Journal of Organizational Change Management, Organization, Organization Studies* and *International Studies of Management and Organization*. Andreas has taught courses on management consulting for both graduate students and practising consultants.

# Acknowledgements

The initiative to write this book was taken in relation to a workshop on knowledge production in management held at the Stockholm School of Economics in the spring of 2004. The editors had invited an international group of colleagues for two days of sharing experiences. The workshop was triggered by our joint wish to celebrate the academic work of and with Professor Bengt Stymne in connection with his formal retirement from the chair in organizational theory at the Stockholm School of Economics.

Bengt Stymne has had a long career as initiator and head of several research institutes, research groupings and programmes. The effect of such roles has been a dissemination of values and practices with regard to how to practise research and teach management and organization theory. His pioneering work with developing participative and problem-based teaching and learning, both at the undergraduate and graduate level, has stimulated many colleagues and can also be seen in the chapters in this volume. The practice of research has been at the forefront of Bengt Stymne's way of teaching research methods – where reflections about our learning by doing have created stimulating academic environments.

Some 30 present and former colleagues presented papers about their own personal approaches to the question of how to conduct research about managing organizations. We found these papers highly interesting and saw the possibility of using several of them as the texts in our teaching. Texts like these may be used in many ways. When designing the content and structure of this book, the editors have had courses in qualitative research methodology and the research processes in mind. Experienced-based learning is particularly difficult in the area of research. Therefore, this is the type of book we think is needed – where graduate students can get insights into the research process from more experienced researchers.

Editing a book like this is a research enterprise in itself. Many people have been involved in the process – from the workshop up to the point where we can present the book to the reader. The editors wish to thank all colleagues who have contributed to this book by working with us to develop the idea of research as a social practice by reflecting and writing about their experiences.

We also want to thank all colleagues that participated in the workshop for their presentations and comments on the topic of producing management knowledge: Kenneth Abrahamsson, Niclas Adler, Johan Berglund, Lars Bergman, Rolf H. Carlsson, Jan Edgren, Per-Jonas Eliæson, Peter Hägglund, Christian Junnelius, Peter Hyllman, Ragnar Kling, Pär Larsson, Sophie Linghag, Åke Magnusson, Ulf Malmquist, Cassandra Marshall, Sinikka Ortmark Almgren, Åke Philips, Martin Rogberg, Andrew Schenkel, Annika Schilling, Pierre Schou, Svante Schriber, Guje Sevón, Mary Walshok and Bernhard Wilpert.

A special recognition goes to Anita Söderberg-Carlsson for her professional efforts, for being our copy-editor and for the hundreds of things she did to make the workshop a success. Thank you Anita, you did it again!

We also wish to thank the following institutions for their financial support of the workshop and to the work of the book: the Swedish Council for Working Life and Social Research (FAS), the Swedish Agency for Innovation Systems (VINNOVA), the Scandinavian Institutes for Administrative Research (SIAR) and the Prince Bertil's Fund.

Jan Löwstedt and Torbjörn Stjernberg
Stockholm, December 2005

# Introduction

*Jan Löwstedt and Torbjörn Stjernberg*

The process of producing management knowledge is so much more than applying a certain method to an empirical situation. It is also a social process full of interactions with company representatives, colleagues, reviewers, editors of journals in which you want to publish, funding agencies, etc. This is the reason why this book has been written – to share the experiences of doing such research about managerial issues.

The authors of this book are all people who are convinced that the process of becoming a knowledgeable producer of management knowledge is an ongoing learning process that can best be guided by learning from real cases of research. This book is not, therefore, another normative book about how to do management research. It is a book with tales from the field in which a group of researchers describe how they have been practising their research and the role methods have played in these endeavours. The ambition is to give the reader a flavour of the full range of issues, problems and interesting dilemmas that she or he will meet on the journey from the beginning of a project to when it is time to deliver the results.

The contributions differ somewhat in form. Some of the authors give a broader view of their research programmes and experiences, such as Earl, Kolodny and Shani, Stymne and Löwstedt, and Stjernberg. Others give a more close-up view of their experiences of one particular study – illustrating, in depth, examples of and experiences from doing management research guided by ideas from a particular approach, such as Anell, Blomberg, Bolander, Tillberg and others. The chapters also differ regarding the areas being researched: from micro-oriented studies of recruitment, consultancy work and people in small business, to comparative studies of issues and cases in schools, industry and also between countries.

It is our ambition to describe a spectrum of research approaches, practices and ideas – dealing with these approaches as a sharing of our experiences, rather than as providing normative advice. The book is therefore a volume about management research seen from the insiders' perspectives and hopefully it could be read as learning opportunities from case reports from research projects.

In the first chapter, we describe research work as a 'messy' practice and highlight a number of dilemmas and issues we have to handle as management researchers during a research project. We (the editors) think that it is appropriate to say something about the pillars that support the platform of values that guide our research. Following the introductory chapter, we have structured our book into five parts: The researcher as producer of knowledge, Approaches to knowledge production, From data to theory, Co-producing management, and Concluding management knowledge.

## The researcher as producer of knowledge

What is the object of study – management knowledge? And how can one approach this field? Michael Earl shares his experience from entering the field – experience that also led to the development of a research methodology where the interaction with the professionals in his field became entwined with the theoretical development. Thus, Earl's approach entails a strong emphasis on the research's relevance for both the knowledge about and the practice of management.

Academic knowledge is expressed in seminars and lectures orally. However, the process of writing brings a deeper quality to the work of expressing knowledge. In the process of writing, we consider and reconsider our formulations, the analysis becomes sharper, and inconsistencies are brutally evident. But not only this. David Sims also argues that through the writing we also produce ourselves. He shares several examples of how his thoughts have evolved in the process of reflecting and writing.

## Approaches to knowledge production

If the chapters in the first part may be characterized as senior and very well-known researchers' reflections about how they approach the field of management theory and how they reflect and write based on their meeting with the field, the chapters in the second part are much more focused on approaching a particular study and working with a specific methodology for producing management knowledge. Most of these chapters draw on one specific study; for several of the authors, this is their PhD thesis. But rather than describing the methods used in the study, these texts contain descriptions of the researchers' steps, deliberations and reflections about their chosen approaches to research practice.

In the analysis of stockbrokers, Jesper Blomberg works from observations and interviews in order to build an understanding of how each of the participants view and understand their work. Using a phenomenographic approach, he compares the different ways stockbrokers use to express the essence of the role and the tasks of their job with the rather large differences in the brokers' effectiveness, as interpreted through the courtage they earn.

Penilla Bolander's object of study is the talk of recruiters at meetings after having interviewed job applicants. Her study uses a combination of discourse analysis and ethnomethodology. She realized that talking is also a kind of negotiation about the meaning of the arguments used to support or dismiss a certain candidate. The analysis of how things are discussed was shown to be very important for the understanding of the suitability of the job applicant.

Observations of meetings, as well as day-to-day, practices are important when using an ethnographic approach, as Ulrika Tillberg shows in her chapter about three schools. Organizational identity and organizational structure are shown to be important explanations of differences in how the teachers view their roles and their interactions with other teachers, with students and with the principals of the schools. Meetings, the way students and subjects are talked about, and the way Tillberg is introduced into these schools all show that data can exist everywhere and in any form when trying to understand and communicate about organizations using this approach.

In his studies of management consultants' use of collective knowledge and tools, Andreas Werr used interviews, participant observations and simulations. It is the experiences from simulating the process of writing a proposal in particular that he focuses on in his chapter, where similarities and differences between the approaches of six consultants from two consulting firms, one international and one local, are analyzed. Werr discusses how, during the simulations, the verbal protocols describing the thought processes of the consultants gave valuable information. Using a cluster analysis, he found that the similarities had to do with the methods that the consultant had internalized as well as the firms' routines.

## From data to theory

Torbjörn Stjernberg builds on experiences from several studies, but primarily from his thesis work done in the 1970s, when discussing his approach to using interviewing as a tool for knowledge production. His emphasis is on the interview as a relationship between the interviewer and the interviewee and as a simultaneous process of data collection and analysis, not only *about* the interviewee's statements, but to some extent also together *with* the interviewee in a joint search for knowledge. The interview may be seen and used as an intervention in an ongoing organizational change.

Barbro Anell also chooses to share experiences from producing knowledge through analysis of interviews. The focus of her chapter is content analysis – what does the researcher do with the interviews when they are 'on the table'? In Anell's case, content analysis is a search for concepts that help to clarify and organize the material into themes that describe the life-worlds and life histories of managing directors.

In his chapter, Tomas Brytting gives insights into a systematic application of grounded theory. Brytting leads us through the steps from the first categorizing of the data into successively more abstract constructs, thus building a theory of small firms' organizing. These steps include interpretations of data obtained through longitudinal observations and interviews with entrepreneurs.

Thomas Durand shares the strong links to the practice of research, being active both as a management consultant and in the field of academia. His chapter contains an account of the process of developing a particular theoretical framework that helps to give a deeper meaning to management knowledge. The theory – or 'metaphor' as he prefers to call it – is developed through a series of impulses from seminars, reading of classics and encounters as consultant. During this process, the hard work of writing is mixed with sudden revelations and insights.

## Co-producing management

Knowledge exists at both the academic level and in the context where management is practised. There is no reason to see one as superior to the other; instead, knowledge production may be strengthened by using the different sources and methods of knowledge production in cooperation.

In the chapter about organization design, Harvey Kolodny and Rami Shani compare two approaches to knowledge production, one being based on comparisons of organizations' designs in different contexts, and the other being based on collaborative work with the managers, where the use of the knowledge within the firm and the knowledge from the academics mutually strengthen the analyses of design alternatives.

To learn about the processes of organizational change, the research may preferably be carried out close to the interventions by management, employees and/or researchers that lead to the changes, according to Docherty, Ljung and Stjernberg. Action research is both an approach to knowledge production, as well as a set of values, emphasizing the responsibility to the system rather than to individual stakeholders.

## Concluding management knowledge

In Chapter 14, Bengt Stymne and Jan Löwstedt discuss the power of contrast as an approach to be used to overcome ethnocentrism. Quite extensive international research projects are presented and discussed as examples of how comparative research gives new insight into classical issues addressed in organizational studies. It is argued that insights can be won and theories created that would not have been possible with research confined to one geographical or cultural area.

Starting in philosophy of science, Bengt Stymne argues in the final chapter that knowledge production could be seen as an innovative research enterprise. He discusses the role of all stages in the knowledge production endeavour of research, from data collection to communicating the results. Two aspects of organizing this research enterprise are emphasized. One is the importance that method have in linking managerial practice and the inquiry system of the researchers – and the potential the research methods have with regard to leverage innovations in knowledge. The other aspect is the need to 'leave windows and doors open' for new ideas both from practitioners and from other academic disciplines.

It is our hope – and in fact our conviction – that the majority of the readers will find most of the chapters of great interest as examples of research approaches that have a strong foothold in northern Europe and that, hopefully, are both relevant and of interest wherever management knowledge is produced.

# 1 Knowledge production in management

## A messy practice

*Jan Löwstedt and Torbjörn Stjernberg*

## Management as a field of research

There has been an impressive development in the range of issues managers deal with and the knowledge needed by managers over the past 50 years. Organizations have become larger in size, much more complex in their structures and affairs, and more far-reaching in time and space. This widening of scope has been accompanied by a more specialized and deeper knowledge base. Many companies of our times can be described as knowledge- intensive firms acting in an era of globalization. Some management researchers have suggested that this development is occurring less in the character of today's organizations, and more in the perspectives taken in our attempts to analyze and understand the modern organization. Management ideas also tend to infuse many other aspects of modern society, such as schools, health care, art and religion, to mention only a few. Charles Perrow (1972) has described this tendency as the emerging organization society.

Hand in hand with this development, we can see a growth in the number of students in business schools and MBA programmes all over the world (Engwall and Zagmani 1998). The supply of managerial knowledge has increased and involves not only practising managers and business school teachers/researchers, but also management consultants and business advisory firms, journalists and the media, and a motley crowd of management 'gurus' who are carriers of management knowledge. Sahlin-Andersson and Engwall (2002) consider the boundaries to be blurred between those who create, mediate and use managerial knowledge. Still, there are certain distinguishing characteristics of the different actors taking part in the managerial discourse. In academia, the specific competence is the collecting and analysing of data and the focus on problematization and on quality control through peer reviews. In consultation, there is a focus on competent inter-action with clients, and in the media on the simplification and distribution of information to a large audience (*op. cit.*).

Management research, as we see it today, is primarily not research *for* management, but increasingly research *about* management and, more specifically, about the processes in organizations whereby management is exercised. Management training programmes have become widespread among organizations, especially after the Second World War. Luo (2002) finds that there has been a significant expansion of personal development at the expense of training of technical skills. The focus is on the development of the social and cognitive competence of the managers and employees, and not development related to the immediate technical aspects of their job tasks.

Along with this development and the accumulation of knowledge in management, there has also been scientific critique of the role of and claims made by management research. Without entering into this debate, we conclude, in a very generalized way, that management research is less occupied with the collection of facts and figures as representations of organizations and, instead, more focused on developing concepts and language to describe and analyze organizations (Brunsson 1981; see also Simon 1957, who emphasizes his ambition to develop concepts rather than to describe administrative behaviour). Management research is reflexive and interested in new ways of understanding contemporary managerial phenomena. As a consequence of this, management, as a field of knowledge, compounds a variety of competing perspectives and theories emanating from different schools of thought.

This development in the ways managerial knowledge is produced has called for new research methodologies and work practices of the management researchers. During the first decades after the Second World War, claims were made for a management *science*, with a focus on mathematical modelling and the development of sophisticated statistical methods, as means to solve managerial problems. Today, management, or 'business administration' as the subject is often referred to in northern Europe, is increasingly being recognized and integrated in modern social science, often using critical approaches or praxis and/or action-oriented ways of working. As a consequence, the demand for training in methods for the production of knowledge in management must shift focus.

## Management research as a messy practice

Early on, studies of managers showed that managerial work is far from the planned and controlled activity that is associated with the verb 'to manage'. On the contrary, managerial work is better characterized as a fragmented, ad hoc-oriented way to operate in often quite unpredictable circumstances (Carlsson 1951; Mintzberg 1973). To be successful, you have to be able to handle the duality of expectations on normative control and the specific needs unique to specific local requirements. Similarly, the work of management researchers could be described as a messy practice. The everyday work of the researcher is much more devoted to handling the dilemmas generated by practical problems and the tension between competing ideals than on what is recognized in most theories found in books on research methodology.

Courses on research methodology have traditionally been occupied with the techniques of the methods at hand, rather than with the blending and using of methods as part of a research practice and as part of the relation to the studied organizations. Although there has been a shift in emphasis from statistical methods and mathematical modelling towards the more qualitative methods common in today's social science, the courses and textbooks still tend to focus on the methods per se.

Most management researchers would agree that the thrill of doing research in organizations is related to the opportunity to experience what is happening out there, what people do, and their rationales behind their doings. First-year doctoral students, as well as undergraduate students doing project work, may be surprised, though, when they find that the methods suggested in the textbooks seldom fit with the situation at hand. Their work will in most cases require compromises, thus diverging from the ideals of the methods used. Doing research and producing management knowledge is by many means a social process that is interactive in character and must adapt to the subject of study and the subjects being studied. As teachers and practising researchers, the authors of this book have felt a need for a text more in line with the messiness of day-to-day management research – a book with more personal reflections about the *practice* of research.

This volume provides examples of the practices in a community of researchers linked together by a common history, and by shared values underlying our research practice. We have put together a volume guided by the ambition to show and discuss what we do when we approach a research opportunity, and how we then try to transform this opportunity into production of knowledge. The various contributions differ somewhat in form. Some of the authors give a broader view of their research programmes – such as how their entire research career has evolved in steps from curiosity stemming from their own managerial experiences into knowledge validated in interaction with other managers. Other examples discuss comparative research and collaborative, action-oriented research projects. Still others stay close to the experiences in a particular study – illustrating, in depth, examples of and experiences from doing management research guided by ideas from grounded theory, ethnomethodology, ethnography, etc. Some of the contributors to this book take a specific technique (interviews, think-aloud exercises, content analysis, cluster analysis, etc.) as the point of departure for their reflections about their research work.

It is our ambition to describe a spectrum of research approaches, practices and ideas – dealing with these approaches as sharing of our experiences, rather than as providing normative advice. It is a volume about management research seen from the insider's perspective. The book may be seen, speaking with John van Maanen (1988), as a series of 'tales from the field'.

The aim of this first chapter is to highlight some of the dilemmas or issues we have to handle as management researchers. This is not to say that every contributor to the volume would subscribe to every sentence presented. Each author represents his or her lived experience as a management researcher. Still, we think that it is appropriate to say something about the pillars that build the platform of values that guides our research. One may see this chapter as a way of describing some fundamental values guiding us in our attempts to manage the messiness of everyday research. As Nobel laureate in economics Gunnar Myrdal (1968) advised researchers – in order to be trustworthy, we should not try to claim to be objective but instead show the values that may affect the results of our research.

The first issue discussed is the notion that management research is a social process, where the researcher is an actor that has to deal with expectations and constraints placed not only by the research subjects but also by funding agencies, collegial and societal norms. Further on, we state that knowledge in management, as in most social sciences, is not a cumulative international body of knowledge but is better characterized as both local and international (a 'glocal' practice) due to the fact that research is situated in time and space. The influence of zeitgeist is therefore discussed as the third issue. Furthermore, we discuss the ethics of knowledge production processes, which relates to the need for distance and for maintaining the integrity of the researcher, as well as of the subjects involved. The chapter concludes with a discussion about the products of research and the duality of the messy practice that we consider the knowledge production process to be.

## Knowledge production as interaction in social systems

Research is a practice in a web of expectations and constraints, which means that a researcher is a manager of social as well as intellectual processes. Therefore, to succeed with a research project, the researcher not only needs access to sources of data in the empirical world, but also needs to develop relations with other actors in the knowledge systems. Viewing knowledge production in management as a social process, rather than 'just' the assembling and analyzing of facts and figures, raises issues about the relationships between the actors in the knowledge system. The knowledge production process is not only in the hands of the researcher and the research subject(s) but is also dependent on funding agencies, fellow researchers for support or peer reviews, societal norms and expectations, etc.

From this (social) perspective, the relation to the research subject is also of major importance – not least for those researchers working with a collaborative or action-oriented approach. The crucial success factors in these projects are most intimately linked to the interest the project manages to create among its collaborating partners.

In research with a more traditional relation to its research subjects, and a lower degree of involvement for the participating organization, the results could be of less explicit relevance to the particular organization in focus. In these cases, the recognition from fellow researchers is a more salient criterion of success. The scientific journals and publishing houses are an important part of the knowledge and career systems of the management researcher and peer reviews are always required for successful publication. To these direct relations with other actors in the everyday work of the researcher, the system of mediators and co-producers of management knowledge can be added. Management consultancies and other types of business advisory firms, the media and, last but not least, business schools are important in this system, through the expectations and constraints that infuse the goals and actions of the researcher.

What is common for all contributions to this volume is that research is conducted in an interactive mode with those who are the focus of the research. Doing empirical work in micro-oriented studies, the researcher and participating organizational members become an interlinked social knowledge system, even though the degree of involvement with the research subjects varies.

## Management research as a glocal practice

Research is a practice about some practice. As researchers, we should be helped in our attempts to understand the practice we study by a better understanding of our own practice as researchers. We are embedded in communities and networks that share interests, research problems, theories, tools and ideals. Together, these interests, problems, etc. constitute our research practice (cf. Brown and Duguid 1991, 2001). This practice means taking into account the expectations and constraints formulated in several systems of knowledge and values. The literature on research methods may guide us, but the stories and tales about what we actually do in particular research projects may be more relevant for the development of our research practice – and of us as researchers.

Brown and Duguid (2001) distinguish between networks of practice and communities of practice. As researchers, we are involved in many international and national networks, often organized in forms like the US-based Academy of Management, the Nordic Academy of Management (NFF), the European Group of Organization Studies (EGOS), and in closer organizational units, such as the Research Centre for People and Organizations (PMO) at the Stockholm School of Economics.

Thus, research is truly international in the sense that we cannot sustain high quality research without strong international links, thus being global (which until now has had a strong Western, especially Anglo-Saxon, dominance). Global dissemination of knowledge – open to everyone – is a traditional ideal in academia. However, the abundance of such open information forces us to be selective in our attention, thus relating, in some sense, to local influences; local geographically, but more importantly, cognitively. The communities that we belong to, and in which we primarily share our experiences, are often local in the sense that, although they are international, they consist of small groups of people who do joint research projects, share practices and interact intensively. This is exemplified by a study of the use of references in the publications from researchers at different business schools and departments of management in universities in Sweden. Engwall (1994) shows in this study that there are both general patterns and local traditions regarding the references used. One such example is the common references to Herbert Simon, Richard Cyert and James March (all of whom happened to be part of one such local research community, at Carnegie-Mellon University in the 1950s and 1960s) that were used by most Swedish research groups until the beginning of the 1990s.

Examples of references used more locally at this time by management researchers include Pettigrew (1973) and Weick (1969, 1979) at Gothenburg University, and Buckley (1967), Crozier (1964) and Rhenman and Normann (1994) at Lund University, due to the influences of SIAR (Scandinavian Institute of Administrative Research) developed in Lund in the early 1970s (Engwall *op. cit.*). Another example is Eric Trist, Fred Emery and Philip Herbst (linked to the Tavistock Institute), who had a strong influence in the 1970s on the group that the authors of this chapter belonged to, the Centre for People and Organization (PMO). Thus, there is a specialization between different research groups. This specialization is not necessarily directed to references to local research, but to a local use of a certain body of research literature, as exemplified above. These relationships in research are therefore both global (e.g. international) and local. The combined global and local character of modern management phenomena has been given the term 'glocal' (see Hedlund 1986; Hedlund and Rolander 1990).

The specialization may be seen as linked to a particular community and a particular time, thus it is not only glocal, but also limited in time to a particular zeitgeist, searching and forming selectively its roots by digging through sediments of earlier research communities. The interest in developing and applying phenomenographic approaches (Marton 1981; Sandberg 1994) among some scholars at Gothenburg University is an example where the roots in phenomenology lead back to philosophers such as Husserl and Heidegger. The glocal character is exemplified by Sandberg now being based in Australia after having had some impact in the Stockholm School of Economics while working there, as shown by the contribution of Blomberg in this volume (Chapter 4). When looking into the patterns of collaboration in any research field, it is our expectation that you would find common references, manifesting particular schools, with roots in a few innovative researchers that have criticized old paradigms and in the process become the node of other strong research communities that gradually come to show more and more of what Kuhn (1962) called 'normal science', institutionalized through a growing network of students, colleagues, conferences and journals. Since most members are members of several such communities, the wider networks of researchers that such glocal communities reach are considerable.

## Management research is situated in time and space

The term 'zeitgeist' is indeed relevant when describing the development of research over time – some research questions are easier to fund one year, others another, and some topics draw a lot of attention from the research community, and as we become interested in them, so do other researchers. The funding of work-life related studies in Scandinavia is a good example of this strong influence of the changing interests over time. In the late 1960s and the 1970s, the focus was very much the democratization of work – leading to the formation of research groups such as our own *Centre for People and Organization* (PMO), as well as to the establishment of institutes such as the Ontario Quality of Work Life Institute, and the Swedish Centre for Working Life. While PMO has survived the changing interests of funding agencies by focusing on new topics, such as the effects of the IT revolution, interest in promoting and studying learning organizations, and in areas such as knowledge work, management consultants, school management, company mergers, etc., the other two institutes were dissolved when the agencies funding them changed their priorities. Today, we are living in a time when the primary issues of interest for funding organizations seem to be the development of the economy through innovations systems, clusters, etc. Social responsibility was an important keyword in applications for funding in the late 1970s and 1980s. Interestingly, social responsibility, now termed 'corporate social responsibility' (CSR), and ethics have come back as areas of high priority.

Not only funding agencies change their research priorities as time goes by; research approaches also follow the zeitgeist to some extent. In the 1970s, action research was a way of learning by being close to the subjects being studied. It meant a strong emphasis on working not only with management but also with the employees and their unions in an attempt by the researchers to participate in the development of the system being studied, thus learning about the dynamics of change. Today, being close to the studied subject is still highly valued, but the approaches seem more often inspired by traditions in the field of ethnography. The term 'climate', frequently used in the organization development (OD) approaches of the 1970s, has been replaced by the term 'culture' – covering similar but not identical aspects. Schein (1969, 1992) bridges the two traditions of the uses of the terms but, as shown by Kunda (1992) and Alvesson and Berg (1992), culture may indeed also have other interpretations.

Thus, there are theories and schools of thought that are more popular at a certain time. By utilizing the concepts and the frameworks of the communities you value, as a young researcher, you associate yourself with the development of a particular research area even if your own contribution may be meagre. In a sense, you are borrowing the legitimacy of the research community 'in vogue'. This may be excused, in our view, as long as the concepts and perspectives are in fact instrumental as tools for describing and analyzing the empirical phenomenon in question.

We have used the term 'zeitgeist' to describe the influence of the dominating ideas in a particular time. Research is always conducted in a tension between values and the dominating ideas of different knowledge systems (academic, practitioners, society, etc.). Another way of expressing this – and doing it with a more positive tone – is to say that research is always embedded in the ongoing discourse that forms current research agendas. For the individual researcher or the research group, however, there is implicitly (or explicitly) a narrow line between opportunism and being impressionable to the concerns of the time.

The academic discourse is more general than any of the research projects embedded in the discourse – and develops as a result of the input from projects into the discourse. However, this input is not only scientific results, but also commonly felt societal problems, socially constructed in the sense that these societal problems exist as definitions and understandings generally shared and often contested. Examples that have had very strong influence on the research agendas are problems of a lack of motivation, lack of influence at work and gender inequality. All of these three examples have, as problems, existed parallel in time – and none has been solved in such a way as to make the problem irrelevant. Still, as focused on in academic discourse, they have been sequential rather than parallel, and the concepts and models guiding the different research traditions have differed – even if, as the examples show, the problems overlap.

## Ethics of the knowledge production process

An ethical condition for research – as for most, if not all, activities in society – is to respect the individual's integrity. This places demands on the research practice. The concern for integrity and trust affects what the researcher decides to publish. There may exist results that are not publishable because persons may be harmed. Every organization is characterized by power differences – and in particular persons that are in some sense vulnerable need to be protected. In the academic community, debates about the strengths and weaknesses of our academic leaders are common, and generally do not lead to sanctions. In many corporations, however, similar comments about managers would be judged as a sign of disloyal attitudes. Therefore, even if the interviewed person may have given his or her consent to publish information, as a researcher, you must make your own judgement about whether publishing that information could be harmful. A comment made in oral interaction is usually given other interpretations when it appears as written text. A comment that may seem innocent in the light of other comments made in the same interaction may appear differently when taken out of context.

The emphasis on the ethics of knowledge production comes at a cost. It may lead to a reluctance to participate in debates, and a reluctance to publish spectacular and controversial research results. The world is a complex one, which makes arguing for one particular view of the world difficult.

Viewing the practice and the practitioners of the organizations studied as co-producers of knowledge also has other implications of which you as a researcher must be aware. One such implication is that the relationships developed during the research process are not only relationships about the sharing of information, analysis and conclusions – but also relationships about loyalty and mutual influence. As a researcher, in the process of doing research, you tend to see the world a bit like those you are doing research with – you tend to 'go native', and more so, the more you interact. This is a problem – noted especially by researchers in the ethnographic tradition – and is perhaps even a precondition for action research, in the sense that action research requires some degree of shared interests and values with those predominant in the system you are studying.

But the close interaction also has an effect on the people in the organizations you are interacting with. The researcher goes native, but the natives may at the same time 'go academic', as mentioned in the chapter on action research later in the book. Problematizing, questioning – not least questioning authority – and an open and honest search for knowledge may have costs for people in organizations where other values are predominant. In the studies of the fates of 'souls-of-fire' conducted as a longitudinal follow-up of organizational developments of the 1970s, we found examples where change champions to some extent shared more of our academic values than the shifting business values of the organizations that employed them as middle managers. The careers of several of these change champions became problematic after change of higher management, and thus changes in the ideals on which to base the organization (Stjernberg and Philips 1993).

The potential value of research demands a critical and questioning attitude to both the data and the perspectives in the organizations involved in the studies, as well as to the perspectives of dominating research communities. Illuminating, questioning and 'problematizing' may be seen as tacit skills of good researchers – tacit because they are difficult to describe and teach.

The close cooperation between the researcher and the subjects whose world is under examination makes for a fuzzy distinction between researching and learning. Research is a balancing act between getting familiar with the problems and people involved in research and the need for distance in order to problematize and make critical interpretations. Our argumentation is therefore not only a quest for respect for the integrity of the research subject but equally for the integrity of the researcher.

Thus, there may be situations and studies that you, as a researcher, should stay away from because they may challenge your own integrity or that of the research subject. An example of this can be when you do not share the basic values that guide the practice you want to study. In this sense, research is truly guided by deep personal values. Honesty to yourself and to your subjects, i.e. your partners, in the research setting you are studying requires a mutual and shared sense of a true search for knowledge. This means that doing research in a criminal organization, for example, or in a racist organization, would be impossible to do in a collaborative manner, since it would mean breaking the trust that has to be developed in order to get valid data. An alternative research strategy, although highly controversial, would be to do a Gunther Walraff (1970, 1979) type of covert study. Such examples may be easy to rule out as partners in a collaborative research project, but many organizations, and many persons that you need to collaborate with in any organization, may have values or act in ways that you find violate your own personal values. There is no simple answer for how to involve yourself, or not involve yourself, in collaborative research or other interactions in such situations. The decision must be your own, and the support in that personal decision process may come from the discourse in the research communities of which you are a part.

In our own research community, a guiding formulation for how to conduct research is: 'Conduct your research in such a way that your research subjects or partners are willing to engage in research also in the future.' This implies not only living up to the norm of trust and concern for the individuals involved, but also a demand for relevance. The people involved as co-producers of knowledge must be able to see some potential value in this knowledge. At the same time, as a researcher, you need to be able to distance yourself from a naïve empiricism by questioning and problematizing what is taken for granted in the system being studied.

## The product of research . . .

The contribution of management research is not foremost to describe existing knowledge about contemporary phenomena but to create new knowledge and insight into relevant problems. As suggested by Bengt Stymne in the concluding chapter in this volume (Chapter 15), research can be described as an innovative system. Our contribution should not primarily be to prescribe what actions to take, nor should it only be to produce accurate representations in facts and figures. Instead, we may take part by contributing new concepts and theories as *tools* to explore and understand the phenomena under study.

When looking back from a certain point in time, there is a risk we will be disappointed and only remember the more seminal contributions of a mere few of a large number of researchers. However, the product of management research is not limited to those seminal results that are often referred to. The product of management research, and organizational research in general, must be much more than that. It is not only in collaborative research designs that research subjects become a part of the knowledge-producing system. An often overlooked aspect of the interaction with people in organizations is the potential for learning among all those involved. The product of research efforts in the area of management is therefore not merely the final report or project results presented to a wider audience through books or scholarly articles.

Research is a process of social interactions that produces both intended and unintended learning. The professional researcher must therefore not only know when and how to handle his or her tools in the process, such as theories, methods and research techniques. He or she must also be able to use them in a process whereby they become part of a wider learning process. Again, this is not only required by those conducting collaborative research aimed at 'actionable knowledge'. It is a quest for all of us who believe in producing 'knowledge-in-action', situated in 'glocal' managerial and research practices. From the perspective that knowledge production is a social and glocal process, it has importance for the enlightenment of not only research colleagues, but also for the enlightenment and empowerment of people in the organizations researched. The insights gained are fed into other parts of our knowledge systems, such as consultancy firms, the media, etc.

'The product of work is people' is a well-known idea, formulated by Phil Herbst (1975). At the workshop instigating this volume, one of the authors of this chapter made an analogy to Herbst in the formulation – 'the product of research is researchers'. One very obvious argument for this, from a Scandinavian perspective, is that a large proportion of the research being done in the field of management studies is done by PhD students as their thesis work. Thus, an important product of research is also new generations of researchers. A more subtle aspect of the importance of research for the development of the researcher is discussed in this volume in the chapter by David Sims, where he describes the writing process as 'the production of self'.

One aim of this book is therefore to convey experiences from research on management and organizational issues. As will be shown, the research focus and interests vary in the chapters that follow. There is however an important element of common ground in the contributions – the willingness of the authors to share their experiences and learning from their research processes with the reader. We have conference traditions where the focus is not only on sharing our research results, but also our experiences about the practice of research. This is much more of an oral tradition than what we find when reading academic texts. Workshops and conferences enable us to articulate our experiences through dialogue of a character difficult to capture in writing. The texts in this volume cannot match the inter-active character of dialogue as a means of sharing experiences. But, to use Kaplan's (1964) distinction, they are written primarily with the ambition of sharing our logic in use, rather than attaining the reconstructed logic that characterizes our normal style of writing.

## The duality of a messy practice

In this introductory chapter, we have sketched out some of the values and practices that characterize some of the issues that shape our view on the production of managerial knowledge. These values are signified by a highly interactive relation to the members of the organizations studied. The values, as they are presented here, are *our* (the editors) values and the practices are *our* practices. However, several of the contributing authors have served as a source of inspiration and several also as our tutors and partners in our socialization into the values and ideals that guide our research practices. Others may, as more junior colleagues, have been important for our development by challenging our thoughts and by exploring alternatives and further developments of these research practices.

The chapter began with a discussion of research as a practice guided by normative ideals. These normative ideals were contrasted against experiences from the everyday work of the researcher and found to be rather 'messy'. But the messy research practice has a foundation in values and traditions that are difficult to formulate but that mirror the zeitgeist and the glocal community of the researchers.

There is no need to take a position of 'either/or' here, but instead one should recognize the duality inherent in the issues of managerial research discussed in this chapter. Every researcher and every research project is embedded in systems of thoughts and values concerning dilemmas such as responding to academic and praxis, a quest for relevance, responding to issues of deep personal interest for the researcher and to issues popular among the funding organizations, treating information with ethical care and using the information as part of the chain of reasoning needed to substantiate the research results. Occasionally one finds colleagues, research subjects or other participants in the knowledge production process taking a firm position for or against one or the other of the ideals. It is our conviction that the interactive work practices of everyday management research are complex and situated in unique and often peculiar circumstances that a competent researcher must resolve by recognizing the duality of these contexts. They are all important aspects of the knowledge production process that have to be handled. It is our hope that this chapter has generated some ground for reflection about these issues.

# References

Alvesson, M. and Berg, P.O. (1992) *Corporate Culture and Organizational Symbolism: An Overview*, Berlin: Walter de Gruyter.

Brown, J.S. and Duguid, P. (1991) 'Organizational Learning and Communities-of-Practice: Toward a Unified View of Working, Learning, and Innovation', *Organization Science*, 2, 1: 40–57.

Brown, J.S. and Duguid, P (2001) 'Knowledge and Organization: A Social-Practice Perspective', *Organization Science*, 12, 2: 198–213.

Brunsson, N. (1981) 'Företagsekonomi – avbildning eller språkbildning', in N. Brunsson (ed.) *Företagsekonomi – sanning eller moral?* Lund: Studentlitteratur.

Buckley, W. (1967) *Sociology and Modern Systems Theory*, Englewood Cliffs, NJ: Prentice Hall.

Carlsson, S. (1951) *Executive Behaviour*, Stockholm: Strömbergs.

Crozier, M. (1964) *The Bureaucratic Phenomenon*, Chicago, IL: University of Chicago Press.

Engwall, L. (1994) 'Säg mig vem du umgås med . . .', in B. Rombach (ed.) *Med hänvisning till andra*, Stockholm: Nerénius & Santérus Förlag.

Engwall, L. and Zagmani, V. (1998) 'Introduction', in L. Engwall and V. Zagmani (eds) *Management Education in Historical Perspective*, Manchester: Manchester University Press.

Hedlund, G. (1986) 'The Hypermodern MNC: A Heterarchy', *Human Resource Management*, 25: 9–35.

Hedlund, G. and Rolander, D. (1990) 'Action in Hierarchies: New Approaches to Managing the MNC', in C.A. Bartlett, Y. Doz and G. Hedlund (eds) *Managing the Global Firm*, London and New York: Routledge.

Herbst, P. (1975) 'The Product of Work is People', in L.E. Davis and A.B. Cherns (eds) *The Quality of Working Life*, Vol. 1, New York: Free Press.

Kaplan, A. (1964) *The Conduct of Inquiry: Methodology of Behavioral Science*, San Francisco: Chandler Publications.

Kuhn, T. (1962) *The Structure of Scientific Revolutions*, Chicago, IL: University of Chicago Press.

Kunda, G. (1992) *Engineering Culture: Control and Commitment in a High-Tech Corporation*, Philadelphia, PA: Temple University Press.

Luo, X. (2002) 'From Technical Skills to Personal Development: Employee Training in US Organizations in the Twentieth Century', in K. Sahlin-Andersson and L. Engwall (eds) *The Expansion of Management Knowledge*, Stanford, CA: Stanford Business Books.

March, J.G. and Simon, H.A. (1958) *Organizations*, New York: Wiley.

Marton, F. (1981) 'Phenomenography: Describing Conceptions of the World Around Us', *Instructional Science*, 10: 177–200.

Mintzberg, H. (1973) *The Nature of Managerial Work*, New York: Harper & Row.

Myrdal, G. (1968) *Objektivitetsprobemet i samhällsforskningen*, Stockholm: Rabén & Sjögren. (For a discussion of Myrdal's work in English, see Streeten, P. (ed.) (1998) *Value in Social Theory: A Selection of Essays on Methodology by Gunnar Myrdal*, London: Routledge.

Perrow, C. (1972) *Complex Organizations: A Critical Essay*, Glenview, IL: Scott Foresman.

Pettigrew, A.M. (1973) *The Politics of Organizational Decision Making*, London: Tavistock.

Rhenman, E. and Normann, R. (1994) *Om målformulering och effektivitetsmätning i statsförvaltningen*, SIAR-S 55.

Sahlin-Andersson, K. and Engwall, M. (2002) 'Carriers, Flows, and Sources of Management Knowledge', in K. Sahlin-Andersson and L. Engwall (eds) *The Expansion of Management Knowledge*, Stanford, CA: Stanford Business Books.

Sandberg, J. (1994) *Human Competence at Work: An Interpretative Approach*, Göteborg: BAS.

Schein, E.H. (1969) *Process Consultation – Its Role in Organization Development*, Reading, MA; Addison-Wesley.

Schein, E.H. (1992) *Organizational Culture and Leadership*, San Francisco, CA: Jossey-Bass.

Simon, H.A. (1957) *Administrative Behavior*, New York: Macmillan.

Stjernberg, T. and Philips, Å. (1993) 'Organizational Innovations in a Long-term Perspective: Legitimacy and Souls-of-Fire as Critical Factors of Change and Viability', *Human Relations*, 46, 10: 1193–1219.

van Maanen, J. (1988) *Tales from the Field*, Chicago, IL: University of Chicago Press.

Wallraff, G. (1970). *13 unerwünschte Reportagen*, Köln: Kiepenheuer Witsch.
Wallraff, G. (1979) *The Undesirable Journalist*, New York: Overlook Press.
Weick, K.E. (1969) *The Social Psychology of Organizing*, Reading, MA: Addison-Wesley.
Weick, K.E. (1979) *The Psychology of Organizing*, Reading, MA: Addison-Wesley.

# Part I
# The researcher as producer of knowledge

# 2 On issue-driven research

*Michael Earl*

## Introduction

To be invited to write a chapter on research strategies is a novel experience for me; I have tended to 'just get on with it' without considering whether I should be contributing to theories of management research. This partly is explained by my background. I entered academe after eight years in industrial management, having no formal training in research. Immodestly, I could claim to have produced two well-received dissertations at undergraduate and postgraduate level and so I was not afraid to start research. No doubt I was helped in this bravado by not knowing what I didn't know.

Indeed, in my first post at Manchester Business School, I arrived with a big question based on my recent experience as group systems manager in a telecommunications company. I soon discovered in teaching that this question was a big *issue* on management agendas more widely and before long it ranked very high for over two decades on issue lists compiled from chief information officers (Dickson *et al.* 1984; Niederman *et al.* 1991). The issue was how to do strategic or long-range planning of IS/IT applications and investments.

Of course, my more experienced colleagues at Manchester Business School quickly responded to my research idea with what I regarded as irritating obstacles. Indeed, had I still been in business I probably would have dismissed them as 'academic'! Feedback to me included questions like, did I have a *model*, what was my *hypothesis*, did I have my *dependent and independent variables* sorted out, was it possible to *operationalize* these variables, which *discipline* is underpinning this research, etc. I suspect I replied by saying, 'I don't know yet, but this is a real issue I am interested in'.

But was it an issue? Or issue-driven research? Given my business background and associated managerial bias, an issue for me quite simply has been a question of management practice or policy that functional or general managers would recognize as both relevant and important. Now you could say that any research is driven by, or implies, a question. I would venture that my orientation has been to look at management questions, answers to which can inform or improve practice and make a contribution, however small, to theory development.

There perhaps also has been another characteristic. In order to be synergistic with teaching and with being able to advise organisations, I have been drawn to contemporary questions and current phenomena. This inevitably has the potential of falling victim to a fad or engaging in rapid and superficial enquiry. So if the aim is to be published in serious outlets and contribute to knowledge, issue driven research does have to be done with care, even though some compromises may be necessary.

It is this concern with being grounded in practice (some might say organizational reality), with contributions to knowledge in both applied and theoretical senses and with an eye on the contemporary, which has influenced my own research journey and an associated search for acceptable methodologies, mostly through learning by doing.

The corollary of what I have just written is that bad research, or at least bad applied research, can be recognized by several diverse characteristics, including: providing unreliable guidance for practice, making no contribution to theory development, having ephemeral value, displaying lack of care and no recognition of limitations, and, of course, being rejected by peers.

The 'recipe' I have evolved over the years has been one of *triangulation*. This is not a novel idea or term, but here I mean use of multiple – three to be precise – methods in combination. I will demonstrate it by reference to four of my previous studies, all from my principal research domain, the strategic management of information resources.

## Strategic information systems planning

This study (Earl 1993) examined practices of strategic information systems planning (SISP) in the UK. A topic high on chief information officers' (CIOs) agendas over the years, I sought to examine the question of what SISP methods were effective. Obvious challenges, besides those of sample design, sample size and so on, arise. How do you recognise SISP, how do you study it, what might be meant by effectiveness and how do you assess it?

Answers to these challenges can be found in the original paper. Prior strategic management and MIS literature provided ideas, propositions and descriptions of sub-issues, but most of the prior research suffered from several of the following defects:

- Too much anecdotal evidence.
- Production of high level frameworks which described the problem rather than resolved it.

- Use of case studies from which reliable generalizations were difficult to derive.
- Lack of transparency of how effectiveness was assessed, unless it was done subjectively by the researcher or the IT function.
- Little commonality about the SISP processes being described.

I decided on a three-pronged research study. First, I wrote up six case studies of UK firms that had been engaged in SISP. Some were firms I had been involved with in a consulting role; others I approached for the first time. Evidence was collected by interviews, analysis of documents and obtaining copies of IS strategic plans. I chose to *begin* with case studies for five reasons:

1　To develop a rich picture of SISP since prior studies mainly seemed simplistic.
2　To 'get a handle' on how to examine what I already knew from experience was a complex management process.
3　To refine issues, questions and propositions to examine in a later stage.
4　To explore how SISP effectiveness might be assessed.
5　To assess whether context, particular sector and organization structure should influence later stages of the research.

To a large extent, these aims were met. The most significant learnings were:

1　SISP had to be thought of as a combination of method (techniques, formal methods, implicit methodologies . . .), process (procedures, politics, relationships . . .) and implementation (both expected and unexpected outcomes and trajectories of actions).
2　Effectiveness could be seen in at least three ways: managers' perceptions of the activity being successful, reported concerns with SISP, and ability to identify IT applications which could yield competitive advantage.
3　The perceptions of method, process and implementation and of effectiveness might vary with stakeholder group, the three key groups being general managers, line managers and IS managers.

In other words, case studies confirmed the complexity and interesting nature (both theoretical and practical) of SISP, generated detailed research questions and helped refine research methodology to follow. It is worth noting that commentators and later workers often commented on the importance of the above learnings, especially the first and third.

The next stage of the study involved field studies in 21 UK companies. By field studies, I mean investigation of organizational experiences to a reduced intensity than case studies in order to widen the sample size. I interviewed one senior IS executive, one line (user) manager and one general manager in each firm – plus collected documentary evidence on methods, processes and outcomes. Semi-structured and closed questions were used, probing the areas suggested by the three key learnings from the case study phase.

Subjective content analysis, albeit around prior questions, propositions and ideas, was carried out on all the data (actually while on sabbatical at the Stockholm School of Economics) and sense-making and pattern-detection were far from easy ... until I sought to group highlights of method, process and implementation. The result was a taxonomy of five SISP approaches, each with distinguishing characteristics, particular strengths and weaknesses, some suggestive associations with context, and apparent success factors.

In other words, the field studies presented more of a 'universe' of data, achieving a balance between breadth and depth, and generated a framework through which practitioners could assess their firm's approach and ask useful questions to aid improvement. The framework also contained propositions for other researchers to test *and* a language for further study. Also, three success scores were feasible: respondents' self-reported perceptions of success, respondents' reports of concerns experienced, and which approaches seemed to have most propensity for generating competitive advantage applications of IT.

However, this work was inductive and subjective. So I added a third stage: running workshops with firms from the field studies, at least one per approach. I asked them to consider which of the five approaches they thought described their firm's experience best. The three stakeholder groups were present in each workshop. Rarely was agreement initially achieved. Different stakeholders had different views!

I then invited the workshop to re-think by discussing two questions:

1   What had been most emphasized in that firm's SISP?
2   Who had had most influence on the SISP process?

Then agreement was achieved and clearly we had two key distinguishing characteristics of a SISP approach. This then led me to use statistical tests (analysis of variance) to assess whether differences between approaches were significant and whether differences between stakeholders were significant. Only the former difference was significant.

Apart from suggesting perhaps obvious tests of significance, the real value of the workshops was to validate also in a qualitative way – and with more anecdotes – the taxonomy and qualities of each approach. In essence, they provided validation.

The study overall therefore comprised three stages (Figure 2.1). Stage one was necessary to refine both the scope of the study and the research methodology. Stage two comprised much more structured and disciplined fieldwork. Stage three involved verification by feedback and by statistical analysis. I will now develop, with other examples, this implied triangulation and its rationale.

*Figure 2.1*  The three stages in the study of strategic information systems planning (SISP).

## The chief knowledge officer

As knowledge management evolved as a management idea in the 1990s, maybe as an organizational phenomenon, such an interesting melange of business strategy, information systems, organizational behaviour and change management (not to mention more philosophical questions) was irresistible as an area of enquiry. I had carried out and published two opportunistic case studies on strategic initiatives which I had labelled as knowledge management (Earl 1994), but they had been based on descriptions of two fascinating and successful strategic thrusts in the recent history of a reinsurance firm and a chemical company.

A key question was where to start research in a new area of practice where it was important to capture the essence of this new phenomenon, rather than, as many have done, examine previously existing initiatives which were rebadged as knowledge management. I had conducted a study of chief information officers in 1993 (Earl and Vivian 1993) and it struck me that the newly emerging role of chief knowledge officer (CKO) could be both useful and interesting to study – both to help CKOs and CEOs and as a lens or portal on what firms actually were doing under the label *knowledge management*.

The resultant paper (Earl and Scott 1999) defines what we accepted as a CKO in designing the study and hazards a good guess that we studied 21 of the 24 CKOs that we knew to exist in the world at that time. Again, we adopted a three-stage methodology.

First, we interviewed all the CKOs with structured and semi-structured questions on what they were doing, their concerns and frustrations, their successes and measures of success, their career backgrounds and expectations and their learnings to date. These we presented in the paper. What struck us, however, was how *interesting* these CKOs were: bright, reflective, adventurous, broad-gauged, and from quite diverse backgrounds, both in terms of discipline and previous jobs. Because of this and because we wanted to know 'what on earth is a CKO' (Earl and Scott 1998), we chose, with help, to apply a psychometric test on personality. This produced quite a consistent picture, which was surprising since they had been mostly appointed by CEOs into a role with no prior description or specification. The next question was: would our CKOs recognize their psychometric picture and the nature of the job we had discerned in our interviews?

Once again, therefore, workshops were deployed in New York and London for the participants. The psychometric pictures were not rejected and our descriptive data on the role of the CKO was easily recognized. However, our attempt to derive the 'model CKO' generated substantial discussion and argument. Fortunately, we recorded key or interesting words the CKOs frequently used and I have to confess that it was as I was walking down Madison Avenue that the four labels in our published model came to me. (Was I on the sunny side of the street?) Fortunately, they seemed to be consistent with the psychometric data.

This study, therefore, comprised once again three stages, but not identical to those deployed in the SISP research (Figure 2.2). Stage one was quite well structured because the object of our study was well defined and, being a very contemporary phenomenon, we could keep our questions simple. Stage two introduced more formal analysis suggested by stage one. The final stage again aimed at verification, but actually led to revision of our model.

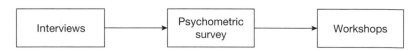

*Figure 2.2* The three stages in the chief knowledge officer (CKO) study.

## E-commerce and IT

At the height of the 'dotcom era', writers and consultants suggested that e-commerce was generating 'new business models' (for example, Tapscott 1966; Evans and Wurster 2000). Less attention was paid to the impact of e-commerce on the management and practices of IT, yet IT platforms and systems underpinned e-commerce. Thus an important question for IT management practice was: were there new challenges for the IT function posed by e-commerce and were new responses emerging which might have long-term value in managing IT and suggest revisions to existing theories of IS development?

To start, a set of exploratory interviews and three deeper case studies were conducted to explore a new and relatively undocumented phenomenon. Prior reasoning suggested three categories of firm to explore: start-ups, incumbent businesses and spin-out businesses. We also visited some e-commerce consultancies. This induction might suggest different contextual or contingent factors at work or indicate generic trends and practices. It was soon clear that an entrepreneurial attitude was common, new rules were evolving and some seemingly appropriate practices and policies emerging (Earl and Khan 2001).

Next, and very rapidly in order to capture firms willing to participate as confidence was waning in the 'new economy', we conducted interviews and collected documents from further sites in the UK and USA in the spirit of field studies.

Again, some sort of validation of the inductive picture we derived from the first two stages was required and, again, we sensed the willingness of actors to give us time was eroding fast. So we conducted a workshop with one large organization who had each type of e-commerce organization in our stratified sample, and we also ran two workshops with CIOs coping with e-commerce initiatives. In some ways, these events combined validation or feedback with dissemination and education. They gave us confidence to publish our results and recommendations.

Although the pressures of what was being called 'Internet time' drove some of our research design choices, we evolved a three-stage process again (Figure 2.3). Stage one was by design exploratory due to the multi-faceted and fast-moving activity being studied. Stage two examined characteristics discovered in stage one in a larger sample. Stage three sought verification and to a degree consideration of the consequence of our 'results'.

*Figure 2.3* The three stages in the e-commerce and IT study.

## Strategies for knowledge management

Here the story (perhaps a nice word in this case) is one of retrospective sense-making – or a rationalization of an unplanned journey. The result was a taxonomy of knowledge management strategies in use, with suggestions of how to select a particular strategy for a particular organization (Earl 2001).

As reported above, I wrote two case studies in 1989 and 1990 of what I then saw as business strategic thrusts based on the management of knowledge.

Both teaching cases and research cases were published (Earl 1989, 1990). In Skandia International (an opportunity which arose in my aforementioned sabbatical at the Stockholm School of Economics), the competitive strategy in the reinsurance business was based on the capture, storage and dissemination of market knowledge involving elements of information systems, organization design, product-market choices and new roles design. In Shorko Films (an opportunity afforded by a consultancy study for Courtaulds PLC), a turnaround strategy was based on the capture, storage and analysis of process control information, new work organization, product-market choices and new investment in manufacturing equipment.

The analysis and suggestive theory development was based on just these two case studies – and while the knowledge management initiatives easily could be classified as 'strategic', they also were quite specialized. So generalizations had to be induced at a high level.

It was not until the CKO study mentioned earlier (Earl and Scott 1999) that more systematic evidence was collected; or to be more circumspect, a wider sample size was addressed. Interviews with our 21 CKOs provided descriptions and subjective evaluations of different kinds of knowledge management. In a way, we were mapping knowledge management by an interview-based survey. And as other managers suggested their firms were doing interesting things under the label of knowledge management, I visited them rather in the spirit of a geographer's field visit. At least four of these were particularly influential in subsequent thinking, and one became a deep, longitudinal case study (Earl and Nahapiet 1999).

In parallel, and following the CKO study, the researchers in that study (Earl and Scott 1999) founded a CKO network. Although its lifespan was short, we did hold some workshops on initiating knowledge management strategies and on how the CKO can achieve sustainable impact. Patterns about crafting knowledge management strategies and diverse 'schools' of knowledge management began to emerge. This led me to examine all the data I had collected since 1989, supplemented by a few secondary sources, and the production of the 2001 paper.

The critical observer may well see this 'project' as a higgledy-piggledy journey, a classic case of undesign and 'stumble and lurch', a multi-year exercise in 'bricolage' or an outrageous case of expost rationalization. I can only plead 'guilty'. However, I find it perhaps interesting that in a period of enthusiastic adoption and experimentation of a management idea (some would say 'fad') when most published work was based on single or few case studies, conceptual exercises or critical management theory, 'thought leadership' books or re-badging of related work-in-progress, this journey yielded field-based empirical evidence and a framework to guide practitioners and stimulate further work by researchers.

Moreover, although based on rationalization, again there were three stages, even if they were not wholly linear (Figure 2.4). Stage one can be seen as unanticipated discovery and learning about a management idea that was just emerging at the time. Stage two, although opportunistic, allowed development of ideas and further evidence generation. The third stage, a by-product of knowledge-sharing among CKOs triggered the need for classification through a taxonomy and highlighted critical dimensions of knowledge management strategies.

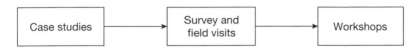

*Figure 2.4* The three stages in the retrospective study.

## A theory of triangulation?

If issue-driven research is to produce knowledge, then the relevance that drives it has to have rigour to underpin it. Relevance and rigour are often seen as contradictions or opposites. I am easily persuaded that obsession with rigour at all costs generally produces research results that have at best arm's length connection with relevance. Equally, much so-called 'practical', 'relevant', 'managerial', 'timely' or 'accessible' research is so superficial or unreliable that it needs a health warning for practitioners and policy-makers at least as much as for academics.

So I am obviously going to claim that the triangulation I have described here offers a way to navigate through these challenges that can produce publishable articles and guidance for practice. But what is the basis for this triangulation other than suggesting three stages which imply three lenses, three perspectives and three attempts at the research question? I suggest that there is a logic and, I admit, as in much of my research described above, it is based on inductive reasoning.

The three-stage structure of the four projects described above suggests not only a generic three-pronged 'methodology' for issue-driven research, but also the basis of triangulation. Each stage builds on, and is dependent on, the previous one – with possible iteration as well. In the pursuit of alliteration, I label these stages exploration, examination and exposition (Table 2.1).

### Exploration

The purpose here is reconnaissance, with at least four aims in mind. One is to see whether this particular research or enquiry (or issue) is as interesting

*Table 2.1* Triangulation for issue-driven research

|  | *Exploration* | *Examination* | *Exposition* |
| --- | --- | --- | --- |
| Nature | Reconnaissance | Testing | Verification |
| Character | Trawling | Surveying | Feedback |
| Purpose 1 | Confirm worthiness | Bounded evidence | Data validation |
| Purpose 2 | Evolve methods | Test propositions | Validate interpretation |
| Further benefit 1 | Grounding in realities | Widen database | Gather reflections |
| Further benefit 2 | Spin-off case studies | Capture graphical details | Capture finesses |
| Typical method | Case studies | Field studies | Participant workshops |
| Alternative method | Interviews | Questionnaire surveys | Secondary testing |

or important as one thinks. Another is to explore whether it is researchable and thus also seeks to establish or refine the overall research methodology. A third is to ensure grounding in the issue and in the organizational and business realities. A fourth is to capture both deep and raw examples, para-doxes or issues before employing more structural investigation. Synonyms for exploration could be digging, induction, immersion, familiarizing, quick learning or, more pejoratively, trawling.

The overarching goal is to confirm worthiness of the research question – perhaps both in terms of contribution to knowledge and influencing or improving policy and practice. At the same time, one is discovering or confirming appropriate methodology.

Case study investigation is the archetypal method here and, as a result, teaching case studies or research mini-cases can be by-products. If one is stepping into more uncertainty than usual, or needing to acquire rapid induc-tion (as for example in the e-commerce research described above), then a programme of interviews can be a substitute.

It is not novel to suggest that case studies are a useful first stage in research, although Yin (1984) argues persuasively that case study investigation can be a complete research method in its own right. Nevertheless, case studies are an effective, if laborious, means of scoping empirical enquiry.

It could be argued, validly, that the need for this exploration stage in my triangulation model arises because of orientations to new or contemporary management ideas and practice, or because there is little relevant prior research upon which to draw. However, I could argue also that any search for grounded theory, the exploration of new areas and pursuit of theory generation (Glaser and Strauss 1967), will benefit from this stage. But it is not enough.

### Examination

Here, ideas, propositions, and even hypotheses are tested on a wider, and usually stratified, sample of organizations or individuals. Often driven by questions, both structured and less structured, in some senses the *issue* or research question is probed further. The investigation in this stage is tighter and more bounded than in the exploration stage: propositions underpin questions, structured and semi-structured questions outnumber open ones, measures – for example scores, rankings, assessments – are sought. The researcher is concerned with focus, but remains alert for contextual, deeper or surprise data. Synonyms for examination might include testing, probing or surveying.

The primary purpose is testing propositions, with perhaps some 'fact-finding'. However, this stage is also required to widen the database, that is to say, increase the sample size, if possible with defined sample character-istics. In short, this is where the core data for analysis and/or interpretation are collected. So the examination stage can include the use of descriptive and analytical statistics, of content analysis, of pattern generation methods or of various sense-making and interpretation approaches. It also provides further opportunities for capture of more graphical or soft data such as examples, quotations, war stories and so on.

The typical methods deployed for data collection can be summarized as field studies or surveys. By field studies, I mean multiple case studies of more restricted enquiry than exploration-style or classical case studies, where often the focus is on dependent variables within a sample framed by categoriza-tion of independent variables (see some discussion by Benbasat 1987). The research studies into strategic information systems planning and e-commerce described earlier might be examples.

By surveys, I mean both analytic surveys, which aim to test a theory, and descriptive surveys, which aim to identify the characteristics of a specific population (Gill and Johnson 1991). The research on chief knowledge officers described earlier essentially deployed the survey method.

It could be argued that this stage comprises a weak or sometimes semi-strong form of hypothesis testing, not in the classical hypothetico-deductive mode (Popper 1959) adhered to by proponents of scientific method, but in a more pragmatic evidence-building sense, where some induction and inter-pretation are allowed to leaven deduction and discipline. Data and their analysis are permitted and recognized to be suggestive or probabilistic. Thus the third stage of triangulation, exposition, becomes crucial.

*Exposition*

This stage may be better thought of as one of elaboration, explanation and validation. It is all three and in these senses, 'exposition' seems appropriate other than in just its alliterative quality. When it involves workshops, it essentially has the character of feedback, both to participants and in return back to the researchers. So its nature is verification of the findings and of implications or recommendations.

However, through detailed presentation and discussion, such workshops also tend to provide validation of the data – in at least four ways. Participants usually exercise a critical eye on the *practical* side of the investigation, especially construct validity; namely do whatever operationalization or measures of the concepts or constructs being examined seem reliable or reasonable? Some participants also may have a keen eye for causality and thus will be assessing internal validity of any associations being made. Typically, they will alight on too uni-dimensional a view or on the need for some contingency thinking. Likewise, some will question research design, especially sample construction, and thus be concerned with external validity. Above all, managerial participants will be concerned with face validity, that is to say 'does it all make sense?' This last concern can be interesting if results appear counter-intuitive.

Workshops also provide an excellent opportunity to discuss and assess implications for policy and practice and to consider further, related questions for research. Participants can validate, or stimulate amendment of, the researchers' interpretations and attempts to answer the 'so what' questions.

Of course, if workshops typically include managers, then these events fit well with the oral tradition of managerial life. So even at this stage, there is an opportunity to gather reflections and capture finesses – quotations, caveats, for instances . . . – for the eventual formal output.

The ideal format of the exposition stage therefore is participant workshops. Indeed, these are an effective way of communicating research results to the practical world. Occasionally, however, either in the examination stage or in the exposition stage, the opportunity or need for some secondary testing becomes apparent. This was the case in the strategic information systems planning study described earlier. Emergence of stakeholder differences in perception of SISP approaches in use led to the idea of testing for stakeholder differences by analysis of variance tests.

This notion of secondary testing could be seen as a case for iteration, that is, going back to a previous stage and doing more work (or taking more care). The drive for 'results' can be a deterrent to iteration, but in some ways the research on knowledge management strategies described earlier was a journey of iteration which in retrospect seems to also fit the triangulation model.

## Reflections and beyond

The term *triangulation* usually refers to the practice of ensuring there are three data points, borrowing from trigonometry. Thus it can be applied to any sort of data collection where there may be potential differences according to position, time, perspective, etc. of the data object. Here, however, I am arguing for three distinct stages of enquiry into the sort of research in which I have been primarily engaged. Thus it is important to try and characterize this sort of research.

It seems to me to have four essential characteristics:

1 It is concerned with management practice.
2 It aims to contribute to theory development as well as practice improvement.
3 It examines current or contemporary issues in business and management and thus there may be limited prior research of a specific nature to guide one.
4 It is concerned with relevance – will managers or policy-makers find it useful? – and rigour – is it clear when and how it can be relied on and will peer reviewers accept it?

These characteristics suggest at least four more conceptual questions. First, is this sort of methodology most appropriate for the more applied areas of social science research, in particular in business schools? After all, it is issue-driven, it involves opening up the black box of organizations and it is likely to be managerial in attitude. Issue-driven research perhaps requires research of an evolutionary nature, which begins with exploration, then requires more careful examination and finally benefits from several facets of validation in the exposition stage. This three-stage approach gradually refines an issue into questions and gradually adds rigour to relevance.

Second, does it suit the European research tradition? At least in management and business research, North American research values seem to lead researchers towards more formal methods and safer or narrower domains. Laboratory experiments, theorem proof, simulation and questionnaire surveys outweigh more adventurous or more qualitative methods such as case studies, longitudinal research, action research or scholarly analysis which are often favoured in Europe. Against these two contrasting positions, perhaps this model of triangulation provides a 'middle way'. In particular, it can inject some deduction into induction and add quantitative analysis to qualitative.

Third, is triangulation a means of discovering *grounded theory* (Glaser and Strauss 1967)? The idea of grounded theory can be seen to be theory development grounded in real-world data. If this view is taken, triangulation is worthy of consideration. More correctly, grounded theory is concerned with exploring new areas not covered by existing theories. This goal maps on to the very idea of issue-driven research. It is less about verifying and incrementally adding to existing theories, and more about discovering new theories. Practically, grounded research involves building theory out of qualitative data, exploring differences in datasets, ascertaining patterns of behaviour and generating propositions, frameworks and ideas – all of which may be further examined by appropriate next steps and perhaps in an iterative manner. Importantly in all four examples of research I described, the results are more 'theory' than 'proof'.

Thus in my own research journey, I may have discovered for myself both the rationale for grounded theory and one means of developing it.

Finally, as today's researchers are taught, it is important not only to understand questions of ontology, epistemology and methodology that arise in research, but to appreciate the caveats and limitations which therefore inevitably arise in any chosen social science research. Issue-driven research can appear atheoretical, managerialist, positivist and 'suspect' in a variety of ways. My arguments and propositions underpinning the triangulation model have ignored many such dilemmas. However, I am clear that the model implies at least as much qualitative endeavour as quantitative, involves interpretative and subjective work, contains implicit (but hopefully careful) compromises – for example, between rigour and relevance – and never should be seen as a finishing point.

And on this last claim, perhaps this chapter is inviting readers to either encourage or discourage me from a next step in this particular 'theory development' or is inviting others to take it further.

## References

Benbasat, I. (1987) 'An Analysis of Research Methodologies', in F.W. McFarlan (ed.) *The Information Systems Research Challenge*, Boston, MA: Harvard Business School Press.

Dickson, G.W., Leitheiser, R.L., Wetherbe, J.C. and Nechis, M. (1984) 'Key Information Systems Issues for the 1980s', *MIS Quarterly*, 10, 3, 135–139.

Earl, M.J. (1989) 'Shorko, S.A., Case Study CS93/3', Centre for Research in Information Management, London: London Business School.

Earl, M.J. (1990) 'Skandia International, Case Study CS93/2', Centre for Research in Information Management, London: London Business School.

Earl, M.J. (1993) 'Experiences in Strategic Information Systems Planning', *MIS Quarterly*, March, 1–24.

Earl, M.J. (1994) 'Knowledge as Strategy', in C. Ciborra, and T. Jelassi (eds) *Strategic Information Systems – A European Perspective*, Chichester: Wiley.

Earl, M.J. (2001) 'Knowledge Management Strategies: Toward a Taxonomy', *Journal of Management Information Systems*, 18, 1.

Earl, M.J. and Khan, B. (2001) 'The New Face of IT: How E-commerce is Shaping Perceptions and Practices', *Sloan Management Review*, 43, 1: 64–72.

Earl, M.J. and Nahapiet, J.E. (1999) 'Skandia, Case Study CS97–001–00', London: London Business School.

Earl, M.J. and Scott, I.A. (1998) *What on Earth is a CKO?*, London: London Business School and IBM.

Earl, M.J. and Scott, I.A. (1999) 'The Chief Knowledge Officer: A New Corporate Role', *Sloan Management Review*, 40, 2: 29–38.

Earl, M.J. and Vivian, P. (1993) 'The Role of the CIO: A Study of Survival', London: London Business School and Egon Zehnder, January.

Evans, P. and Wurster, T.S. (2000) *Blown to Bits: How the New Economics of Information Transforms Strategy*, Boston, MA: Harvard Business School Press.

Gill, J. and Johnson, P. (1991) *Research Methods for Managers*, London: Paul Chapman Publishing.

Glaser, B.G. and Strauss, A.L. (1967) *The Discovery of Grounded Theory: Strategies for Qualitative Research*, Chicago, IL: Aldine.

Niederman, F., Brancheau, J.C. and Wetherbe, J.C. (1991) 'Information Systems Management Issues for the 1990s', *MIS Quarterly*, 15, 4, 475–500.

Popper, K. (1959) *The Logic of Scientific Discovery*, London: Hutchinson.

Tapscott, D. (1966) *Digital Economy: Promise and Peril in the Age of Networked Intelligence*, New York: McGraw-Hill.

Yin, R.K. (1984) *Case Study Research: Design and Methods*, London: Sage.

# 3 Writing as reflexive knowledge production and as self-production

*David Sims*

Writing does not simply reflect knowledge that we wish to convey. It is one of the means by which knowledge is produced. The intellectual work of knowledge production takes place through conversation, including with the self, and writing is a means by which we discipline the conversations we have with ourselves. Writing is also an expressive activity in which we are aware of presenting ourselves. When academics write they know that their readers will not only judge their work; they will also make judgements about the author. We write as part of our presentation of ourselves (Goffman 1959).

Knowledge production and self-production are inter-related activities. The knower and the known are too closely intertwined for the production of knowledge and self to be separated. Writing can be part of a process of reflexive knowledge production. We write in order to be able to inspect our thought processes, and in order to allow others to do so, to improve the quality of our thinking, and in order to be able to offer others the opportunity to make use of some of our thoughts. We also write for the mixture of motives for which we speak; we write to entertain, to get attention, to be seen in a particular way. Our writing is not directed exclusively to the content or the style. In writing this piece now, my wish to gain your attention and to keep you reading goes alongside my wish to clarify my own thoughts and to contribute to yours on the process of writing as knowledge production. Either may become more dominant at a particular time, but neither can be allowed to overpower the other. The thought processes involved in writing are at the heart of the intellectual endeavour – they are what enable reflections to be more than fleeting, deliberations to build on earlier deliberations, and reframing to be something more purposeful than a continual and undirected pouncing on any alternative way of constructing ideas. But all of this is to no purpose if the reader is not sufficiently engaged to keep reading and to stay in the conversation.

We are all in the process of producing two different corpuses of work. The first of these is writing about topics such as (in my case) people in organizations. This is aimed at knowledge production. We are engaged in an often painful search for words that express as precisely as possible a multi-faceted, complex and ultimately indescribable world. We may yearn for the easy life that we imagine our colleagues in areas that are more naturally amenable to quantitative analysis have, memorably described as 'physics envy' (Clegg 2002). This is typical of any kind of hard work; we know how hard the work that we do is, and imagine that others' work is easy in comparison. A similar prejudice is to be found with surgeons, plumbers, lawyers, taxi drivers and indeed most of the diverse groups of working life.

The other corpus of work that we are engaged in is that we are all writing our own stories. All of us lead storied lives (Ochberg 1994). We create meaning for ourselves through the retrospective activity of telling stories about the past, the current activity of playing a part according to the story that we see ourselves as currently engaged in (Sims 2005a), by writing ourselves into others' stories (Edwards 2000), and the prospective activity of writing the next chapter of our story (Sims 2005a). Each of us is our own personal novelist. Some weave more everyday plots for themselves than others. Some seem to lose the plot and become caught up in the fantasies of their own stories. The British politician, novelist and liar Jeffrey Archer is a good example of this latter category. He seemed to enter a world where his view of his own life was as fictional as his novels. Others have a more mature and honourable relationship with their way of telling their story. This chapter discusses the aspects of writing that are self-production.

At their best, these are not two distinct activities; good intellectual work in the study of people in organizations engages in knowledge-production and self-production simultaneously, and this is what reflexive knowledge-production means. The understanding that we gain while writing casts its illumination in two different directions. In one is the knowledge that we wish to advance. In the other is the identity of the person who wishes to see that knowledge advanced, the writer. Those who we respect most keep these activities in balance with each other. Those who focus on knowledge production at the expense of self-production are likely to become repetitive and ungrounded. As they disappear more fully into their area of study, so they lose touch with why they are in that area, and with what they cared about that took them there initially. We may have a grudging admiration for those whose message is unsullied by contact with external realities, but we may also wonder why they are not more interested in dialoguing with the world around them. They have lost touch with who it is who is doing the writing. Those who focus on self-production at the expense of knowledge production are likely to end up seeming self-obsessed, and may also produce little knowledge. As they disappear more into their exploration of themselves, so those selves may seem to others more abstract, more self-absorbed and more disconnected than is healthy. They have lost touch with what it is they are writing about.

## Writing for knowledge production

Writing is a peculiarly challenging activity, which is often seen as the definitive task of the intellectual. In the past there were academics who wrote almost nothing but were believed by others to be major intellectual figures. Such people have all but disappeared. Many have mourned the passing of the non-writing intellectual, and also pointed out that some great minds of the past have spent long periods of time without writing. Einstein, it is often said, would not gain tenure these days.

Why is so much value placed on writing? Part of this is undoubtedly the coming of an audit culture. If people are not producing something which can be counted and audited, are they doing anything? Writing gives a physical product, a deliverable, to academic work.

But there is a better reason why writing is so highly valued in academic circles. In our early school work in mathematics many of us were told to 'show our workings'. Writing is the means by which we show our workings. I could speak much of the content of this paper without too much trouble, and certainly much more easily than I can write it. But by writing I am showing my workings, laying out my reasoning, both to myself and to my readers. The spoken word is ephemeral, and only limitedly challengeable. By the time I have been speaking for 15 minutes the finer points of what I wish to say will have been lost. If I am reasonably competent in handling discussion I can probably slide around any inconsistencies, and lapses in reasoning, any failures to back my ideas with argument and data. By the time anyone can pick us up on our spoken words, no one can really remember what was said. If I have written it, however, it is much easier to challenge. By writing I am opening my ideas up to interrogation by others.

I am also opening them up to interrogation by myself. Most of us are amazed when re-reading first drafts of materials at the amount of rubbish we are capable of writing. On occasions we may find ourselves wondering what idiot wrote a particular sentence or paragraph, before the awful truth dawns on us. Re-reading and improving our own material is a core activity for academics, and one of the hardest tasks for many. This is partly because it is less interesting than much of our reading. We know more or less what it is going to say – because we wrote it. But I think it is more because of the painful realization that our thoughts as stated in a first draft are not always of very good quality. The hardest work for many of us comes in that tussling with the first draft, trying to rid it of some of the poor quality thinking and improve it. But the thoughts slip around as we try to manipulate them. We are faced with difficult decisions about whether anyone will notice little slips of reasoning within our work. The temptation is to assume that, if anyone reads it at all, they will do so only quickly. That is when we realize that there is seriously hard intellectual work to be done in writing.

In addition, as we revise our work, we are not a static thinker revising a fixed document. We are learning at the same time as revising. We are continuing the process of thinking about our topic while revisiting the text that we wrote. So writing does not simply reflect our thinking, it constitutes it. As the writing is made more precise and apposite, so we lose the particular kind of clarity that ignorance gives us, the ability to make clear and simple statements about areas which we know deserve highly nuanced forms of expression. By writing, we have taken ourselves to the position where we know too much to be able to make the simplistic statement with comfort.

I have not yet mentioned the most frequently quoted reason for academic writing, which is that we need to offer our thoughts to others. While it is undoubtedly important to open our thoughts and our research to interrogation by colleagues, we hope to survive that interrogation sufficiently well that others develop an interest in what we have to say. We hope that they will read us, and be influenced by our writing. Beyond this, we hope that this reading may lead to that great aspect we noted above of intellectual work – conversation. Intellectual work demands that people converse, and good intellectual work demands that they converse well. Writing is the means by which intellectual workers begin such conversations, which may then continue either in writing or in speech.

## Writing for self-production

Like our discourses about knowledge, much of our discourse about how we produce ourselves is usually unwritten. We tell stories, make guest appearances in other people's stories, daydream ourselves into new situations and so on without the need for pen and paper.

There are times when we write for self-production without knowledge production. For example, when we write an application for a job, or revise our *curriculum vitae*, we are producing a self. The conventions of job application usually require a fairly consistent and coherent self, with a personal story which explains how the whole of the person's higher education and working life has been single-mindedly preparing them for precisely the job applied for (Sims 2002). In writing these documents we are usually all too aware that there are other ways that the story could be told. However, if we want the job, we manage to write application letters that suggest a cogency and a singleness of purpose which does not reflect how most of us fccl about our lives.

In this paper we are more interested in the self-production which happens within the context of intellectual work. Are our academic writings exercises in self-production too?

> I can't write without a reader. It's precisely like a kiss – you can't do it alone.
>
> John Cheever (1912–1982)

Academic papers are often spoken about as if they were written by and for disembodied minds. They are the expression of pure reason, a distillation of science, written to a tried and trusted formula, without the need for self-presentation or for asking the reader to engage emotionally.

We all know that this is completely untrue. We have no reason to suppose that our mind could be engaged without our emotions. We know that our emotions often lead our mind. So we get excited about one idea, angry about another idea, sense a total indifference to a field of thought, fall in love with some ideas and so on. All of this will affect our response to a piece of writing.

Given that we know this, and given the quotation from John Cheever above, what sort of production or presentation of self is going on when we write our academic papers? I would suggest that there is always a reader that we have in mind, and that we will be taking care of the way we come across to that reader. Sometimes we may imagine a particular person who we know reads the target journal, other times it will be more generalized. But in any case, we will be trying to make some kind of impression on the reader, for example by writing in a way which is meant to entice them, amuse them or impress them with our erudition. We have notions of what we would like the reader to think both of us and about the subject by the time they get to the end. More forcefully, we often have fears about what they might think of us, and we will engage in damage limitation exercises to decrease the likelihood of negative responses. The academic author is not so different from other authors. We suffer all the same problems: the writer's block, when we do not believe we are ever going to achieve fluency again; the isolation, when we are trying to work through some difficult section, while feeling that if we do not manage to say something clever about it, no one else will ever care; the insecurity, when we have no sounding board to tell us whether we are currently producing a stream of pure genius or pure garbage; the demand to produce, when it does not seem to matter how good or bad our work is, but only that so many words need to be produced to achieve a level of output which will keep us fed.

But even more interesting, from my perspective, is the question of what we are writing about. Surely we are focused on the production of academic knowledge, not the production of self?

On one memorable afternoon at the Stockholm School of Economics, in a seminar with staff and postgraduate students, we started to look at how we each came to be doing the research that we are doing. The policeman's son was doing work on the police, the teacher's daughter was studying processes of learning, the doctor's son was studying health systems, the child who could not get his parents' attention was studying how people got others to pay attention to them, the person who had been accused of laziness as a child was studying motivation, and so on. One way or another, everyone was studying something closely associated with their childhood, something to do with their own story. This leads me to suggest that our academic knowledge production is closely related to our own stories of ourselves. Our stories of ourselves as academics are intertwined with the rest of the story that we have of ourselves, of who we are, what we care about, where we are going, and so on. We care about what we write not only because it keeps us employed, but also because it is one of the ways in which we express who we are, who we wish to be taken to be, and who we would like to see ourselves becoming.

This last enterprise is sometimes more successful than we expect. Our academic writings are often identified so closely with us that, as others respond to them and see in them things that we were not aware of, these writings do not simply reflect us, but also create us. Others come to see us in terms of the ideas they have read from us, and we too share their view and develop and change according to those ideas. Academic writing becomes one of the ways in which we produce ourselves.

## Reflexive knowledge production

I recently heard the following said about someone being appointed to a professorial chair in a UK university:

> We had no choice but to appoint him. His list of publications looks great, and the research grants too. But it is a typical ambitious c.v. for someone who is really good at picking what the next big topic is going to be and getting in there not so early that they have to do much of the groundwork, but early enough so that they can make a contribution fairly quickly without having to think it through in depth, and then get out. You end up saying – 'so what does he actually care about' – but you never get an answer to that one.

Recent arguments about research in management (Gibbons *et al.* 1994; Tranfield and Starkey 1998) have stressed the iterative nature of management research. It is suggested that research is only management research if it iterates between worlds of theory and practice. That is not to argue that a highly theorized piece of economic or sociological research might not be very useful, or to argue that we might not learn a lot from a relatively untheorized action research project, but that it only counts as management research if it visits both of those worlds.

I would argue that good research exhibits a similar duality around reflexive knowledge production – that it is research that takes seriously both the production of knowledge and the production of the self of the holder of the knowledge.

It is the reflexive character of knowledge production that means that knowledge is grounded in a person. The idea that there can be knowledge of a human, personal, contextualized activity like managing without that knowledge having such a grounding is not convincing. It is rather like suggesting that you can take trigonometric readings of the position of a mountain without being quite sure where you and the theodolite are located. For the knowledge production to be of real value it has to be to some extent reflexive; it has to work for the situation and the person that generates it. The development of knowledge in management has been disappointing so far (Bennis and O'Toole 2005), and I would suggest that lack of reflexivity is a major reason for this. Without considerable awareness of who it is who is seeking the knowledge, and of the effect of their personal position and agenda on what they find, we are likely to end up simply with more of the correlations between two variables, neither of which necessarily exist, that currently disfigure the pages of many highly rated management journals. It is work, of a kind, but it fails the test of being intellectual work. If our research continues in that vein, we are condemned to the continuous repetition of triviality.

On the other hand, it is also possible for the reflexivity to become too much of an end in itself, for self-production to dominate knowledge production to such an extent that there is no real interest in the research. The narcissism of the researcher (Brown 1997) is taken as the justification for the research, and there is no real expectation of needing to test rigorously whether a person's ideas are well founded; the sincere belief of a researcher that they have discovered 'their truth' is taken as sufficient. Several postmodern schools of argument have gone down this path, although it should be clearly distinguished from the careful and scholarly work of others in 'new paradigm' research (Reason and Rowan 1981; Reason and Bradbury 2001). The author who is engaged in nothing but self-production may be interesting in all sorts of ways, and possibly even to others, but they are not engaged in the intellectual work of management research.

## Of millstones, bastards and velveteen rabbits

In this section I will reflect on three of my recent publications to see how my claims above relate to them. In a paper on a narrative understanding of the pressures suffered by middle managers (Sims 2003), I considered the pressure on middle managers to tell convincing stories to three different audiences – their superiors, their subordinates and themselves – a process in which, I suggested, they found themselves being ground between the millstones. I originally wrote this for a conference on the theme of 'subaltern storytelling'. So I needed to produce some knowledge about the storytelling activities of those in relatively less powerful positions. However, I also wanted to reflect that many very senior people had discussed with me their feeling of powerlessness in ways which would have been a surprise to many of their subordinates. In other words, many people seemed to feel that they were in the middle, even if their colleagues and the organization chart placed them higher than that. At the conference I was given very positive feedback about the coherence of the paper by some people whose opinion I respected, and this encouraged me to revise it for journal publication. At this stage, I spent many more hours developing the ideas, and coming across gaps in my own argument which I found horrifying. But I was kept motivated because I had experienced most of the pressures that I was writing about. As the head of a business school, I had felt the pressures of the middle managers in my paper. So at the same time that I was understanding and presenting my data and analysis, I was understanding my own experience and finding ways to cope with the sense in which my own working experience had left me 'between the millstones'. This is a very short account of a long story; the response from referees and the journal editor led me into many more hours of intellectual work, as I strove to take account of many criticisms and suggestions which seemed valid to me as soon as I read them, but which I would not have come up with for myself. For example, the concept of the vulnerability of stories to attack or non-validation by others had always been part of the paper, but its meaning was far more developed and refined by the end of the dialogues with editors and referees. This illustrates the point above about the value of writing in creating a dialogue with others.

If the paper about middle managers started from knowledge production and developed to encompass self-production, my paper about indignation in organizations (Sims 2005b) worked the other way. I started from a puzzle about how people who maintain a fairly pluralistic discourse about others, and yet lose patience with some of those others to the extent that they do not simply feel they disagree with them, or feel that they have misunderstood them, but that the other has to be described as just 'a bastard'. This paper started from a puzzle which I felt as much for myself (how could I find myself getting so indignant with some of my fellow beings, and have so little interest in understanding their different perspectives?) as for its intellectual puzzlement. Who was this indignant, unreasonable being? And could I change his mind, or at least develop him, or at least come to terms with him, by writing about this topic and trying to understand the hypocrisy which always seemed to be involved with anger? The knowledge production proceeded quite similarly to the previous paper, with presentations to lively audiences followed by solitary writing effort, followed by very exciting interactions with editors and referees. To start off with the title of the paper referred to 'moral indignation'. One of the early audience members argued strongly that the indignation I was writing about was not necessarily anything to do with morals and mores, so the title evolved. The paper drew a characteristic range of responses from referees. On first submission, for example, they all commented on my writing style:

*Reviewer 1*:   The article is written in a lively and engaging style, and is full of ideas which are well linked together.

*Reviewer 2*:   For a paper acknowledging narrative neatness, this is a surprisingly scrappy and repetitive piece of writing.

*Reviewer 3*:   This is a clearly written paper with the potential for publication after some expansions and revisions.

While I have chosen to illustrate the issue with a clear disagreement about the writing style, disagreements about the theoretical developments in the paper were of similar strength. Here, the writer can be considerably helped in making sense by the advice of the editor, particularly if that advice is of such good quality as this:

*Editor*:   The reviewers are divided about whether or not the paper is clearly written. In my view it is clear in some places but not in others. Reviewer 1 gives a very clear summary of the line of the argument, and this could help with rewriting the introduction.'

I agreed with the editor as soon as I had read him, but these were not points that had struck me before. The analysis that reviewer 1 had done of my argument in the paper was, in my view, more than accurate – he had understood it better than I understood it myself when I wrote it. He laid out my argument carefully, and he disagreed with my final step. So in the revised version, one of the things I did was to show much more clearly how my data led me to that final step. This means that the writing process had been helped by a referee who had seen my argument more clearly than I saw it myself, an editor who pointed out to me what a good summary this was, and then by my own efforts to explain myself better to an unknown other who was dialoguing with me.

The velveteen rabbit (Sims 2004c) came about by a different route. On my way to work I heard an account of an old American children's story, about a velveteen rabbit which only came to life when loved by a child. I was immediately struck by the parallels between this and many situations I had seen in organizations which seemed to come to life when they were loved more than they could reasonably expect by some of their members. Examples came flooding to mind, and again I wrote a conference paper on the basis of it. The discursive processes of academic debate with colleagues about the paper were similar, but in this case the extent to which the story re-wrote me is even more apparent. As I thought through the examples that I was using of the way in which some people's love for their organizations seemed to bring those organizations to life, I felt that the theories that I had held for many years about reification and personification of organizations did not work. In a section of the paper entitled 'Led by a rabbit' (page 211), I said:

> I acknowledge the power of this dilemma with some reluctance. I have spent some 25 years writing and thinking about organizations as individual and social constructions, and I am reluctant to have my mind changed by the resonances of a children's story. However, while I can still rehearse the arguments against reification, the narrative truth and sense-making power of the idea that people can bring an organization to life by loving it convinces me far more. I give examples in this chapter of organizations being loved to life. I might not have recognized these before I was both liberated and captured by the Velveteen Rabbit.

I go on to describe some of the train of thought which this led me into, and continue, in a section entitled 'Dialogue with a rabbit' (page 212), thus:

> I would now argue that the anti-personifying view is based on a model of organizations as mechanisms, which has been the sociological orthodoxy but which has never persuaded people not to treat organizations more like persons. The feelings of love, hate or indifference that so many have felt for their organizations over time are soundly based in experience, and are not simply a category error.

This was part of the eventual, published paper, but formed no part of the original conference paper. When I gave the original paper, I had been asked whether what I was saying might lead to personifying of organizations. The more I thought about it, the more I thought the question was right in what it implied about the paper but wrong in the way it expected me to respond;

the paper and the logic of the story were right, and the prohibition on personification wrong. Thus my whole frame of thinking, and my view of my identity as an organizational researcher in relation to my materials, was changed by the act of writing, by questions from others about my writing, and by an internal thought process which resulted from those questions. This was writing as knowledge production, but producing a knowledge which would have completely surprised me when I started to write that paper. It also produced a self in which I understand the relationship between the writer and their materials quite differently. I was written by that paper as much as I wrote it.

Another debate was around my use of the word 'love' for the feelings that people developed for their organizations. One of the reviewers suggested that it was too broad and ill-defined a concept; how about 'cathexis'. At this point, other readers and the editor supported my view that love might be ill-defined, but so were the feelings that I was trying to describe here. The looseness of the label seemed entirely appropriate, although I do not think I had been conscious of that until it was challenged. So I strengthened the argument to show that there was a range of emotions involved just like the range of emotions covered by the word 'love', rather than anything that could be more tightly defined, like cathexis. My knowledge production was thus, I think, enhanced by the critical comment from the reviewer, albeit in the opposite direction from that which he was arguing. My self-production as a straight-talking person who did not wish to hide behind academic jargon was also challenged by his comment, and I believe that those who supported my resistance to changing the word 'love' also understood how important it was to my self-production.

## Conclusion

This paper has argued that good work in management research cannot proceed without attention being paid both to knowledge-production and self-production. I have given examples from my own writing experience to illustrate how writing works as a discourse for me through which knowledge is produced. I have discussed some of the ways in which writing sparks off discussion and then further thought, and the ways in which it often involves both reconstruction of the writer's thinking and the writer's self. In the spirit of reflexivity, I should now ask how the internal and external dialogues of writing have affected the production of knowledge in the present paper, and to what extent I may have been rewritten by it, but I am still too close to it to know. Is it not only my chapter but also my self that has been edited by Löwstedt and Stjernberg?

# References

Bennis, W.G. and O'Toole, J. (2005) 'How Business Schools Lost Their Way', *Harvard Business Review*, 83, 5: 96–104.

Brown, A.D. (1997) 'Narcissism, Identity and Legitimacy', *Academy of Management Review*, 22: 643–686.

Clegg, S. (2002) 'Why Distributed Discourse Matters', in L. Holmes, D.M. Hosking and M. Grieco (eds) *Organizing in the information age*, London: Ashgate, 4–12.

Edwards, L. (2000) *A narrative journey to understanding self*, unpublished M.Phil, London: Brunel University.

Gibbons, M., Limoges, C., Nowotny, H., Schwartzman, S., Scott, P. and Trow, M. (1994) *The New Production of Knowledge: The Dynamics of Science and Research in Contemporary Societies*, Thousand Oaks, CA: Sage.

Goffman, E. (1959) *The Presentation of Self in Everyday Life*, New York: Anchor.

Ochberg, R. (1994) 'Life Stories and Storied Lives', in A. Lieblich and R. Josselson (eds) *Exploring Identity and Gender: The Narrative Study of Lives*, Thousand Oaks, CA: Sage, 113–144.

Reason, P. and Bradbury, H. (eds) (2001) *Handbook of Action Research: Participative Inquiry and Practice*, London: Sage.

Reason, P. and Rowan, J. (1981) *Human Inquiry: A Sourcebook of New Paradigm Research*, Chichester: Wiley.

Sims, D. (2002) *Careers as Prospective Story Telling: A Narrative Understanding*, paper presented at the European Group on Organization Studies, Barcelona.

Sims, D. (2003) 'Between the Millstones: A Narrative Account of the vulnerability of Middle Managers' Storying', *Human Relations*, 56, 10: 1195–1211.

Sims, D. (2004) 'The Velveteen Rabbit and Passionate Feelings for Organizations', in Y. Gabriel (ed.) *Myths, Stories and Organizations*, Oxford: Oxford University Press, 209–222.

Sims, D. (2005a) 'Living a Story and Storying a Life: A Narrative Understanding of the Distributed Self', in A. Pullen and S. Linstead (eds) *Organization and Identity*, London: Routledge.

Sims, D. (2005b) 'You Bastard: A Narrative Exploration of the Experience of Indignation within Organizations', *Organizational Studies*, 26, 11: 1625–1640.

Tranfield, D. and Starkey, K. (1998) 'The Nature, Social Organization and Promotion of Management Research: Towards Policy', *British Journal of Management*, 9, 4: 341–354.

# Part II
# Approaches to knowledge production

# 4   Making sense of stockbrokers' performance

## Reflections about the phenomenographic approach

*Jesper Blomberg*

In this chapter, I will describe how my constructionist epistemological position once made me dismiss most formalized empirical research methods. In my opinion, formalized methods were in conflict with constructionism. But when conducting constructivist empirical research, I gradually started to feel the need for a method that did not conflict with constructivism. I will also describe here how I found such a method, as well as my attempt to apply it to my research. The chapter will focus on the process of learning and applying phenomenography in a specific empirical study. The study aimed at making sense of why the ability to generate trade differed between individual stockbrokers working in the same firm, at the same trading table and with the same type of clients (wealthy private investors). Using the experiences of this study, the phenomenographic approach will be evaluated as a formal constructionist method. The chapter will end with conclusions both regarding phenomenography as a constructionist method and the ups and downs of using formalized methods in constructionist empirical research.

## The epistemological journey

From the very beginning of my work as an organizational scientist, I was interested in the theory of science and questions regarding ontology, epistemology and theories of truth – not as a field of its own, but as a prerequisite for doing good empirical research. When I learned about academic organizational research, I quickly converted. From being a kind of uneducated positivist, taking a naive empiricist position for granted, I became a convinced constructionist. In doing social science, I felt very close to both Weber's sociology and Mead's social psychology. Thus, my research aimed to construct accounts of meaning and motive – action schemes – and not to settle for cause–effect explanations. My philosophical stance was something of a mix of neo-Kantian philosophy of the Simmels kind, a social-phenomenology inspired by Schutz, and the American pragmatism of James and Dewey. And thus, my finding should be viewed as generated from both empirical and logical investigations, and always relative to the interests and perspectives of the researcher and the historical context in which they were produced. I appreciated the post-structural critique, the linguistic turn and the semiotic and discursive theories in vogue, even if I thought some of the formulations took it a bit far.

My neo-Kantian/social-phenomenological/pragmatic position felt more comfortable for me. My then-new epistemological position had two practical consequences for how I viewed and conducted, in my own opinion, 'good' empirical research: First, epistemology had to be an integrated part of any of my research efforts. Second, I usually disliked 'methods' in the more formalized technical sense, because they were usually based on an empiricist objectivism that I did not agree with. In my early years as an organizational scientist, I regarded formalized technical method as contradictory to my constructionist epistemology. I did not only prefer the latter, I believed it was the only position that one could hold, given that one had studied the matter thoroughly. Instead of unreflected use of method, I believed that epistemological reflection, i.e. explicitly building your perspective and research efforts on both epistemological assumptions and empirical impressions, would produce better science. My epistemological journey took me away from formalized method and into the world of reflective theorizing on empirical impressions (see Figure 4.1). My favourite quote at the time was Habermas' (1987: vii) somewhat harsh formulation: 'That we disavow reflection is positivism.'

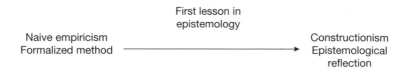

First lesson in
epistemology

Naive empiricism                                    Constructionism
Formalized method    ─────────────────▶    Epistemological
                                                       reflection

*Figure 4.1* My epistemological journey, Part 1.

## A growing unrest

In many ways, the constructionist position I held, and the research I conducted, worked just fine. When meeting opposition from colleagues, I could dismiss the critique rather simply with the argument of their not being very well informed regarding epistemological knowledge. I met the critique about lack of method with the argument that method would make my constructionist research less consistent and unable to produce new knowledge about the empirical subject matter. I could be quite snobbish, stating explicitly at times that if one did not see or understand the implicit philosophical references of my texts one should go back and study these matters before criticizing my good constructionist research efforts.

But is it possible that the critique did affect my view on method after all? Or was it perhaps my once-held positivistic position that somehow spoke back to me from the past? Regardless, I did start to feel a sense of unrest with my own position. I had learned the lesson regarding epistemology, a lesson that in my opinion led to better research than either naive and sophisticated positivism. But wouldn't my research become even better if I could find a method of a more formalized kind, consistent with my epistemological stance? At least I felt a need to find out. In the middle of the 1990s, just before I entered the last few months of work on my thesis, I stumbled upon something different – the phenomenographic approach.

## The phenomenographic approach

Phenomenography was developed by a Swedish educational research group in the 1970s (Marton *et al.* 1977). The phenomenographic approach aims at describing qualitatively different ways in which aspects of reality are experienced (Marton 1981, 1986). Overviews of the development of phenomenography are offered by Marton *et al.* (1984), Ramsden (1988), Dall'Alba and Hasselgren (1996) and Marton and Booth (1997). Although Alexandersson's (1994) count of the uses of the phenomenographic approach amounts to more than 50 doctoral theses and between 500 and 1000 research reports, and although the approach is well established within educational research, phenomenography has had a short history in the field of organizational analysis. The introduction of the approach to organizational analysis is to a great extent a product of Sandberg's work. He has both applied phenomenography in studies of competence and elaborated the approach's phenomenological foundations (Sandberg 1994, 2000).

The phenomenographic approach to interpreting texts has similarities with both traditional content analysis and semiotic analysis, but there are also some important differences. Compared to content analysis (Krippendorff 1980; Weber 1990), the phenomenographic approach relies less on counting words, sentences or any other sub-unit of a text, and relies more on making intuitive interpretations and different types of (phenomenological) reflections upon, and logical investigations of, these interpretations.

Compared to semiotic analyses (Eco 1979; Fiol 1990), the phenomenographic approach offers a less formalized method. Instead it can be said to be more inductive. It aims at being as faithful or sensitive as possible to the interviewee's own conceptions of the studied phenomena (Marton 1986; Sandberg 1994: 64). The more formalized semiotic analysis produces a rather specific structure representing the text's underlying meaning, but this structure does not necessarily inform us in a way that is consistent with the interest of a specific study. Compared to formalized semiotic analysis, phenomenography is more flexible in regards to different use and research purposes.

How I ran into phenomenography can best be described as – by chance. I happened to read Sandberg's dissertation from 1994, which applied a phenomenographic approach to the study of competence among engine optimizers at Volvo Cars. The point of departure in the dissertation thesis was an introduction to the phenomenographic approach and a discussion of how it could work as a tool to understand competence at a workplace. The rest of the book was an application of the approach used to analyze the competence of the engine optimizers. Since the main reference in my almost-finished dissertation was to the social-phenomenological work of Alfred Schutz (1962, 1964, 1966) and phenomenography has explicit links to phenomenological epistemology, it was logical to enter a dialogue with the author (Sandberg), who at that time had been recruited to a post-doctoral position at our school. Jörgen Sandberg's ambition was not only to introduce phenomenography to organizational research. He also wanted to critically examine and develop the approach's connections to phenomenology.

It did not take me long to recognize that my view on constructionism with epistemological roots in neo-Kantianism, pragmatism and, above all, Schutz's social-phenomenology was different from Sandberg's. Sandberg was much more influenced by phenomenography's quest to find the 'faithful' conceptions of reality in the studied actors' life-worlds. This ambition was also well-aligned with the early writings of Husserl (1962, 1970a), where phenomenology is used to construct an absolute ground for scientific knowledge, a project Husserl later at least partly abandoned (Husserl 1970b). I was convinced that, like all other approaches and methods, phenomenography always produced results that were just as much a consequence of the researchers' explicit and implicit knowledge, interests, assumptions, use of methods, etc. In my opinion, neither phenomenological epistemology nor phenomenographic method could detect 'essence' or some objective/absolute truth. At best, a rigorous use of epistemology and method could increase the researcher's control between the first-degree constructions of the empirical world studied and the second-degree constructions that the researcher produced in the form of her or his results. Sandberg and others who practised phenomenographic research often responded to my somewhat critical remarks by saying that I should not dismiss phenomenography before I had tried it. So I decided to do just that.

## Studying the life-worlds of stockbrokers

As part of a larger research project focusing on the actors and their competence and interaction on financial markets (Blomberg 2005), I set out to understand why some stockbrokers were so much more successful than others in generating trade and thereby generating both courtage revenues[1] for the brokerage firms they worked for and income for themselves. My pre-understanding was that stockbrokers probably conceived their work in qualitatively different ways. This thesis stemmed from my earlier research of other types of work (Blomberg 1995), but was also consistent with the standard results of phenomenographic studies. As with the early use of phenomenography in classroom research, my plan was to use phenomenography in the stockbrokerage firm's trading room. And similarly to how pedagogic research tried to understand why pupils learned different things with different speed in the same classroom, I wanted to understand why stockbrokers in the same trading room generated different amounts of trade and revenues. The standard result from the phenomenographic classroom studies was that pupils learned differently from one another because they conceived their life-worlds in the classroom in qualitatively different ways. Normally, the phenomenographic method resulted in the construction of three to six qualitatively different conceptions of the studied actors' life-worlds. My guess was that, with the help of phenomenography, I would be able to construct three to six qualitatively different ways to conceive stockbroking in the trading room.

My study showed an interesting, but far from simple, correspondence between a stockbroker's success and the way that stockbroker perceived his or her work. Thus, in this respect, there is a strong similarity to the general pattern of results found in phenomenographic studies.

## The empirical study

The study was conducted in a stockbrokerage firm that operates on the Stockholm Stock Exchange (SSE). The empirical material was to a large extent collected/constructed through ethnographic observations and interviews. The phenomenographic part of the study focused on 14 stockbrokers who worked next to each other around the same trading table. They all participated in the same morning meetings, listened to the same analysts, all used the same type of monitors, and were all informed by the same on-line news services. They also dealt with the same type of clients (wealthy private investors). Formally, their work situations were very similar.

The 14 brokers were interviewed one by one in a room next to the trading room. The interviews took place in the 1½-hour period immediately preceding the opening of the exchange. The interviews were conducted during two months when the SSE was characterized as strong and stable. As is usually the case in phenomenographic studies (Marton 1981, 1986; Dall'Alba and Hasselgren 1996), the interviews were highly unstructured and geared towards producing an as rich, detailed and concrete a description of the interviewee's work world as possible (Kvale 1996). Each interview was transcribed before the interpretative work started. The transcribed interviews would then constitute the main material in trying to construct different conceptions of stockbroking.

These conceptions could be thought of as important results in themselves. They could be viewed as important information about a relatively unstudied type of job. But my ambition was higher; these conceptions might also be able to explain, or in some way make sense of, the varying ability of stockbrokers to get their clients to trade in stock.

The ability to generate trade and revenues differed considerably between the brokers studied. As will be shown below, the top-performing broker out-performs the lowest performing broker by more than eight times, and the top two brokers' yearly courtage revenues amount to over seven times as much as the bottom two. Whether one looks at the variation in courtage revenues on a weekly, monthly or quarterly basis, the same pattern emerges. Also, the top three high-performing brokers for the year in question were on top the year before the study was conducted as well as the year after. Thus, the performance records show a clear and fairly stable difference in performance between the brokers.

## Ideal types vs phenomenographic conceptions

I wanted to make another detour from the most direct and widest route through the phenomenographic landscape; I wanted to construct ideal types from the brokers' own stories of their work. Ideal types, in Weber's and Schutz's sense of the concept, are *not* the same as approximative simplifications of a complex reality. The ideal type is a deliberate exaggeration of some aspects of reality (Weber 1947; Schutz 1962, 1967). This is very different from the phenomenographic ambition to construct conceptions that are as 'faithful' to the studied actors' life-worlds as possible. The ideal type implies an active constructionist doing with the empirical material what his or her interest, research questions, assumptions and theory demands. Phenomenographic research implies a more passive inductionist approach, letting the empirical material speak for itself. I just could not bracket the standard arguments against this kind of inductionist/grounded approach (see Chalmers (1999) for these arguments), and I therefore wanted to mix ideal-typical logic with a phenomenographic approach in my interpretative work.

The first step in the interpretative work was therefore to construct ideal-typical stories or narratives of stockbroking from the transcribed interviews with the brokers.

The interpretative strategy used to extract ideal types from the interview data was: (1) to maximize the consistency within each story; (2) to maximize the differences between them; and (3) to construct as few stories as possible but which, taken together, exhaust the ways stockbroking was described by the brokers.

The constructed stories were 'initial' and 'pragmatic' in the sense that the interpretative work did not follow a formalized technique used to remove all intuitive interpretations. On the contrary, the interpretative work followed, and was motivated by, a pragmatist and phenomenological epistemology. This epistemology postulates that *all* interpretations are *always* intuitive, and that scientific rigor is *not* enhanced by the use of methods that try to avoid intuition but by those that begin with making the intuitive interpretations explicit (James 1981; Husserl 1964; Schutz 1962: 99–117; Spiegelberg 1982: 678–715).

Both pragmatism and phenomenology (as well as Kant) postulate that ongoing experience, 'the stream of thought', always consists of a united or synthetic consciousness (Schutz 1967: 45–53; 1966: 1–14). This implies that any analysis of experience, as stories, conceptions or in any other form, should start with the formulation of one or several entities characterized by synthetic unity. Once they have been made explicit, these entities can be carved up in the analysis, not the other way around. Or as James puts it:

> . . . instead of starting with the mind's supposed elements (which are always abstractions) and gradually building up, I have tried to keep the reader in contact throughout as many chapters as possible, with the actual conscious unity which each of us at all times feels himself to be. [. . .] But as I wished to disentangle psychology as far as possible from any close alliance with ultimate questions of metaphysics, I have limited my contention of unity to what is empirically verifiable, namely to the unity of each passing wave or field of consciousness.
>
> (James 1981: 1483)

The synthetic, partly intuitive ideal types that were constructed could be formulated as four stories of stockbroking. See Boxes 4.1, 4.2, 4.3 and 4.4.

**Box 4.1**   *The drama of complexity*[2]

My work is really demanding, both mentally and physically speaking. Each day is unique and has its own challenges. There's all the background information about everything happening in and around the business world. I have to follow the TV news from early in the morning, read the papers on my way to work, and then listen carefully to the analysts and my colleagues, all before the exchange opens. At the same time, I have to check the news on the monitor. All this information has to be taken in and processed before the exchange opens. But this is just the beginning – at nine o'clock the real work begins. The first one or two hours are usually more intense than the rest of the day, something can happen and change everything at any time during the day. You make decisions all the time – who to call, what to recommend, how to react. You have to follow the exchange's movements on the monitor, keep an eye on the news, recommend different transactions to different clients, and listen to your clients' information, all at the same time. Being able to do this efficiently is what makes you a good stockbroker. I love my work. It's very challenging, and I learn a lot every day.

**Box 4.2**   *The tragedy of boredom*

My work is really simple. I really don't understand why it's so well paid. If you know how to talk to your clients, and after a couple of years it isn't very hard, all you have to do is to give the impression that you know something they don't. The work runs itself. Each day is more or less the same. You sit in front of your monitor, you listen to the 'noise' in the trading room, and you talk to your clients over the phone. What to say is evident from what your colleagues are doing, and they're doing the same thing you are. You don't need any specific information or to be able to do any advanced type of analysis. It's like selling vacuum cleaners or any other simple product. If it weren't for the money, I would never keep this job. But for now, I can't afford to do anything else.

**Box 4.3** *The comedy of competition*

It's like playing an interactive combat game on your computer with your friends. When I get news on my monitor I immediately evaluate it, not the news itself but how my competitors might be reacting to it. Sometimes it's a 5-second news item; sometimes it's a 15-second one. By that I mean that it is possible to make some money on it in the next 5 or 15 seconds, after that it's too late – the others are giving or have given the same recommendation to the same type of clients as I have. I have a pretty good picture of which brokers I am playing against. There aren't that many brokers at that many stock brokerage firms who deal with the same type of stocks and clients as I do. A good stockbroker is one who is a good competitor in the game. If I'm faster than anyone else in judging how my competitors will react to a specific item of news, and in getting clients to do business, then I'm the best. It's a fun game.

**Box 4.4** *The tale of industrial wisdom*

To me stockbroking is all about understanding the world, and making something out of that understanding. It's pretty easy to get stuck in the short-term noise, to only try to make money on the latest piece of news or trend. I'm conservative, maybe too conservative, but I want to understand what's going on out there in industrial life. I've always been interested in analyzing companies; I have my favourite branches and my favourite companies. I could never recommend that a customer sell or buy based on short-term noise alone. Working as a stockbroker gives you a chance to improve your understanding of companies and of life itself.

## Faithful but not simply induced

It is quite obvious that it would be hard to combine these four stories into one consistent description of stockbroking. To conceive stockbroking as both playing computer games with friends and understanding the logic of the industrial world would be somewhat paradoxical. And to conceive stockbroking both as a challenging intellectual activity and as the equivalent of 'selling vacuum cleaners' seems rather contradictory. Despite these contradictions, all 14 stockbrokers did express all four ideal types to some degree. Taken together, the four stories can be said to be faithful to the brokers' descriptions of their work, but in the ideal-typical form, not one of them is faithful to any one broker's description. The stockbrokers' descriptions were neither consistent nor 'pure'.

However, in order to construct interpretations – to make sense – of each individual stockbroker's performance, measured in accumulated courtage revenues, I had to investigate how each stockbroker's description related to the four stories. I knew that the four stories were extracted from the brokers' descriptions, but I didn't know how much the typified four stories resembled each broker's description. To determine the extent to which each broker's description related to each of the four stories, the phenomenographic approach seemed to offer a very suitable method. Phenomenography offered me a tool to find out how each stockbroker's description of work resembled the four ideal types. Maybe I could have conducted some kind of similar analyses without phenomenography or any other type of method, but with a method like phenomenography my interpretations would follow a more structured, describable process and thereby be more transparent. If phenomenography worked, my earlier unrest for not using 'method' would hopefully calm down. See Figure 4.2.

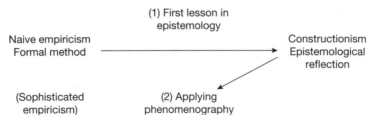

*Figure 4.2* My epistemological journey, Parts 1 and 2.

## The benefits of phenomenography

Phenomenography aims at being as faithful or sensitive as possible to the interviewee's own conceptions of the studied phenomena (Merton 1986; Sandberg 1994: 64). The interpretative method used did not need to be very precise, as long as it enabled a rough estimation of the extent to which each of the 14 stockbrokers' descriptions resembled the four stories of stockbroking. My impression of phenomenography is that it lacks precision, which, in this (explorative) study, was an acceptable drawback. See Box 4.5.

As a result of the phenomenographic analysis, the transcribed interviews were clustered as illustrated in Table 4.1. The information in Table 4.1 was only regarded as a hint or rough interpretation of how each broker conceives his work. In the following analysis the numbers in Table 4.1 were not treated

---

**Box 4.5**  *Phenomenography in action*

The phenomenographic analysis of the transcribed interviews started with acquiring a general grasp of each broker's conception of his work. This was done *not* by focusing on particular statements themselves, as in most forms of content analysis, but by focusing on the meaning of statements in relation to surrounding statements and to the transcript as a whole. The transcripts were then sorted into groups according to how much my impression of each broker's conception resembled each of the four stories constructed earlier. The second step was to shift the focus from each individual broker's conception to the relations between them. Transcripts were compared both within and between groups. In some cases, the interpretations were adjusted and the conceptions were judged to have more or less resemblance with the different ideal types than previously. In these cases, the broker's conceptions changed places in and/or between the groups. Finally, each conception was analyzed again by breaking up the transcript and trying to impose other interpretations on smaller and smaller units of text. Why had I interpreted each transcript as more or less similar to the four types? Was there any way I could change my impression? Steps two and three were then repeated until I could not find any way to change my interpretations.

The interpretative work involved a lot of rereading of transcripts and a lot of moving of each transcript in relation to the other transcripts and to the four stories. In this way, the first pragmatic and preliminary interpretation was tested according to a phenomenological variation analysis (Schutz 1962: 113–115; Spiegelberg 1982: 696–699). There are points of similarity between this last step of the analysis and traditional content analysis, such as focusing on the meaning of individual statements, but there is at least one major difference. In the phenomenographic approach, it is a repeated step in an interpretative process that starts with an attempt to construct preliminary impressions of the unity of consciousness of the studied brokers. These repeated last steps lead to reinterpretation of the conceptions and thereby regrouping of the transcripts.

---

as 'social facts' (Durkheim 1991: 103–110) or as statistical 'objective structures' (Bourdieu 1977: 21, 1984: 258–259, 507). They were treated for what they were – rhetorical devices that sometimes efficiently express meaningful accounts. An important role these numbers filled was to fuel the analysis that followed.

Table 4.1 A rough interpretation of the resemblance between the individual brokers' conceptions and the four typified stories, on a scale of 1 (almost none) to 5 (very close)

| Broker | The drama of complexity | The tragedy of boredom | The comedy of competition | The tale of industrial wisdom | Accumulated courtage | Years as broker[3] |
|---|---|---|---|---|---|---|
| a | 3 | 1 | 3 | 5 | 8816 | 5 (5) |
| b | 3 | 1 | 5 | 5 | 6885 | 15 (15) |
| c | 4 | 1 | 4 | 3 | 3871 | 10 (14) |
| d | 3 | 2 | 1 | 5 | 2793 | 16 (16) |
| e | 1 | 5 | 2 | 2 | 2002 | 13 (13) |
| f | 1 | 4 | 2 | 4 | 2002[4] | 20 (20) |
| g | 4 | 2 | 3 | 3 | 1849 | 3 (3) |
| h | 3 | 3 | 2 | 3 | 1737 | 7 (12) |
| i | 5 | 1 | 4 | 2 | 1693 | 3 (3) |
| j | 2 | 1 | 3 | 5 | 1358 | 1 (3) |
| k | 1 | 4 | 1 | 5 | 1270 | 15 (15) |
| l | 3 | 1 | 2 | 5 | 1027 | 1 (38) |
| m | 2 | 2 | 3 | 3 | 1013 | 4 (15) |
| n | 5 | 1 | 3 | 1 | 198 | 0.25 (10) |

Although the empirical base was much too small to fulfil positivistic demands on material appropriate for statistical analysis, a quick look at the numbers in Table 4.1 offered some preliminary interpretations. First, one was struck by the relative similarity between the top and bottom of the list. But one could also see that the top-performing brokers' descriptions have higher total resemblance to the four stories than the lowest-performing brokers. It was possible to detect more correlations between courtage and how the 14 descriptions relate to the four stories. However, these correlations could not be described as strong. Other quantitative data, such as the broker's age and the number of years he had worked as a broker, did correlate more strongly with the accumulated courtage. Moreover, such results were of limited interest in themselves; they did not fulfil the constructionist's demands for an interesting interpretation that uncovers 'underlying meanings that would otherwise remain imperceptible' (Fiol 1990: 378). Instead of being quasi-positivist, and treating bad statistics on a sample that was too small, I continued the interpretative work according to another strategy and looked at individual cases in an attempt to construct interpretations on a level below quantitative data and below discourse.

By looking more closely at the stories of high- and low-performing brokers, and comparing brokers that had worked as brokers for a similar number of years, a pattern of differences between the stories of individual brokers began to emerge. Both within some individual brokers' descriptions and between brokers' descriptions, there seemed to be a contradiction between 'work' and 'social interaction'. By bringing in theories that treat work and interaction as contradictory, two opposing types of conceptions of stockbroking, or two types of stockbrokers, could be constructed (Blomberg 2004). My interest in making sense of brokers' economic performance, my empirical impressions and my choice of method and theory enabled me to construct *the socialized interactional broker* type and *the objectified instrumental broker* type (see Figure 4.3). The former appeared to outperform the latter. By comparing different experienced brokers and analyzing their stories with the help of Habermas' reading of young Hegel (Habermas 1984: 181–208, 1988: 149–203, 303–370; McCarthy 1988), I was also able to construct a processual account for how these two types of brokers could develop out of a typical inexperienced broker.

How these results were reached, and their relevance and implications, are described and discussed in detail elsewhere (Blomberg 2004). What the main point is here, though, is that the construction was just as much a result of the phenomenographic empirical study as of the chosen theories. Without the quantitative measurements of the brokers' economic performance, without the brokers' 'faithful' descriptions of their work, without the phenomenographic analysis of how these descriptions resembled the four ideal

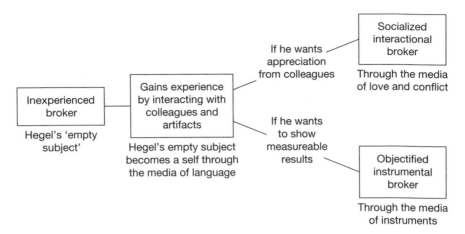

*Figure 4.3* The development of two opposing types of conceptions of stockbroking.

types of stockbroking, and without the help of Habermas' and Hegel's theories of work and interaction, the above results would not be attainable. Therefore, the empirical study and the theory-driven analysis conducted cannot be regarded as purely phenomenographic; rather, it is an example of the mixed discourse of constructionism. It has its epistemological foundation in neo-Kantian philosophy of knowledge, in American pragmatism and in social-phenomenology.

## Phenomenography as a method

In my opinion, and I believe the conducted study of the stockbrokers supports this opinion, a strength of phenomenography is its flexible character. Since it lacks precision, one can use it in many different ways. It is not as transparent as, in my opinion, and I believe the study of the stockbrokers supports this opinion, one of the strengths of counting words or sentences might appear to be, but this lack of transparency invites the researcher to be more creative. According to more positivistic and empiricist positions, a method's lack of precision and flexibility is regarded as bad – it leaves the research open to the uncontrolled subjectivity of the researcher. Method is regarded as something that should limit the subjectivity of the researcher as much as possible (Chalmers 1999). One of the referees of an early version of the paper in which the conducted study is reported formulated this critique very explicitly:

Phenomenography seems to be less rigorous and less transparent than other interpretative approaches and even worse is the author's decidedly cryptic use of the so-called phenomenographic-approach.

This and similar comments from the same referee led me to rewrite the paper to make my epistemological position more explicit, but also to make my role as a subjective, creative, active constructionist more transparent. In other words, I both motivated the interpretative work more rigorously and made the subjective/creative/less transparent part of it more explicit. The referee disliked the second paper even more. Lucky for me, the other two referees were much more positive toward it and gave me both good advice for improvements and flattering comments. My interpretation of the very different readings of my text is that they were done from different paradigmatic positions. The critical referee seemed to take for granted that subjectivity could and should be eliminated with positivistic methods, while the others seemed to be closer to my own epistemological stance. In my way of using phenomenography, I *made use of* subjectivity without destroying it with positivistic methods, and without denying it by counting verbatims and pretending that the result was objectivity.

My reply to the demand for more transparent method was not to apply a more transparent method. Instead, I made my epistemological position more transparent. In that way, my use of phenomenography had not moved me as far from my earlier view of formal method as I had hoped. I did make use of a phenomenographic approach, but that approach was flexible and did not satisfy positivistic demands for transparency. My defence of this flexibility/lack of transparency was instead more epistemological reflection. (See Figure 4.4.)

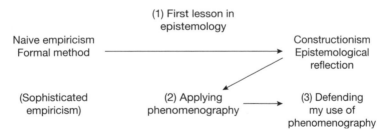

*Figure 4.4* My epistemological journey, Parts 1–3.

## Conclusion

My quest for a 'method' in the formal and technical sense of the word had led me to try phenomenography. This attempt was driven by positive curiosity and expectations of what results phenomenography might generate. It was also driven in part by a discussion and disagreement between me and convinced phenomenographers. Trying phenomenography was also driven by an interest in understanding a specific empirical phenomenon: why did some stockbrokers generate more trade and courtage revenues than others? The experience was good – applying phenomenography worked to enhance my knowledge of the lived-worlds of stockbroking and to make sense of stockbrokers' performance. With the help of phenomenography, I was able to make sense of the differences in the studied stockbrokers' ability to generate trade and courtage revenues. Blending ideal type constructionism, the phenomenographic approach and theoretically generated analysis, enabled me to construct a processual account for how the inexperienced broker can develop into two opposing types of broker: one high-performing and one relatively low-performing. This result has many types of relevance. The brokers themselves, as well as their employers, have expressed an interest in the study. To find, educate and/or develop high-performing brokers is of strategic interest for any stockbrokerage firm. For organizational analysis, the result shows that 'old' questions concerning competence and performance can still generate 'new' answers. For social science, the results show that phenomenography can be used as a method in explorative studies about practical knowledge.

However, my use of phenomenography was not 'method' enough to satisfy the positivist's reading of my text. My defence for the positivist's demand for even more transparent 'method' was not more method, but more explicit epistemological reflection. By explaining my epistemological position, I succeeded at least in making two referees and an editor appreciate my research. The positivist was still unwilling to listen or at least did not like what he or she heard.

In the end, it appears to be hard to find a 'method' that fulfils both positivistic demands of transparency and constructionistic demands for interpretative space. If viewed as a simple one-dimensional trade-off, I know at which end I like to conduct my research. But I do not believe the matter of epistemological position and use of method is or should be a choice between positions that are seen as equally good. My attempt at phenomenography and my dialogues with phenomenographers and positivists have made my position even more non-negotiable than before. To do good empirical science, we need to educate ourselves in both epistemology and method. At least, I cannot see how it would be possible to construct an account, as the one above, of how the inexperienced broker develops into either a high performer or a relatively low performer without the use of a flexible interpretative approach like phenomenography combined with theory-based analyses. We need to know the good and the bad about whichever position we take or method we choose. Knowing this enables us to both construct elaborated 'mixed' positions and to communicate over paradigmatic borders. Instead of not being able to appreciate research conducted in unknown territory, instead of treating everything outside our homeland as strange and frightening, we can educate ourselves and appreciate and help one another to do good research both close to home and out in the wilderness.

I do not think we can or should replace epistemology with method. Trying to do so just means that the epistemology will find its way in through a back door. Instead of employing it, we will become its victims. In this sense, Habermas is correct – to disavow reflection *is* positivism.

Not only taken-for-granted positivism and naive empiricism can victimize us however. Romantic idealism or hermeneutics can trap us too. In the case of phenomenography, one could very well end up justifying an illusory objective phenomenology. This would be to deny our active role as researchers, as constructors. It would also be to deny our interests, perspectives and use of theory. In my opinion, constructionist epistemology, in the neo-Kantian (Köhnke 1991) or in the Schutzian (Schutz 1962, 1967) sense of the term, implies that one should try to use methods in a creative way to overcome the analytical distance between the world of ideas and the world of objects. We should neither try to hide behind beautiful philosophical formulations nor behind formalized empirical methods. Instead, we should make our epistemology at hand and our creative and subjective use of method as transparent as possible.

## Notes

1   Courtage revenues are the fees customers pay the brokerage firm for the stock-broker's service of executing a specific trade on the stock exchange. Fees differ with regard to type of customer (institutional investors usually pay lower fees than private investors). The brokers studied here mainly trade for private customers and, at the time the study was conducted, customers paid a courtage fee of 0.4% of the total value of the specific trade. The courtage revenues typically amount to a predominant part of a brokerage firm's total revenues (in the firm studied, about 95% of total revenues). Generating courtage revenues is therefore of vital importance to any brokerage firm.

2   One might ask, what is romantic about complexity? Or comic about competition? Two types of argument motivate the labels. First, the labels communicate meaning. The brokers who talked about complexity and competition often did so with a tone of voice, expressiveness and style that indicated something more than their spoken words. Complexity was talked about as something that made their work interesting, positive, and lovable, or in a word – romantic. When talking about stockbroking as competition, they did so with some distance and irony. The brokers did not describe competition as a struggle for survival but as a comic game. Communicating this type of meaning by using labels like 'romantic' or 'comic' is, to me, one of the important contributions that narrative approaches have given to organizational analysis. Compare this line of thinking with Bruner (1986), and his distinction between narrative and paradigmatic logic.

    Second, the four labels, the four stories, and the chapter as a whole, paint a picture of stockbroking as rather tragi-comic. This is a nice parallel to how Weber, and his many followers who used the ideal type, thought of this methodological device. An ideal type is nothing on its own (without ontological status). Considered together with other types and with empirical experiences, however, they are as objective as any other form of methodological or theoretical construct. Stretching this parallel somewhat, one could argue that the idealization of stockbroking in terms of different dramatic formats, including the more complex format of tragi-comedy, is an interpretative and narrative theory underlying the logic of the chapter.

3   The numbers in parentheses indicate how long each broker has been working in finance or banking, though not as a stockbroker.

4   The two stockbrokers that share the fifth place also share customer accounts. This means that there is no way for them or for anyone else to differentiate their accumulated courtage. Here, they are treated the same way as they are by the brokerage firm. Their total courtage is divided into two equal parts (4004/2 = 2002).

# References

Alexandersson, M. (1994) *Metod och medvetande* (Method and Conciousness), Göteborg: Acta Universitatis Gothoburgensis.

Blomberg, J. (1995) *Ordning och kaos i projektsamarbete – en socialfenomenologisk upplösning av en organisationsteoretisk paradox* (Order and Chaos in Temporary Partnerships – A Social-phenomenological Resolution of an Organization – theoretical Paradox, with English summary), Stockholm: EFI.

Blomberg, J. (2004) 'Appreciating Stockbroking – Constructing Conceptions to Make Sense of Performance', *Journal of Management Studies*, 41, 1: 155–180.

Blomberg, J. (2005) *Aktiemarknadens aktörer – ett organizational finance perspektiv*, Malmö: Liber Ekonomi.

Bourdieu, P. (1977) *Outline of a Theory of Practice*, Cambridge: Cambridge University Press.

Bourdieu, P. (1984) *Distinction – A Social Critique of the Judgement of Taste*, London: Routledge.

Chalmers, A.F. (1999) *What is the Thing Called Science?* Maidenhead: Open University Press.

Dall'Alba, G. and Hasselgren, B. (eds) (1996) *Reflections on Phenomenography – Towards a Methodology?*, Göteborg, Sweden: Acta Universitatis Gothoburgenisis, Studies in Educational Sciences, 109.

Durkheim, E. (1991) 'Sociologins metodregler', in *Tre klassiska texter* Göteborg: Korpen. (First published in 1895.)

Eco, U. (1979) *The Role of the Reader: Explorations in the Semiotics of Texts*, Indianapolis, IN: Indiana University Press.

Fiol, C.M. (1990) 'Narrative Semiotics: Theory, Procedure and Illustration', in A.S. Huff (ed.) *Mapping Strategic Thought*, Chichester: Wiley.

Habermas, J. (1984) *Den rationella övertygelsen – en antologi om legitimitet, kris och politik*, Stockholm: Akademielitteratur.

Habermas, J. (1987) *Knowledge and Human Interest*, Cambridge: Polity Press.

Habermas, J. (1988) *Kommunikativt handlande – Texter om språk, rationalitet och samhälle*, Göteborg: Daidalos.

Husserl, E. (1964) *Ideas of Phenomenology*, Dordrecht, Netherlands: Kluwer Academic Publishers. (First published in 1907.)

Husserl, E. (1962) *Ideas: General Introduction to Pure Phenomenology*, London: Collier Macmillan. (First published in 1931.)

Husserl, E. (1970a) *Logical Investigations*, Vol. 2, London: Routledge and Kegan Paul.

Husserl, E. (1970b) *The Crisis of European Sciences and Transcendental Phenomenology*, Evanston, IL: Northwestern University Press. (First published in 1936.)

James, W. (1981) *The Principles of Psychology*, Cambridge, MA: Harvard University Press. (First published in 1890.)

Köhnke, K.C. (1991) *The Rise of Neo-Kantianism: German Academic Philosophy between Idealism and Positivism*, Cambridge: Cambridge University Press.

Krippendorff, K. (1980) *Content Analysis: An Introduction to its Methodology*, Beverly Hills, CA: Sage.

Kvale, S. (1996) *Interviews: An Introduction to Qualitative Research Interviewing*, Thousand Oaks, CA: Sage.

Marton, F. (1981) 'Phenomenography: Describing Conceptions of the World Around Us', *Instructional Science*, 10: 177–200.

Marton, F. (1986) 'Phenomenography: A Research Approach to Investigating Different Understandings of Reality', *Journal of Thought*, 21: 28–49.

Marton, F. and Booth, S. (1997) *Learning and Awareness*, Hillsdale, NJ: Erlbaum.

Marton, F., Dalgren, L.O., Svensson, L. and Säljö, R. (1977) *Inlärning och omvärldsuppfattning* (Learning and Conceptions of the World Around), Stockholm: Almquist & Wiksell.

Marton, F., Hounsell, D. and Entwistle, N. (eds) (1984) *The Experience of Learning*, Edinburgh: Scottish Academic Press.

McCarthy, T. (1988) *The Critical Theory of Jürgen Habermas*, Cambridge, MA: MIT Press.

Ramsden, P. (ed.) (1988) *Improving Learning: New Perspectives*, London: Kogan Page.

Sandberg, J. (1994) *Human Competence at Work: An Interpretative Approach*, Göteborg: BAS.

Sandberg, J. (2000) 'Understanding Human Competence at Work: An Interpretative Approach', *Academy of Management Journal*, 43, 1: 9–25.

Schutz, A. (1962) *Collected Papers I: The Problem of Social Reality*, The Hague: Martinus Nijhoff. (First published in 1951.)

Schutz, A. (1964) *Collected Papers II. Studies in Social Theory*, The Hague: Martinus Nijhoff.

Schutz, A. (1966) *Collected Papers III: Studies in Phenomenological Philosophy*, The Hague: Martinus Nijhoff. (First published in 1941.)

Schutz, A. (1967) *The Phenomenology of the Social World*, Evanston, IL: Northwestern University Press.

Spiegelberg, H. (1982) *The Phenomenological Movement: A Historical Introduction*, third edition, The Hague: Martinus Nijhoff.

Weber, M. (1947) *The Theory of Social and Economic Organization*, New York: Cambridge University Press.

Weber, R.P. (1990) *Basic Content Analysis*, Newbury Park, CA: Sage.

# 5 Studying everyday life

## An ethnomethodological and discourse analytic approach

*Pernilla Bolander*

## Introduction

How does selection take place in organizations? This was the general question that a research project I started in 1997 attempted to answer (Bolander 2002). In reviewing previous research, I had found that considerable effort had been put into producing knowledge, in the form of prescriptive models, about how selection should be accomplished. However, there was a dearth of in-depth studies of how selection actually does take place. To conduct such a study, with a particular focus on internal decision-making in selection, therefore became the aim of my research.

In this chapter I will describe how I conducted this study. I will briefly outline my two main sources of methodological and theoretical inspiration, namely ethnomethodology and discourse analysis, and describe how they were integrated to form a coherent approach to studying decision-making in selection. I will also describe how I used this approach to analyze two different types of empirical material, i.e. interview data and observation data.

## In search of authenticity in the interview society

When starting my research on selection, I decided to begin by conducting a broad interview study. The purpose of this study, at least initially, was to interview selectors in order to examine how selection takes place in a large number of organizations. According to Atkinson and Silverman (1997), the fact that I quickly turned to interviews when approaching my research question was no coincidence. They argue that we live in an interview society where large parts of the information we have of the world comes from face-to-face interviews. Interviews play a predominant part in such different phenomena as talk shows, news and, indeed, qualitative social research (Silverman 1993).

A main characteristic of this interview society is that the interview is seen as a method for revealing the 'authentic'. That is, we believe that we, through the interviewee's account, can discover what is *really* going on, what *really* happened, what the interviewee is *really* feeling in her hearts of hearts, and so on. Lately, it has been argued that this search for the authentic and the widespread use of the interview to this end is problematic, at least in qualitative research (Silverman 1993, 1998a; Atkinson and Silverman 1997). Some of the reasons for this will be discussed below.

The search for the authentic is based on the idea that there exists an authentic self with authentic experiences. Furthermore, it is believed that this authentic self is at least partially hidden beneath the surface of things. The purpose of the open-ended, in-depth interview is to bring the authentic out into the open. It is assumed that you can uncover the individual's lived experience if only you can establish 'rapport' and achieve inter-subjective depth. In this confessional atmosphere, the interviewee will ' "reveal" the contents of his or her mind' (Atkinson and Silverman 1997: 310).

According to this view, what makes an account given during an interview feel authentic is that it actually *is* authentic. After all, the account has been given by the person most qualified to give it. As both subject and object of the narration, the narrator is 'assumed to have a uniquely privileged insight into a realm of private experience' (Atkinson and Silverman 1997: 315). Atkinson and Silverman maintain that this is a romantic and individualistic perspective. They argue that people appear to us to be their most authentic selves when we recognize *ourselves* in what they say, that is, when they reproduce cultural scripts (Silverman 1993: 96). In talk shows as well as research interviews, interviewees present apparently unique biographies that nonetheless are predictable, as they are constructed through the repetition of rehearsed narratives of experience. As Atkinson and Silverman (1997: 316) put it, 'the personal is inescapably social in its forms of telling'.

Interview talk is formed not only by the broader social and cultural context in which it takes place; it is also shaped by the specific interactional context. Conversational practices and patterns of exchange form the interaction that takes place (Silverman 1993; Baker 2003; ten Have 2004; Rapley 2004). Accordingly, interviews are not only and simply about the interviewees' experiences, actions, thoughts and feelings outside the interview situation, even if these experiences, actions, thoughts and feelings are precisely what is talked about. Some would argue that interview data also reflects how versions of experience, etc. are 'locally and collaboratively' produced by both the interviewer and the interviewee (Rapley 2004: 16). Some would go even further and argue that the interview cannot offer any information about any other reality than the interview situation itself.[1]

The search for the authentic and the use of the interview to this end is thus problematic, as the accounts offered during the interview are contingent on the broader social context and, more directly, the interview setting as such. In other words, the accounts are accredited with a status that they do not live up to. Another perhaps more serious problem concerns what researchers do with the accounts once they have been collected. A researcher that interviews in order to uncover the interviewee's authentic self tends to try to be true to this authentic self in the analysis and presentation of the data, which then comes to focus on how people 'see things'. There is a risk that the researcher gets stuck in reality reporting, in simply recounting the interviewee's account and assuming that 'lay accounts can do the work of sociological explanations' (Silverman 1993: 200). For example, a researcher might ask selectors to describe how they go about selecting candidates and use their accounts to draw conclusions about how selection 'really' takes place, without considering how, when and why selectors characterize the selection process in *different* ways.

This line of reasoning does not, however, necessarily lead to the conclusion that interview research is fruitless by definition. Open-ended interviews have traditionally been offered as an alternative to objectivist approaches. While objectivist approaches have used standardized interviews to measure and analyze pre-defined variables in order to elicit facts, subjectivist approaches have used open-ended interviews to focus on the interviewee's perspective and on how the interviewee constructs meanings. Given this bi-polar and oversimplified definition of the situation, researchers are faced with the 'unappetising choice between treating accounts as privileged data or as "perspectival" and subject to check via the method of "triangulation" with other observations' (Silverman 1993: 197). Silverman argues that this is an incomplete picture of the alternatives the researcher stands before:

> Analytically, [the apparent identification of non-quantitative social science with the open-ended interview] appears to accept that the only alternative to treating organizational structures as 'real' even 'natural' facts is to focus on an individual's private experiences of organizational life. It thus leaves vacant the vast terrain of socially organized practices that cannot be reduced to either 'objectivist' organizational structures or 'subjectivist' individual meanings.
>
> (Silverman 1998a: 10)

In the following, we will take a closer look at this terrain.

## Studying reality-constituting practices in everyday life

The terrain referred to in the quotation above is one that ethnomethodology has done much to map. Some basic characteristics of this terrain seen from an ethnomethodological perspective focusing on what should be studied and how (Silverman 1993; Gubrium and Holstein 1997, 2000) will be discussed below.

A fundamental question within ethnomethodology is how members[2] 'construct, manage, and sustain the sense that their social worlds exist as factual and objectively "there"' (Gubrium and Holstein 1997: 7). Ethnomethodologists are particularly interested in the procedures and practices through which reality is constituted – in the members' practical 'ethnomethods'. The *hows* rather than the *whats* of reality construction are put at the centre of attention (Gubrium and Holstein 1997, 2000). In other words, ethnomethodologists ask themselves how the life-world is produced rather than what it is made up of, what it subjectively means or what perspective members have on it.

Members' methods for reality construction can readily be studied in everyday life. From an ethnomethodological perspective, research 'is fundamentally about understanding the routine rather than what appears to be exciting' (Silverman 1993: 30). Ethnomethodologists tend to study the ordinary procedures and practices of everyday life *in situ*, that is, in their original place. The empirical material is often made up of so-called naturally occurring data, where the label 'natural' is used to indicate that the talk, social interaction, etc. is produced independently of the actions of the researcher (Potter 2004a: 205).[3]

The question is how everyday life can be analyzed, for in 'the natural attitude', the observer 'simply believes that "as he sees things, so they are"' (Heritage 1984: 41). In order to see that which in everyday life is 'seen but unnoticed' (Garfinkel 1967) and problematize that which in everyday life in taken-for-granted, the observer must therefore create a certain distance to that which is being analyzed. One method for creating this distance is phenomenological bracketing (Schutz 1970; Gubrium and Holstein 2000; Denzin 2002).

> In our everyday life . . . we accept as unquestionable the world of facts which surrounds us as existent out there. . . . But by a radical effort of our mind we can alter this attitude, not by transforming our naive belief in the outer world into a disbelief, not by replacing our conviction in its existence by the contrary, but by suspending belief.
>
> (Schutz 1970: 58)

As is made clear in this quotation, bracketing does not involve questioning the existence or substantiality of reality. Rather, it involves setting these questions aside in order to enable an examination of how reality comes to be experienced as objectively existent (Heritage 1984: 41). In other words, bracketing is a method for focusing on the *hows* of reality construction.

The need for distance is also expressed in an often-repeated ethno-methodological maxim: 'beware of confounding the topic of your studies with the resources for studying them'. Members' resources, i.e. accounts, explanations, etc. should not be treated as the researcher's resources. The researcher's role is not to use members' resources as explanatory devices, but to study these resources as a topic – to analyze how they are used by members in creating a sense of objective reality. For example, a researcher interested in how selection decisions are made might observe occasions where selectors assess candidates and notice that certain attributes, say flexibility and social competence, are referred to frequently in the discussions. The researcher could use these attributes to explain why some candidates are selected while others are not, i.e. a candidate is selected if she is flexible and socially competent. This, however, would be confounding topic with resource. Alternatively, the researcher could treat these attributes as a topic, asking for instance how they are given meaning in a specific situation or how they are referred to so that they can be said to provide grounds for a certain selection decision.

If the maxim is neglected, Gubrium and Holstein (1997: 43) warn, the researcher places herself 'on the same analytic plane as those being studied', which only results in reality reporting. This does not imply, however, that ethnomethodologists regard members' accounts as untrue, wrong, irrational etc. Rather, the act of setting topic and resource apart renders etnomethodological indifference possible.

> Ethnomethodological studies . . . describe members' accounts of formal structures wherever and by whomever they are done, while abstaining from all judgments of their adequacy, value, importance, necessity, practicality, success, or consequentiality.
>
> (Garfinkel and Sacks 1970: 345)

The same stance is expressed in another ethnomethodological maxim: 'don't argue with the members'. The purpose of research is not to compare members' accounts with an external reality in order to determine whether they are accurate or not, or to make judgements about whether members' activities are rational or irrational. The purpose is, rather, to examine 'the procedures by which the actors themselves arrive at these and related judgements' (Heritage 1983: 120).

## Analytic bracketing

As discussed above, ethnomethodology focuses on the *hows* of reality construction. Gubrium and Holstein (1997, 2000) have argued that an exclusive interest in *how* is problematic:

By focusing on the *hows* of indigenous accounting and explanation at the border of reality and representation, ethnomethodologists risk losing track of the *whats* that anchor matters of local concern. . . . As the substantively meaningful aspects of local culture are shunted aside in order to concentrate on constitutive interactional activity, the content of lived experience becomes almost incidental. Setting substantive differences aside risks turning lived experience into a homogeneous world of members' representational practices, shorn of meaning and emotional content.

(Gubrium and Holstein 1997: 107)

In other words, the authors argue that phenomenological bracketing and a one-sided interest in *how* risks excluding an interest in what is being constructed, under what circumstances and with what resources. The result is a description of a machinery of interaction which is devoid of context. What is being studied, whether it is selection or something else, and when and where becomes uninteresting. While retaining a strong interest in the *hows* of reality construction, Gubrium and Holstein identify a need to also focus on the ethnographic details of everyday life: 'it is also imperative to engage the overarching issues of what meanings are available for construction, how circumstances condition the construction process, and the manner in which the animatedness and sheer scenic presence of the process brings all this to life' (ibid., p. 121). What is required, then, is a method that focuses alternately on *how* (constitutive activities) and *what* (substantive conditions), and on the interplay between them.[4] They call this method 'analytic bracketing' (ibid., pp. 118–122). For example, for a researcher interested in decision-making meetings, this method would involve asking not only, say, how the meetings are opened and closed, how the participants demonstrate that they are following rules and procedures and how the participants establish facts, but also what these particular meetings are about, in which organizations they are played out, who the participants are, what the rules and procedures consist of and what specific facts are established.

Whether research is guided by phenomenological bracketing or analytic bracketing directly affects the choice of methods for analysis. Many ethnomethodologists have used conversation analysis as a means to focus strictly on *how* (Heritage 1984; Atkinson 1988; Silverman 1998b). Discourse analysis is one alternative for those working with analytic bracketing (Gubrium and Holstein 1997, 2000). While conversation analysts will analyze a text to explore the structural properties of talk, discourse analysts will, as we shall see below, analyze it with respect to both the procedures through which social reality is constructed and the resources drawn on in this process.

## Discourse analysis

As discussed above, discourse analysis is one alternative for those looking for concrete procedures and techniques that can be used to achieve analytic bracketing. Discourse analysis is a broad term that covers a variety of specific perspectives and procedures (Alvesson and Kärreman 2000; Wetherell *et al.* 2001; Phillips and Jørgensen 2002; Grant *et al.* 2004). A unifying theme for organizational discourse analysis is that it focuses on 'how the everyday attitudes and behaviour of an organization's members, along with their perceptions of what they believe to be reality, are shaped and influenced by the discursive practices in which they engage and to which they are exposed or subjected' (Grant *et al.* 2004: 3). The type of discourse analysis that will be discussed here was developed by Potter and Wetherell (Potter and Wetherell 1987, 1994; Wetherell and Potter 1988, 1992; Potter 2004a, 2004b). As used here, the word discourse stands for 'language use in everyday text and talk' (Phillips and Jørgensen 2002: 118).

A basic point of departure is that discourse is action-oriented, that is, put together to perform actions, and that it is used constructively, that is, to construct different versions of events, persons, objects, etc. (Potter 2004b; Hepburn and Potter 2004). A specific phenomenon can be accounted for in different ways depending on what the speaker wishes to achieve. Thus, in discourse analysis the question is not how a certain text compares with reality, but rather how the text is organized, consciously or unconsciously, in order to construct and stabilize a factual version of reality. For example, when selectors are interviewed about the selection process, they may describe the selection process in different ways depending on the circumstances (such as what questions they are responding to). Thus, the question is not if a particular description is an accurate account of actual selection processes, but how the description is organized to construct a certain picture of the selection process.

For purposes of analysis, a distinction is made between two types of questions:

> On the one hand, studies have been concerned with the general resources that are used to construct and enable the performance of particular actions. This style of work . . . attempts to map out broad systems or 'interpretative repertoires' which are used to sustain different social practices (Potter *et al.* 1990). . . . On the other hand, studies have concentrated more on the detailed procedures through which versions are constructed and made to appear factual.
>
> (Potter and Wetherell 1994: 48–49)

In terms of Gubrium and Holstein's (1997, 2000) vocabulary, then, discourse analysis is interested in both *what* – in the discursive resources, known as interpretative repertoires, used in a certain context – and *how* – how actors construct and make a certain version of reality appear factual. Potter and Wetherell (1994) point out that the distinction is heuristic rather than strict; one area or the other is emphasized, but the two are complementary to one another. Thus, their distinction matches well Gubrium and Holstein's conception of analytic bracketing.

The following two sections will take a closer look at each of the areas in discourse analysis. Before proceeding, it might be useful to say something about the types of data used. Generally speaking, discourse analysis can involve the detailed study of any text or talk. However, some types of materials are more appropriate than others when approaching a particular question (Potter 2004b). Interviews provide an arena for participants to draw on discursive resources, and interview data is thus suitable for focusing on *what*. Naturally occurring data, on the other hand, is particularly appropriate for studying participants' situated constructive work and focusing on *how*.

## Identifying interpretative repertoires

The concept of interpretative repertoires was first used by Gilbert and Mulkay (1983, 1984). They were interested in how scientists described the process of producing scientific knowledge. In an analysis of different types of accounts, among them interviews with scientists, they found that the scientists talked about the same actions in quite different ways in different contexts and on different occasions. Instead of treating this variation as problematic, Gilbert and Mulkay framed variation as the object of study. Their goal became to identify the different ways of talking about scientific work, i.e. the repertoires used by the participants, and to analyze when and where the repertoires were used and for what purposes.

The concept was subsequently adopted and elaborated within the field of discursive psychology (Potter and Reicher 1987; Wetherell and Potter 1988, 1992; Wetherell 1998; Edley 2001). It has been described in the following way:

> In dealing with lay explanations the analyst often wishes to describe the explanatory resources to which speakers have access and to make interpretations about patterns in the content of the material. The interpretative repertoire is a summary unit at this level. Repertoires can be seen as the building blocks speakers use for constructing factual versions

of actions, cognitive processes and other phenomena. Any particular repertoire is constituted out of a restricted range of terms used in a specific stylistic and grammatical fashion. Commonly these terms are derived from one or more key metaphors and the presence of a repertoire will often be signaled by certain tropes or figures of speech.

(Wetherell and Potter 1988: 172)

Edley (2001: 198–199) states that there are no simple rules for identifying the interpretative repertoires used in a specific empirical material. One basic condition, however, is that the analyst is familiar with the material, and a prerequisite is thus that the transcribed material is read repeatedly. The feeling that one has 'heard this before' is a sign that the contours of the repertoires are starting to appear.

Wetherell and Potter (1988, 1992) have provided some more concrete guidelines. First, they suggest that the analyst prepare for analysis by sorting the material according to themes that have been identified as interesting (Wetherell and Potter 1992: 100). Second, searching the material for systematic variability in content and structure is an important element (ibid., 101–102). As Gilbert and Mulkay's (1983, 1984) studies suggested, variation is important since it indicates that objects and events are being constructed in different ways to perform different actions. In other words, patterns in the variation point to patterns in which repertoires are being drawn on. It is important to note that the analyst is searching for variation in the whole material, both between and within different interviews (Wetherell and Potter 1988: 177). Third, the variability should be noticeable not only to the analyst, but also to the participants (ibid., 178). Specifically, participants tend to use different repertoires in separate parts of the text. However, sometimes inconsistent repertoires are mixed in the same stretch of discourse, and in these cases, participants orient to and deal with the inconsistencies, for example through the use of disclaimers (ibid., 176).

## Analyzing how versions are constructed and made to appear factual

When analyzing how factual versions are constructed, four issues are central: function, variability, rhetorical organization and fact construction. A basic assumption in discourse analysis is that discourse is a medium for interaction (Potter 2004a). People do things when they talk – they explain, make excuses, motivate, convince, blame, etc. Accordingly, discourse analysis is largely an analysis of *function*, i.e. of what is being done in a particular stretch of discourse (Potter and Wetherell 1987; Wetherell and Potter 1988; Wood and Kroger 2000).

As mentioned above, the search for *variability* is an important element when identifying interpretative repertoires. It is also essential for interpreting function (Wetherell and Potter 1988; Potter 2004a):

> As variation is a consequence of function it can be used as an analytic clue to what function is being performed in a particular stretch of discourse. That is, by identifying variation, which is a comparatively straightforward analytic task, we can work towards an understanding of function. We can predict that certain kinds of function will lead to certain kinds of variation and we can look for those variations.
>
> (Wetherell and Potter 1988: 171)

Thus, the analyst can draw conclusions about function by analyzing variation. What is the reason for the variation? Why is the text organized in this particular way? When and why are certain words and expressions used?

*Rhetorical organization* refers to how one version of a certain phenomenon relates to other versions of the same phenomenon, in particular how a version is organized in order to make it persuasive and undermine alternatives (Potter and Wetherell 1994; Gill 1996; Potter and Edwards 2001; Potter 2004a). Which details are highlighted in the accounts and in what ways? Which details are toned down? How does this strengthen and/or undermine?

Making a certain version persuasive is to a large extent about organizing accounts to strengthen their facticity. The aim is to make the account appear to be an authoritative version rather than one among many possible versions. *Fact construction* focuses on discursive devices used to demonstrate the facticity of accounts through externalization (Edwards and Potter 1992; Potter 1996; Edwards 1997). Stake inoculation, corroboration, repetition, and detailed description are a few examples of these discursive devices.

## How does selection take place in organizations?

After this rather abstract discussion, it's time to go back to the beginning. In the first stage of my project on selection, I conducted 28 interviews with selectors on the subject of the external recruitment of middle managers and specialists. I asked each interviewee to define the start and end of the selection process and to describe what happened in between. I also asked follow-up questions concerning, for example, the use of selection instruments, factors that the interviewee saw as important in assessing candidates, and steps that the interviewee experienced as difficult. The interviews were tape-recorded and transcribed.

At first, my analysis of the interviews focused on describing how selection takes place. I expected there to be considerable differences between prescriptive models for selection and selection practice, but my analysis resulted in a standard description of selection that could be found in any textbook on the subject. However, although there were few differences between the selectors in what they did, for example what activities were undertaken or which selection instruments were used, there seemed to be differences in how it was done (see Box 5.1). Personality tests were thus used in both organizations, but in different ways. The first quotation seems to reflect a view on tests as a straightforward categorization device, whereas the second refers to tests as a point of departure for the unstructured interview.

I therefore analyzed the interviews again, this time trying to identify each selector's underlying perspective on selection in order to see if these perspectives could explain the differences I had found. At this stage another problem arose, namely that the variation within the interviews was strong. A particular selector could for example at one point describe selection as a completely rational process and a few minutes later speak about the importance of emotions in making selection decisions (see Box 5.2). By down-playing some of this variation I managed to formulate a preliminary description of four perspectives on selection, but I was not satisfied with my analysis.

---

**Box 5.1**

In the following quotations, two selectors describe the use of personality tests in their organizations:

> There are a number of questions that the candidate answers and this results in a profile that shows the candidate's strengths and weaknesses. There are four types of personality. Either the dominant type, or the type that works through influence. Or the third profile, which is called stability, or the fourth, which is adaptation.

> The test results rarely, or rather never, come as a surprise. But I still think that tests are useful in certain circumstances, since they result in a special type of discussion during the interview. Instead of asking the candidates who they are and what they have done, you can ask them about the description that you already have, whether they agree with it. It's not a deep psychological test, but it's a starting point for a good conversation.

---

**Box 5.2**

The following two quotations are both from an interview with one particular selector. The first was uttered in response to an early question about how selection took place in the selector's organization, the second in response to a question about criteria for successful selection:

> You have to make sure, all of the time, that you've pushed your feelings away. Professional considerations have to be decisive. You collect enough information to have a solid ground for your decision and then you make the decision.

> Some things can't be avoided no matter what, since it's a question of people judging people. In one way or the other, I have to like the person sitting before me if we are to work together. Chemistry, in other words. And it's difficult to know what chemistry is, but it's a feeling you get somehow. I mean, people work a lot and spend a lot of time at work and so you have to feel that it's fun.

In the first quotation, the selector is describing the selection process in a way that emphasizes objectivity, professionalism and information processing. In the second, the selector is instead emphasizing the importance of chemistry and emotions.

---

While still working with the interviews, I started collecting more data. My interest in ethnomethodology, which originated from a PhD course in interpretive approaches, had grown over the course of the project. I was drawn to the idea of using naturally occurring data to explore how selection is actually accomplished, not just talked about. I wanted to study examples of how selectors together discuss candidates, establish what they are 'like' and make selection decisions. This focus was also motivated by the review I had done of previous studies, which showed that few studies had focused on ongoing 'behind-the-scenes' decision-making processes in selection. I contacted two organizations in the IT business in which I was given access to meetings that were held following employment interviews. The purpose of the meetings, in which HR specialists as well as managers and colleagues participated, was to decide whether candidates were to be offered employment (see Box 5.3). In this in-depth observation study, I attended four meetings in each organization. The meetings, which each lasted approximately 15 minutes,

**Box 5.3**

The meetings typically started when one of the participants asked a question like, 'so what did you think?'. The participants would then one by one express their opinions of the candidate. They discussed the technical competence and the personal attributes of the candidate, as well as the form and the content of the employment interview. Finally, one of the participants concluded the meeting by formulating the decision reached. The following extracts, from an organization herein called IT Bank, give an indication of what the meetings were like. Recruiting manager Urban and HR specialist Cecilia are discussing a candidate named Janis.

Extract 1

*Cecilia*:  What did you (.) think?
*Urban*:   Well, I guess I thought (.) I'd say yesss.
*Cecilia*:  Yes, mm, mm.
*Urban*:   [laugh] I wouldn't say it's someone I got terribly excited about. It wasn't. I suppose I'm a little hesitant and I think he (.) was a little hesitant too. And also, he hasn't worked with (.) Cobol for a while.
*Cecilia*:  No. But on the other hand he had done so until '98.
*Urban*:   Mm. He's probably a bit rusty since he hasn't worked with either DL1 or DB2. . . .

Extract 2

*Urban*:   . . . Then there's his personality that's a little
*Cecilia*:  Yes. What did you think about that?
*Urban*:   Well, considering [laugh] the group, it's composition, maybe we shouldn't add one more like that.
*Cecilia*:  I thought so too, that he would match the gang perfectly, I thought [laugh]!

Extract 3

*Cecilia*:  Still I must say I felt he <u>grew</u> during the interview.
*Urban*:   Yes, he did. He isn't so

*Cecilia:*   He wasn't so (.) I was about to say, dry as I thought from the beginning, sort of [laugh]. There <u>were</u> some things there somewhere, I thought. It

*Urban:*   Yes, he isn't entirely

*Cecilia:*   He told me later that he had (.) worked with DL1 . . .

*Urban:*   But he didn't say that (*Cecilia:* No, no) while he was sitting here. And when we talked about that stuff, none of that <u>was</u> brought up. (*Cecilia:* No) And I asked, tried you know (.) I guess he should have talked a bit more about it.

*Cecilia:*   He couldn't sell himself. He should be able to do so. (*Urban:* No) He was very well-read in Greek history. (*Urban:* Yes, yes) And he was very knowledgeable in that area but (.) (*Urban:* So) he was <u>not</u> charismatic.

*Urban:*   No, he isn't (.) No, that's right.

Extract 4

*Urban:*   No, we'll see what we had (.) Is it on Thursday we're seeing (*Cecilia:* Mm). We'd better wait.

*Cecilia:*   Yes (.) So we're saying no, then.

*Urban:*   Mm.

were tape-recorded and transcribed following the transcription conventions described in Wetherell and Potter (1992).

About this time I participated in a workshop on qualitative methods held by David Silverman. In a consultation he suggested some readings, of which Gubrium and Holstein's (1997) book was one. Their description of analytic bracketing caught my attention for several reasons. First, it gave me an idea of what I would focus on in my analysis of the interview transcripts on the one hand and the meeting transcripts on the other. The analysis of the interviews would focus mainly on *what*, i.e. on the content of the selectors' discourse. The analysis of the meetings would focus mainly on *how*, i.e. on the selectors' constructive work. Second, it gave me an idea of how I could combine the two analyses so that they would enhance each other. Seen from this perspective, each material would help me understand the other better. Third, it pointed towards discourse analysis which provided me with concrete guidelines on how I could analyze the data.

Working with the interviews once more, I concentrated on identifying the repertoires on selection used by selectors in different contexts to justify, evaluate and explain the selection process. This involved making two choices. First, I abandoned the individual as the unit of analysis and began searching for patterns in the whole material. As I was no longer trying to 'categorize' each interviewee, the variation that had bothered me previously became a clue rather than something to be down-played. Second, I viewed the selectors' accounts not as descriptions of how selection actually takes place or as reflections of selectors' underlying perspectives, but as different ways of talking about selection. The analysis resulted in eight repertoires on selection (see Box 5.4).

---

**Box 5.4**

The table below lists the different repertoires on selection as well as key words associated with each repertoire.

| The repertoire selection as . . . | Key words |
| --- | --- |
| an emotional meeting between people | feeling, feel, like, chemistry, intuition, gut feeling |
| matching the candidate with the organization | fit in, match, long-term, reciprocity, honesty, organizational culture |
| play-acting | sell, strengths and weaknesses, read between the lines |
| putting the right person in the right place | traditional, criteria, attributes, objectivity, efficiency |
| forming a professional judgement | professional, experience, own judgement, learning, adjust, exceptions |
| making a financial investment | cost, investment, worth |
| an organizational concern | organizational change, strategic decision, profile, right employees |
| securing support | different parties, no benefit of the doubt, cooperation, agree |

The following two quotations illustrate, respectively, the repertoires *Selection as play-acting* and *Selection as forming a professional judgement*. The first was a response to a question about the potential difficulties of selection, the second to a question on how candidates are assessed.

Well, naturally each person wants to call attention to his strengths. But we all know that all individuals have strengths and weaknesses, and of course we want to find out what the weaknesses are and see if we can live with these weaknesses or if it's something we can develop or change. And I suppose that's the most difficult thing with selection, finding out the weaknesses in the person. . . . I try anyway to find it out during the interview phase. Most people, I'd almost say 100 per cent of those who apply, don't lie. However, sometimes you want to hide certain truths. . . . It's like we said, they try to sell themselves and we try to sell the company.

Let me tell you, I'm often asked this question. But I mean, I pretty much know what kind of person I want. . . . When you've worked in a company for a while and know the company well it's much easier to see. And also, I suppose it's because I've worked with these kinds of questions for 20 years, so it's something I can feel in my bones.

On the basis of the interviews, I demonstrated how the repertoires were used flexibly to describe selection in various ways, for example to characterize the process as both emotional and rational, which is important to HR specialists who tend to 'oscillate between the "personnel" and "management", the "caring" and "control" aspects of the function' (Legge 1995: 14).

In the analysis of the meeting transcripts I followed an analytical strategy suggested by Widdicombe (1993: 97), which involves attending to the ways in which things are being said as a 'solution' to an implicit 'problem' and in the analysis trying to understand what the problem and solution are. In this case the problem for the participants was to reach 'reasonable' selection decisions, a process that involved formulating tentative and, later, definitive versions of the candidates (see Box 5.5). The analysis resulted in a description of the main activities in decision-making in selection, which, I argued, are assembling versions of the candidates, establishing the versions of the candidates as factual, and reaching and motivating selection decisions. Taking the analysis one step further, I looked at what constitutes the selection process across its main activities. In other words, I investigated the methods

**Box 5.5**

The following two extracts are from a meeting in an organization called IT Consultant. Recruiting manager Oskar, consultants Camilla and Nils, and HR specialists Sophia and Ove are discussing a candidate named Jonas. In the first extract, which is from the beginning of the meeting, the participants are starting to explore which attributes Jonas has and what it means that he has these attributes. By the time they reach the end of the meeting, shown in the second extract, they have formulated a definitive version of Jonas as a generalist who will not fill a 'specific gap' in the organization's competence structure.

Extract 1

*Oskar:*   Can I start? Uh (.) I kind of think that he is (.) he is a generalist. And I can't find (.) the exact spot where he fits in or what he knows. He is probably good at a lot. (*Ove:* Yes) He is a good person, you could probably put him onto anything (.) really. But at the same time (.) I feel that what (.) it could also turn out that he (.) isn't good at anything and doesn't fit in anywhere. (*Sophia:* Mm) That's my (.) misgiving.

*Ove:*   Mm, mm.

*Oskar:*   Uh (.) I also thought (.) that some of his assertions and answers to questions were (.) very general or generally held. Of the type, 'yes, you talk about certain things with a couple of people'.

*Ove:*   Mm.

*Camilla:*   Mm. Like it's not so deep.

. . .

*Oskar:*   Even questions (.) he answered in that way. (*Ove:* Mm) I don't quite know what it means but (.) but (.) it didn't feel quite (.) You didn't get this like 'yes there you have it'. Uh (.) I will say that his social competence cannot be mistaken. . . .

Extract 2

*Oskar:*   Because I don't feel (.) I felt more with Mats that he was perfect. And now Mats has turned us down.

. . .

| | |
|---|---|
| *Oskar*: | Uh (.) But he (.) Mats was <u>perfect</u>. I would have sent him right in to customers, direct use in making business and all that. I don't <u>see</u> that with (.) with Jonas. Therefore (.) |
| *Camilla*: | The <u>run-up</u> will be longer. (*Oskar*: Yes) The run-up is bigger. |
| [pause] | |
| *Oskar*: | And I don't really see the specific (.) gap in our competence (.) where he fits <u>right</u> in. |
| *Camilla*: | Mm. |
| *Oskar*: | If we'll like (.) find something. |
| *Nils*: | No, he is a generalist, definitely. There (.) there is no doubt about that. |

by which selectors actually performed these activities. I argued that decision-making in selection is accomplished through the use of the documentary method of interpretation, through the use of background knowledge, through the use of the retrospective-prospective method of reasoning, and through the use of selection tools that function as sense-making devices.

## Conclusion

The purpose of this chapter was to describe my analytical approach in my research project on selection as well as some of the choices I considered when conducting this project. These choices gradually led me to change my initial view on the status of my interview data and to truly appreciate the richness and possibilities of the naturally occurring data, i.e. recordings of decision-making meetings, that I had collected. Finally, they led me to challenge the essentialist assumption, common in much selection research, that candidates have inherent qualities and that these can be uncovered by collecting information, and, instead, to understand selection as a process where selectors through their discussions with each other arrive at local versions of the candidates and perceptions of their competence.

## Notes

1   Silverman's (1993: 98) reading of Cicourel (1964). See also Baker (2003) and Potter (2004a).
2   The term 'member' is used to refer to mastery of the natural language used in a certain context (Garfinkel and Sacks 1970: 342).

3  The preference for recordings and transcripts of actual interaction does not, however, exclude the use of interviews (see, for example, Baker 2003, ten Have 2004).
4  Gubrium and Holstein (1997: 120) point out that it is still important to separate topic from resource. An interest in *what* should not lead the researcher to appropriate members' resources. Instead, members' resources are always to be interpreted in relation to their activities.

## References

Alvesson, M. and Kärreman, D. (2000) 'Varieties of Discourse: On the Study of Organizations Through Discourse Analysis', *Human Relations*, 53: 1125–1149.
Atkinson, P. (1988) 'Ethnomethodology: A Critical Review', *Annual Review of Sociology*, 14: 441–465.
Atkinson, P. and Silverman, D. (1997) 'Kundera's *Immortality*: The Interview Society and the Invention of the Self', *Qualitative Inquiry*, 3: 304–325.
Baker, C. (2003) 'Ethnomethodological Analyses of Interviews' in J.A. Holstein and J.F. Gubrium (eds) *Inside Interviewing: New Lenses, New Concerns*, Thousand Oaks, CA: Sage.
Bolander, P. (2002) *Anställningsbilder och rekryteringsbeslut* (Recruitment Decisions and Versions of Candidates, with English summary), Stockholm: EFI.
Cicource, A. (1964) *Method and Measurement in Sociology*, New York: Free Press.
Denzin, N.K. (2002) 'The Interpretive Process', in A.M. Huberman and M.B. Miles (eds) *The Qualitative Researcher's Companion*, Thousand Oaks, CA: Sage.
Edley, N. (2001) 'Analysing Masculinity: Interpretative Repertoires, Ideological Dilemmas and Subject Positions', in M. Wetherell, S. Taylor and S.J Yates (eds) *Discourse as Data: A Guide for Analysis*, London: Sage.
Edwards, D. (1997) *Discourse and Cognition*, London: Sage.
Edwards, D. and Potter, J. (1992) *Discursive Psychology*, London: Sage.
Garfinkel, H. (1967) *Studies in Ethnomethodology*, Englewood Cliffs, NJ: Prentice Hall.
Garfinkel, H. and Sacks, H. (1970) 'On Formal Structures of Practical Actions', in J.C. McKinney and E.A. Tiryakian (eds) *Theoretical Sociology: Perspectives and Developments*, New York: Appleton-Century-Crofts.
Gilbert, G.N. and Mulkay, M. (1983) 'In Search of the Action', in G.N. Gilbert and P. Abell (eds) *Accounts and Action*, Farnborough: Gower.
Gilbert, G.N. and Mulkay, M. (1984) *Opening Pandora's Box: A Sociological Analysis of Scientists' Discourse*, Cambridge: Cambridge University Press.
Gill, R. (1996) 'Discourse Analysis: Practical Implementation', in J.T.E. Richardson (ed.) *Handbook of Qualitative Research Methods for Psychology and the Social Sciences*, Leicester: BPS Books.
Grant, D., Hardy, C., Oswick, C. and Putnam, L. (eds) (2004) *The Sage Handbook of Organizational Discourse*, London: Sage.
Gubrium, J.F. and Holstein, J.A. (1997) *The New Language of Qualitative Method*, Oxford: Oxford University Press.
Gubrium, J.F. and Holstein, J.A. (2000) 'Analyzing Interpretive Practice', in N.K. Denzin and Y.S. Lincoln (eds) *Handbook of Qualitative Research*, second edition, Thousand Oaks, CA: Sage.
ten Have, P. (2004) *Understanding Qualitative Research and Ethnomethodology*, London: Sage.

Hepburn, A. and Potter, J. (2004) 'Discourse Analytic Practice', in C. Seale, G. Gobo, J.F. Gubrium and D. Silverman (eds) *Qualitative Research Practice*, London: Sage.

Heritage, J. (1983) 'Accounts in Action', in G.N. Gilbert and P. Abell (eds) *Accounts and Action*, Farnborough: Gower.

Heritage, J. (1984) *Garfinkel and Ethnomethodology*, Cambridge: Polity Press.

Legge, K. (1995) *Human Resource Management: Rhetorics and Realities*, Basingstoke: Macmillan.

Phillips, L. and Jørgensen, M.W. (2002) *Discourse Analysis as Theory and Practice*, London: Sage.

Potter, J. (1996) 'Discourse Analysis and Constructionist Approaches: Theoretical Background', in J.T.E. Richardson (ed.) *Handbook of Qualitative Research Methods for Psychology and the Social Sciences*, Leicester: BPS Books.

Potter, J. (2004a) 'Discourse Analysis as a Way of Analysing Naturally Occurring Talk', in D. Silverman (ed.) *Qualitative Research: Theory, Method and Practice*, London: Sage.

Potter, J. (2004b) 'Discourse Analysis', in A. Bryman and M. Hardy (eds) *Handbook of Data Analysis*, London: Sage.

Potter, J. and Edwards, D. (2001) 'Discursive Social Psychology', in W.P. Robinson and H. Giles (eds) *The New Handbook of Language and Social Psychology*, Chichester: Wiley.

Potter, J. and Reicher, S. (1987) 'Discourses of Community and Conflict: The Organization of Social Categories in Accounts of a "Riot"', *British Journal of Social Psychology*, 26: 25–40.

Potter, J. and Wetherell, M. (1987) *Discourse and Social Psychology: Beyond Attitudes and Behaviour*, London: Sage.

Potter, J. and Wetherell, M. (1994) 'Analyzing Discourse', in A. Bryman and R.G. Burgess (eds) *Analyzing Qualitative Data*, London: Routledge.

Potter, J., Wetherell, M., Gill, R. and Edwards, D. (1990) 'Discourse: Noun, Verb or Social Practice?' *Philosophical Psychology*, 3: 205–217.

Rapley, T. (2004) 'Interviews', in C. Seale, G. Gobo, J.F. Gubrium and D. Silverman (eds) *Qualitative Research Practice*, London: Sage.

Schutz, A. (1970) *On Phenomenology and Social Relations*, Chicago: University of Chicago Press.

Silverman, D. (1993) *Interpreting Qualitative Data: Methods for Analysing Talk, Text and Interaction*, London: Sage.

Silverman, D. (1998a) 'Qualitative Research: Meanings or Practices?', *Information Systems Journal*, 8: 3–20.

Silverman, D. (1998b) *Harvey Sacks: Social Science and Conversation Analysis*, Cambridge: Polity Press.

Wetherell, M. (1998) 'Positioning and Interpretative Repertoires: Conversation Analysis and Post-structuralism in Dialogue', *Discourse and Society*, 9: 387–412.

Wetherell, M. and Potter, J. (1988) 'Discourse Analysis and the Identification of Interpretative Repertoires', in C. Antaki (ed.) *Analysing Everyday Explanation: A Casebook of Methods*, London: Sage.

Wetherell, M. and Potter, J. (1992) *Mapping the Language of Racism: Discourse and the Legitimation of Exploitation*, New York: Columbia University Press.

Wetherell, M., Taylor, S. and Yates, S.J. (eds) (2001) *Discourse Theory and Practice: A Reader*, London: Sage.

Widdicombe, S. (1993) 'Autobiography and Change: Rhetoric and Authenticity of

"Gothic" Style', in E. Burman and I. Parker (eds) *Discourse Analytic Research: Repertoires and Readings of Texts in Action*, London: Routledge.

Wood, L.A. and Kroger, R.O. (2000) *Doing Discourse Analysis: Methods for Studying Action in Talk and Text*, Thousand Oaks, CA: Sage.

# 6 Inside the school
## An ethnographic approach to school management

*Ulrika Tillberg*

In an open field on the outskirts of this mid-sized Swedish city lies the Minerva School. I can see one large and one smaller building in yellow brick, and a third, higher building, which is the gym. There is the characteristic pattern of high and narrow windows in the yellow brick, and the large open schoolyard, children's bikes, untrimmed bushes with small, yellow flowers. Not far off is a residential area with apartments. The architecture is typically Swedish, red and white painted wood.

It is around 10 o'clock in the morning and I pass through the double doors of the main building, trying to find my way. There is a small library and a big lunchroom for hundreds of children. Through the windows in the hall-way, I see out to square areas paved in greyish stone overgrown with weeds. Nobody can use those, I think to myself. Around the corner, small signs posted next to the doors read: Administration, Principal, District Manager, Staff Room, Teachers' Lunchroom. This appears to be the administrative heart of the school. Further down the corridor I see classrooms. Between two of them is a small passage with science supplies: stuffed birds, a model of atoms, flasks, Bunsen burners. Suddenly, the bell rings. Doors fly open and children spill out from the rooms. Jackets, pens, papers, books fill the corridor. The smell of children reaches me, the sweet scent of chewing gum mixed with dust, sweatshirts, sweaty hair, adrenaline. The sound volume is high. The last person into the corridor is the teacher. Laden with a stack of books, she turns and locks the door behind her, then slowly moves towards the staff room. It is recess time at Minerva School.

The office of the principal, Peter, is tiny. When we meet, he shows me that he has the entire curriculum on his computer. I can also see the physical version posted on the wall behind him. He works alone the entire summer to make it work. He tells me:

> Most of my time, I am occupied with appraisal talks, meetings on the student board, computerization, real estate, financial and other issues.

Well, and then some students throw snowballs, and a teacher comes running, and I have to rush out and take care of that too. Discussions of educational leadership is something I wish I had time to deal with [he adds with a sigh]. That's a dream. This is a large school with so many student and personnel duties and loads of paperwork.

During our talk, several people come by with some small matter on their mind. Peter describes to me how he would like the school to work:

More cooperation, an integration of subjects and student age groups. At another school, where I used to teach, they had well-functioning work units. Here, a lot of teachers prefer subject-oriented groups.

I wonder why there should be a dichotomy between the two. Peter continues:

I have tough fights with the teachers. They are stubborn and powerful, and resist changes toward teamwork.

Peter admits that his attempts to make changes led to a backlash and that he was forced to switch from team meetings to subject meetings.

When I ask about his interaction with the teachers and other personnel, it becomes obvious that, as a leader, he has closer work relations with the pupils' support staff than with the teachers. He interacts indirectly with the teachers as a group through representatives on a management board. On the other hand, individually, teachers also turn to him with all sorts of matters. Nevertheless, many co-workers feel he is absent from the school's most important business, the educational process. The relation to the school director is also indirect, since the city's school board introduced another level of management, district managers, a few years back. Also, formally, the principal's position in the organization ranks higher, but in practice is equal to that of powerful teachers and groups of teachers.

The introductory text above exemplifies what the introductions to each of the three cases covered in my study look like. The aim of using this style of writing is to take the reader by the hand and lead him or her into each of the schools, in order to get a feeling for the physical environment, the people and everyday school life. In this chapter, my intention is to share how I have used ethnographic methods to 'get inside the school' and study school management.

## The study in brief and the choice of method

The purpose of this study, conducted in the late 1990s, was to examine leadership in Swedish schools. Examining whether administrators of schools had any possibility of improving how a school works through organizing teachers into cooperative teams was of special interest. Patterns in leadership were analyzed and described based on three case studies. I was curious whether local school management had any impact on cooperation within the school and, if so, how this could be described.

There are at least three reasons for my having chosen an ethnographic approach. Firstly, leadership research has been heavily criticized for not really contributing to our knowledge about this very popular but hard-to-grasp phenomenon (Alvesson and Sveningsson 2003). According to the definition used in my study, 'leadership' includes social interaction, a will to influence in a certain situation, and some goal or goals to be reached. Taking this definition seriously means looking for a method that describes and explores from within. The second reason for choosing an ethnographic approach is that a perspective based on a social constructionist view sees actors as sense-making subjects, rather than objects, in organizations. Thirdly, the theoretical model developed to analyze the empirical material is highly influenced by organizational culture theory, which has its origin in ethnography. A basic thought is that how people think and act in everyday life is to a large extent influenced by shared beliefs of the local school's purpose and ongoing activities. See Box 6.1.

The method used is a comparative case study of everyday working life in three schools, called Minerva (academic school), Merkurius (company school) and Myrten (alternative school). In light of the research questions on leadership formulated in this study, ethnographic case studies seemed especially suitable. One reason is that a small number of cases allow rich descriptions from various angles. The empirical material is collected through observations and interviews with school administrators, teachers and other school staff, and through documents. 'Leadership' is defined as a process where the school management negotiates to gain influence over how important issues are described and handled within the school. The model also assumes that leadership is influenced by local identity and structure. A central assumption in the theoretical model is therefore that identity and structure together constitute the organizational stage upon which everyday work and leadership are played. However, the local stage is related to a more general historical and societal context of schools. This is because local identity and structure receive legitimacy from meta-ideas observed in the general context. Based on the assumptions of the model, analyses of organizational structure, organizational identity and leadership are carried out.

**Box 6.1**    *The theoretical model guiding the study*

A central assumption in the theoretical model is that identity and structure together constitute the organizational stage upon which everyday work, leadership and cooperation are played. However, the local stage is related to the general historical and societal context of schools. The reason for this is that local identity and structure are given legitimacy by meta-ideas observed in the general context. Three such relevant meta-ideas are: the *traditional knowledge school*, the *company-like school* and the independent or *alternative school*. Based on the assumptions of the model, four analyses are carried out: of organizational structure, organizational identity, cooperation and leadership, respectively.

## Characteristics of an ethnographic approach

The word 'ethnography' derives from the Greek words *ethnos* ('people') and *graphein* ('to write'). The word, though, has more than one meaning. First, it denotes the science itself. Second, 'doing ethnography' means using an ethnographic approach in your study. Third, writing up an ethnography means presenting a text with certain characteristics, a 'thick description'.

Before going into detail about my own ethnographic experience, I would like to present my view of what the characteristics and goals of using ethnography in the field of leadership and organization are. Firstly, being rooted in anthropology, where culture is a central concept, an ethnographic approach means applying a holistic view of an organization as a cultural system. In reasoning about what culture is, and how it ought to be studied, Clifford Geertz, an appreciated writer on culture, uses examples from burial ceremonies in Java, as well as cockfighting in Bali (Geertz 1973). In his examples, Geertz shows that in order to understand an event, a good grasp of the whole in which the event takes place, and is given meaning, is needed. The same goes for organization theorists who use ethnographic perspectives and methods. Gideon Kunda (1992) offers a colourful picture of the culture of Tech Corporation, exploring how people are socialized into, and committed to, an engineering culture in California's Silicon Valley. Other authors point out that organizations need to be understood as cultural phenomena that develop, change and legitimize themselves during the course of social interaction (Garsten 1994).

Secondly, studying from within is characteristic of the ethnographic approach. Placing the focus on the locals, whether Balinese (Geertz 1973) or

IKEA workers (Salzer-Mörling 1994), means trying to understand how people make sense of their everyday life, or, as Garsten puts it, 'how employees go about organizing those aspects of the cultural flow as to arrive at a meaningful understanding of the context within which they work' (Garsten 1994: 33). When trying to do research, becoming totally included in a cultural system is neither easy nor healthy. Still, striving for an understanding of how people think, act and reason, in order to learn about that system, is very different from testing some theoretical hypothesis constructed in your armchair.

Thirdly, when sharing time and space working together in occupational groups, management teams or departments, people develop shared understandings and a sense of belonging. Therefore, ethnographic research of organization and leadership often includes stories, myths, symbols and artifacts, as they are seen as manifestations and surfaced shared meaning in the cultural system. In Kunda's story of Tech Corporation, socialization rites, beer busts, logotypes and the Tech building itself are prime examples of these cultural categories.

Fourthly, relations of power and influence, aspects that are of special interest when studying leadership, are central in understanding culture. From an ethnographic point of view, power relations are locally constructed, although they can be influenced by meta-ideas on ideal leadership, etc. Patterns of influence may or may not correspond to formal patterns of power. They should therefore be explored and understood as an empirical and culturally-embedded phenomenon. There is often tension between top-management views and subordinate interpretations and re-interpretations of how things are to be understood. Leadership in a cultural setting may therefore be about the management of meaning (Smircich and Morgan 1982) and taking part in the struggle for the 'right' or 'good' interpretation of what is going on and what to do about it. At IKEA (Salzer-Mörling 1994), the leadership style of the founder, as constructed in the rhetoric of the company, is an important part of the culture. IKEA managers are supposed to walk the talk. Managers are like any employee, wearing the red IKEA shirt, walking around the showroom floor, flying economy class, etc.

In sum, the above are what I feel to be central characteristics for ethnography, and therefore important to be aware of. The goals of doing ethnography include getting a first-hand feeling for the people you are studying (Agar 1980: 69), which requires being out in the field among the people and in the organization(s) being studied. The aim is not to test a hypothesis, but rather to learn and to understand by observation. Finally, writing up an ethnography is also part of the work. This means '[transferring] observations into an account that group members say are possible interpretations of what is going on' (Agar 1980: 81).

## Inside the three schools

My ambition of using an ethnographic approach in this study meant getting close to the three schools and their people, especially the school management and teachers, in order to understand their culture. I visited the schools[1] six-ten times over a 15-month period, from autumn 1994 until the end of 1995. The data used in the study were collected in different ways: through observation, interviews and documents. The aim was to gain a deep understanding of cooperation and leadership processes in each school, using an ethnographic approach to study, and to narrate this understanding. As I wanted to pin down such a hard-to-grasp phenomenon as leadership, a combination of observations and interviews was crucial for the study. The observations were very fruitful and yielded valuable memories of people's faces, body language and ways of expressing values and beliefs, as well as their ways of interacting with each other. Observations focused on both formal and informal meetings, arenas I considered to be the most common and important for leadership and cooperation processes. The interviews enabled me to follow up the observed events, in order to better understand their meaning. Below are a number of excerpts from the thematic ethnographies in the study. The first are from the academic school (Minerva), where we return to Peter, whom you met in the introduction. For contrast, I also provide glimpses from the company school (Merkurius) and its principal, Stefan.

From the introduction we know that both Peter and many of the teachers feel that he is very busy and that people come to him all the time. On the other hand, there seems to be a distance between management and the teachers:

> There is at all the same continuity among the principals as compared to the teachers at Minerva. The principals come and go, but many of the teachers have been around since the school started in 1969.
>
> (Teacher S)

> The principal is not a part of the Minerva spirit. All that lies with the teachers.
>
> (Teacher A)

A key to understanding the principal's position and his prerequisites for leadership is to be found in the culture of the academic school. Most important in this respect is the 'knowledge through the teachers'. At the academic school, this means putting the subjects, and the individual teachers with deep knowledge in subjects such as maths, science, etc., at the forefront. A major story has to do with how the school was started, and how 'a stable cadre of teachers' is still around. Continuity and a strong spirit are therefore related to teachers, not principals. There is a strong bearing on the meta-idea of the specialized professional teacher. One ritual that keeps the subject groups going is the annual Christmas party, where a spoon is symbolically traded from subject group to subject group. In leadership terms, this means that there is a group of teachers, with a number of strong individuals who serve as significant representatives, that has a strong influence on how things are interpreted. One conclusion that may be drawn from this is that the principal, Peter, in practice, does not have a superior position in the school organization. In the academic school, there is no room for accepting a manager-like leader. An example of this is Peter's lack of success in introducing work units. The conference schedule, symbolically enough, is dominated by subject group meetings, and pressure from the teachers forced Peter to abandon his ambition to hold workgroup meetings.

In the company school, there seems to be closer relations between management and teachers, and a different view of the influence of school administrators:

> The principals add character to the atmosphere at a school. If the leader is hierarchical, everything will be hierarchical. Alternatively, many people may be knowledgeable, involved and take responsibility.
>
> (Teacher I)

Every Monday, the school management team meeting is followed by a meeting with all personnel. Often, issues are solved on the spot. It is also a good opportunity for the principal to tell stories and give his view of how the school is working. Also at the company school, a story is told. It is not about the birth of the school, but rather about a crisis situation followed by a need to choose the route into the future:

> 1987–88, we had a crisis at the school, related to a conflict between the principal and the director of studies. Many teachers left the school, and so did management.
>
> (Teacher I)

The story told is about the crisis when the more traditional teachers left, and about the new principal being recruited 'from the outside' in order to 'create a peaceful work environment'. The new road included many changes:

> From 1991 to 1994, Merkurius School went through profound change processes. The processes have led to what we call 'the Merkurius model': small classes, of 16 students, despite restrictions in budget.
>
> (Principal)

'Quality through organizing' is an expression that comes up when trying to capture the culture at the company school. An early idea from the teachers was picked up on by the principal: building teaching teams (work units) around small classes. The teachers even agreed on longer working hours in order to create this new work organization! The individual teacher's role is closely related to the team, and they are striving towards a broader role, teaching two or more subjects, along with having greater responsibility for the students' well-being. In the academic school, these tasks are excluded from the teachers' more knowledge-based identity. The differences in culture can partly explain why the principal's position here is different. It is not as important here to maintain professional distance and autonomy. Rather, part of the culture itself is 'to be modern and changing'. A strong manager-like leader fits rather well with this culture. He is allowed to take responsibility for the overall organization and economy of the school, especially building image and relations with the environment:

> As principal, I am responsible for the whole. An important part of this is the school's economic situation in relation to a holistic perspective on what we do. For management, major tasks include preaching, delegating responsibility and encouraging people to take on development projects, etc.

He also explains how important he considers the external relations to be. The principal uses every opportunity to relate good stories to the teachers, parents, etc. about the school's reputation. People seem to give him credit for what he does, which makes sense, since the good spills over to everyone at the school:

> The school has gained publicity, and also been lauded in a public report in which the tight relation between finances and the educational programme is highlighted.

The ethnographies of the three schools studied are constructed in a similar manner. Physical environment and meeting facilities make up one theme; how the actors ('teacher', 'student', 'management', etc.) are constructed, and how people identify and form groups are others. Also significant are how the school's culture and raison d'être are interpreted by the members. Examples of how the 'teacher' is constructed and looked upon in each of the three schools are given below. In the academic school, the teacher is very much an autonomous specialist, admired for his or her deep knowledge. The specialization factor means the subject logic is very strong, while other duties, such as the caretaking part of pupil relations, are handed over to others in the school.

In the company school, the 'teacher' is a broader construction, both when it comes to subjects (teaching in two or more subjects is desirable) and to being a member of one of the teaching teams (where people find part of their identity), thus integrating teaching with the social side of pupil relations.

In the alternative school, the teacher is constructed as one who 'carries the school', being part of the 'collegium', the consensus-based form of management (and wiping out the border between professional and private life, you can always call a teacher at home).

These and other constructions are intermediated through storytelling within the schools. Therefore, organizational stories or 'sagas' are important. As Clark puts it, a saga is:

> a narrative of heroic exploits, of a unique development that has deeply stirred the emotions of participants and descendants. Thus a saga is not simply a story but a story that at some time has had a particular base of believers.
>
> (Clark 1972: 178)

When the story is given life, a piece of history is transformed and filled with pride and identity for the members of an organization. A typical saga is a collective interpretation of something unique that a group of people has been through together. The birth and crisis sagas of the schools described above are two examples, and include both rational and emotional elements. The rational parts explain how one thing led to another, while the emotional parts can turn a school into a highly beloved institution that people can be very devoted to and willing to fight for. In sum, the stories and sagas in the schools studied are of three types: stories that call attention to and compare 'our school' to others; stories about the school's origin; and stories about actual changes important to the school, e.g. the new curriculum in 1994.

For an ethnographic case description to be comprehensible and readers able to assess it requires not only a satisfying amount of observations, but also that these observations fit together in a trustworthy manner. From an ethnographic standpoint, one can say that a case description should enable the reader to understand the meaning of what is going on (Geertz 1973). This means the description should be 'thick' in content. The text should have colour, shape, taste and smell. Another aspect of a good story is to present two landscapes: one of action, and one of conceptions and images (Forssell 1992).

## Lessons learned

How, then, can differences in leadership between the schools be understood using ethnography? What are the lessons learned?

Using a relational perspective on leadership means shifting the focus from a strong emphasis on the leader as an individual, to viewing leadership as a process and something to be found 'between' people, that is, in the relationships. Therefore, the analysis does not take the principal's formal position for granted. Relations with important actors and groups of actors are analyzed, as are the actions taken by principals in order to lead.

As described earlier, in the academic school, the principal has a position parallel to that of the teachers. The relations are indirect and characterized by distance. In the company school, school administrators' relationships with the teachers are closer and more direct, and his position superior. The third school, the alternative school, exhibits interwoven and colleague-based relations, and a superior position for school administrators. The conclusion to be drawn from this is not that the three school managements are stronger or weaker, or more or less effective, etc., but rather that the ethnographic approach helped me to see leadership in a cultural context, and to realize that management, as well as other actors, had to deal with different belief systems and expectations of leadership.

This has not been my conclusion all along, however, and here it is important to discuss the researcher's role. The criteria for choosing the schools were that they be different but equally 'good' with respect to their reputations. My first impression of the academic school was one of familiarity. I recognized a lot from my own time in compulsory school in the 1970s. After a time, I began to feel that this school was very traditional, conservative and rigid. I felt almost sorry for the principal and perceived his behaviour as weak. The company school, on the other hand, gave me a lot of energy, and I was impressed by their principal's well-developed thoughts on leadership and organizing. Both these schools were easy to gain access to, although the principals had very different ways of acting when introducing me and my study to the rest of the school. In the academic school, Peter posted a list in the teachers' room, where people were to sign up for interviews. Not a single name appeared. I had to suggest that I present the purpose of the study at a meeting, and then contact people. At the company school, Stefan thought someone doing research was good publicity and in line with being modern, and encouraged me to mingle with the teachers in order to give my project 'a face'.

The alternative school was harder to access. The process was much slower there, mostly because decisions were consensus-based and discussed in their so-called Thursday 'collegium'. They were also keen on me having knowledge about the Waldorf pedagogy. Being in the midst of a tough time with criticism from the Swedish National Agency for Education, they wanted to be left alone. The different reactions encountered became a part of the analysis. A lesson learned here was that there is information to be gained in every encounter with the studied culture. 'Data' is everywhere. The ethnographic approach is a way of seeing and using the many different forms of data.

As the study progressed, it was important to shift from being close to being more distant. Anthropologists use the expression 'go native' to describe the condition when you get too close and lose the ability to distance yourself as a researcher. For me, it was a phase I went through, where I noticed that I was emotionally involved and could not see the pros and cons of each school. In the end, I used the possibilities of contrast between the three organizations in order to see what was going on. In ethnographic studies, contrast is an important 'tool', helping one to see and focus on cultural signs and the meanings given to these signs. In traditional ethnographic studies, the researcher's own home culture has been the implicit source of contrast. Here, I used the contrast between the three schools – in addition to implicit contrasts with my own previous school experiences. The theories used were also important to enable distance. For example, I realized that the alternative school was not as strange as I first thought. In some respects, it was like any school; in others, it was different. In the end, I felt much more positive towards the academic school, and discovered the strengths of that culture.

In sum, it was necessary to work through my own prejudice, feelings and preferences, and my role as a researcher. A logbook I kept of my own reflections was useful in this work. This relates to the work of writing up an ethnography. The definition of the words *ethnos* ('people') and *graphein* ('to write') points to the fact that the method and the presentation are inseparable parts of research if you define it as a process of constructing meaning. When I, as a researcher, work in an ethnographic tradition, it is impossible not to *construct* reality when attempting to *represent* reality with my descriptions. All descriptions are to some extent also analyses, since they are interpretations of interpretations. Although I tried to make my observations unnoticed, the researcher's role can never be completely 'objective'. Some degree of involvement in the social interplay is inevitable, and the examples above gave me information not only about the cultures of the schools, but also about the role of researcher. I got the touch and feel of the cultural webs that I could expect the members to also have.

When defining leadership as 'a process where the school management negotiates to gain influence over how important issues are described and handled within the school', it becomes necessary to try to understand the influence of the school's management among other actors, to identify how issue(s) are described and handled, and to understand the cultural web within which these issues are interpreted. The ethnographic approach yielded me a grasp of the leadership of the school management as well as the importance of other actors. The implications for leadership scholars are that leadership should be seen as a culturally-embedded process of influence and power, with a focus on the management of meaning.

In sum, based on studying schools from within, the patterns of leadership found were not in line with the ideal model of school leadership presented in the Swedish curriculum, in the media and in many ongoing debates at the time. Still, the academic school, the company school and the alternative school are all 'good' schools. One lesson to be drawn from this study is that we need to scrutinize the ideals and myths around leadership. Theories and methods for studying leadership are largely influenced by these same ideals and myths. I therefore argue that an ethnographic approach opens up new possibilities in management studies.

## Note

1   The schools used in the study are referred to as: the *academic* school (Minerva)
    – a traditional school located on the outskirts of a mid-sized city in central
    Sweden, with about 520 students and 60 teachers; the *company* school
    (Merkurius) – a more 'modern' school in the middle of a large city, with 600
    students and 50 teachers; and the *alternative* school (Myrten) – a Waldorf-type
    school outside a large city, with 200 students and 40 teachers. The Swedish
    National Agency for Education assisted with the choice of the first two schools,
    and the Waldorf Federation with the third. The alternative school is smaller than
    the other two due to the fact that no larger Waldorf school was available at the
    time.

## References

Agar, M.H. (1980) *The Professional Stranger: An Informal Introduction to Ethnography*, New York: Academic Press.

Alvesson, M. and Sveningsson, S. (2003) 'Managers Doing Leadership: The Extraordinarization of the Mundane', *Human Relations*, 56, 12: 1435–1459.

Clark, B.R. (1972) 'The Organizational Saga in Higher Education', *Administrative Science Quarterly*, 17: 178–183.

Forssell, A. (1992) *Moderna tider i sparbanken: om organisatorisk omvandling i ett institutionellt perspektiv* (Modern Times in the Savings Bank, with English summary), dissertation, Department of Business Studies, Uppsala: Uppsala University.

Garsten, C. (1994) *Apple World: Core and Periphery in a Transnational Organizational Culture*, Department of Social Anthropology, Stockholm: Stockholm University.

Geertz, C. (1973) *The Interpretation of Cultures: Selected essays*, New York: Basic Books.

Kunda, G. (1992) *Engineering Culture: Control and Commitment in a High-Tech Corporation*, Philadelphia: Temple University Press.

Salzer-Mörling, M. (1994) 'Identity Across Borders: A Study in the "IKEA-world"', dissertation, Linköping: Linköping University.

Smircich, L. and Morgan, G. (1982) 'Leadership: The Management of Meaning', *Journal of Applied Behavioural Science*, 18, 3: 257–273.

# 7 Tracing consultants' problem-solving processes

## A simulation approach

*Andreas Werr*

## The problem – are methods used in management consulting?

Today's large consulting organizations, such as Accenture, CapGemini, McKinsey & Co, etc., all invest considerable amounts of both time and money in competence and knowledge development. In all these efforts to develop and share knowledge within the consulting organization, detailed methods and tools, i.e. standardized approaches and checklists for how to carry out specific activities, play a role, although to a varying extent (Hansen *et al.* 1999).

However, research on both systems development and consulting shows that consultants' actions are better described as largely intuitive, based on the actors' prior experience, rather than as guided by structured and detailed methods. Efforts to understand and map the knowledge involved, e.g. in organization consulting, show that it is hard to capture this knowledge in well-structured methods and tools (Rhenman 1968; Karlsson 1975). This directs the focus away from methods to the consultant's intuition and 'feel' for the situation. This tension between large investments in the development of detailed methods and the claimed inefficiency of methods calls for a better understanding of the link between formal and detailed methods and management consultants' problem-solving. More specifically, the question guiding the study to be reported here is: *Do methods influence consultants' problem solving? And – if so – how?*

The approach taken to answering this question focuses on the consultants' problem-solving behaviour, making the methodological focus of this chapter one of understanding human problem solving. The methodological approaches to be illustrated include simulations, verbal protocols and the tracking of information acquisition behaviour. In the following, I will start with a presentation of the process approach to studying problem solving. I will then turn to a more thorough discussion of issues related to the design of the simulation, followed by a discussion of the analysis of obtained data and some conclusions on the research questions posed above. I conclude the chapter with reflections on the methodology and its validity.

## Studying problem-solving processes

The above research question calls for a close study of management consultants' thought processes when dealing with the problems of their clients. This was an interest of organization research in the 1970s, with at least two studies trying to map important elements in the thought processes of consultants when designing organizational structures (Rhenman 1968; Karlsson 1975). The purpose of both of these studies was to identify elements in experienced consultants' problem solving in order to create an efficient method for organization analysis. I thus share an interest in the problem-solving processes with these studies. However, the research question guiding this interest is rather different. While Rhenman and Karlsson were interested in developing a method for organizational design, based on a study of experienced consultants, my interest is in the way in which existing methods are manifested and used in the work of the consultants. Still, these other two studies provide important points of departure for this study, as they provide a wealth of suggestions, experience and reflections on how to study consultants' work in simulations.

While problem-solving processes are constantly ongoing in the work of management consultants, it is also a process which is hard to access, as it takes place in the heads of the consultants and in the direct interaction with the client – an interaction that is regarded as highly sensitive by consultants and thus hard to access. Furthermore, methods are part of what management consultants sell and the means by which they legitimate their practice, making the study of them and how they are used even more sensitive from the consultants' perspective. Inspired by the studies of Rhenman (1968) and Karlsson (1975), which provided rather detailed descriptions of approaches for how simulations could be set up and carried out, a decision was made early on to pursue a simulation approach.

While the studies provided detailed accounts of the practical considerations involved in setting up a simulation with management consultants, less was said about the nature of human thought processes and the ways in which those could be studied. I therefore engaged in a brief excursion into the psychological literature, where the study of individuals' thought processes has a long history in, among other areas, the field of judgement analysis (see e.g. Cooksey 1996). Payne *et al.* (1993) identify two techniques for the study of such cognitive processes – analysis of verbal protocols and analysis of information acquisition behaviour. In the first case, the focus is on the test person's thoughts during the completion of the task of interest; in the latter, on the test person's interest for different parts of the information available for the task. In this study, both methods will be used in parallel.

Ericsson and Simon (1984) distinguish between two types of verbal protocols – 'concurrent verbal reports', which are produced at the same time as the cognitive process of interest takes place (think aloud, talk aloud), and 'retrospective verbal reports', which are produced after the process of interest has taken place, through interviews asking persons to reconstruct their thought processes. The former, concurrent verbal reports, are generally regarded as more reliable, as they directly report what passes through short-term memory, a prerequisite for articulation as argued by Ericsson and Simon (1984).

Concurrent verbal protocols are produced by asking the consultant to think aloud during his or her problem-solving process. Two criticisms are often raised against the validity of verbal protocols. The first concerns whether these can be regarded as comprehensive reports of the information that is consciously taken into account during the process; the second concerns the question of whether the verbalization of thoughts changes the problem-solving process under study. These two issues will be discussed briefly in the final section of this chapter.

## Designing the simulation

Given the choice of a simulation study that captures consultants' problem-solving processes through both verbal protocols and information acquisition behaviour, I had to make a number of other choices concerning the more detailed design of the simulation. Patrick and James (2004) propose four generic stages that process studies of cognitive tasks have to deal with: collection of data, transcription, integration and segmentation of the data into a time-line account, coding, and further analysis and representation of the data. In this section, I will deal with issues concerning the collection of data, including the choice of situation to simulate, the choice of a case to simulate, the way in which case data were to be presented to the consultants, and what data should be captured and how during the simulation process. The activities related to the analysis will be covered in a subsequent section.

### The situation to simulate

The consulting process as a whole is so multifaceted and spread out in time that it cannot possibly be captured in a delimited simulation. I thus had to choose a part of the consulting process as the focus for my study. This part should be one that is perceived as important by the consultants, and to which they could be expected to devote some thought, at the same time as it should involve the use of the consulting companies' methods.

A situation that fulfilled these requirements was the design of a first project plan with a statement of the problem, a delimitation, a proposed approach, some preliminary thoughts about the project's results and an analysis of the threats against the change project. Such tasks are often carried out in connection with the writing of a proposal for a project. These activities had also been identified in previous interviews with consultants as important in the consulting organization. The proposal-writing phase was also deemed suitable as it left it to the discretion of the consultants to apply their approaches of choice. In situations later in a change process, the consultants' choices can be severely limited by choices made earlier in the process.

Furthermore, in writing a first proposal for a project, the kinds of activities of interest here – the application of a general method to a unique situation – are potentially well illustrated. In producing a project proposal, a first adaptation of the general method to the unique situation is carried out. In this process, a complex situation is framed, and its important aspects (problems) are identified, an activity that is assumed to be influenced by the structure and content of the method. Finally, the design of a realistic simulation should be facilitated by the fact that in the early phases of the project the consultant normally has relatively limited information about the organization and its problems. Against this background, limitations in the volume and richness of data in the simulation situation should have only limited effects on its perceived realism.

The task of formulating a first project proposal was also relatively well delimited, which was identified as important by Karlsson (1975). Having used a very general question in his simulation – 'carry out a first general analysis of the problem situation' – Karlsson concludes that a more limited task, such as producing a first project proposal, would have contributed to a higher realism of the simulations.

## The case

The choice of the case providing the background for the consultants' proposal has been identified by both Rhenman (1968) and Karlsson (1975) as critical for the perceived realism of the simulations and thereby their validity. Choices regarding the case concerned both content and form. The content had to match the consultants' approach so that the kind of data in focus in the approach was available in the case. In this study, all consultants applied some kind of business process approach, which made information on workflow important. Concerning the form of the data, this had to be sufficiently detailed and complex to be perceived as realistic. According to Karlsson (1975), this can be achieved with a relatively limited amount of information. In his study, a six-page organization and problem description and a 30-page reference material was deemed sufficient to solve a problem of organizational structure. A more extensive reference base did not change the approach.

As the task in the present study was the production of a proposal sketch, it was realistic that the available information be rather limited. In a real project, the consultant would probably be able to conduct one or at most a few interviews as well as collect some secondary data before completing the proposal. It is therefore important that the information provided in the case makes it possible to obtain a broad and holistic picture of the organization and its problem.

Against this background, a relatively rich description of the case was prepared based on the available information of a process improvement project in a surveying authority. This generated about 20 pages of text, which were distributed to 46 information cards. The case provided a description of an organization having problems with their efficiency. The fictitious client was chief surveyor Gustavsson of a Swedish county, who had problems with the lead times of the surveying office's services. The task for the consulting project, as formulated by the client, was to shorten lead times. The content of the case is briefly summarized in Figure 7.1.

The information provided included both 'hard' data, such as the budget, organizational structure, etc., as well as 'softer' aspects, such as information on the organizational culture and employees' attitudes to change. In writing up the case, I made an effort to be as 'ethnographic' as possible in order to convey a feeling for the organization as well as its culture.

## Presentation of the case

The way in which data is transmitted to the test persons is important not only for the perceived realism of the situation, and thereby the motivation of the consultant, but also for the ability to follow the problem-solving process.

A first choice to make in relation to the consultant's access to the case data is whether this should be made available all at once or in a way that forces the consultant to actively search for the information she believes she needs. Karlsson (1975) chose the former approach and provided his test persons with extensive written material; whereas Rhenman (1968) opted for the latter, making the consultants collect data by asking a company representative. Both approaches were described as successful, but it was indicated that the portion-wise provisioning of data used by Rhenman was more

The surveying authority in the Västmanland County consists of three local offices and one central office employing about 40 persons. The chief surveyor in charge is Gustavsson. The surveying authority's main task is the parcelling of land, as well as activities related to this. These activities are to a large extent publicly funded, but in recent years, the surveying authority has increased its services that render direct income from private clients. There is a desire to further increase this line of business.

The main problem faced by the surveying authority are the lead times for handling cases. The current long lead times are problematic both from a customer service perspective as well as from a cost perspective. Several reasons are indicated for these long lead times; among others, are cases that are submitted with missing information and a lack of interaction between personnel groups, as well as a large number of cases in the system. Some of these problems are linked to the system of financial control, which requires that activities be charged to specific cases.

The need for change is regarded as urgent by chief surveyor Gustavsson, but he also points out that the change process must not disturb the ongoing business. The workload is high and the change process should not interfere with day-to-day work. Work is already disturbed by a new nation-wide IT system currently being developed on a national level for the surveying authority.

Gustavsson describes the personnel as somewhat tired of change. There have been a lot of changes in the past year, some that have led to real change as well as a number of initiatives that were discontinued before any results were obtained.

*Figure 7.1* A brief summary of the surveying authority providing the input for the simulations

suitable when the problem-solving process is the focus of interest. This way of making data available facilitates the tracking of the problem-solving process (Karlsson 1975).

A second choice in presenting the case concerns the media by which information is made available. Should the information be provided in written or in oral form through 'face-to-face' communication? These two approaches are again represented in the studies by Rhenman (1968) and Karlsson (1975). The advantages attributed to the oral transmission of information are that this is perceived as more realistic and requires less preparation in terms of the writing and testing of cases (Karlsson 1975). A drawback, on the other hand, is that the personal interaction between the test subject and information provider introduces a variable in the problem-solving process that is hard to control (Rhenman 1968). As one of the advantages of a simulation study is exactly this possibility of controlling the premises of the process (Weick 1965), the introduction of variables that are hard to control should be avoided as far as possible.

Providing information in written form has the main advantage of support-ing standardization across the different consultants' simulations as well as being easy to reuse. The main disadvantage of this approach is its inflexi-bility. The amount of information as well as its focus may not answer the consultants' questions, which may reduce the realism of the simulation.

For this study, an approach was chosen in which written data was provided step-by-step via a computer at the consultants' demand. The information in the case was divided into small information elements treating a specific theme. The text in Figure 7.1 provides an example of such an information card. The cards were available through a menu at the bottom of each card, as well as hypertext links in the text on the cards. This approach made it possible to follow the information collection process in detail. It also ensured standardized stimuli, which made it easier to identify the possible effects of the method on the consultants' problem solving.

## Data capturing

The approach to data capturing is to a large extent a function of the choices described above concerning the situation to simulate, the scope and level of detail of the case, and how case information is provided. Patrick and James (2004) argue for the use of multiple data sources in trying to understand cognitive processes. Verbal protocols should thus be complemented by, for example, behavioural data. In this vein, during the consultants' work with the task, which typically took two to three hours, three types of data were collected by the researcher:

1   The consultants' written proposal sketches produced during the simu-lations (the outcome of the task).
2   The consultants' verbalized thoughts during the simulations.
3   Information on the consultants' data collection behaviour in terms of what information was looked at, in which order and for how long.

In addition, pre- and post-interviews were used to collect data on the con-sultants' background, their methods and their perceptions of the simulation process (e.g. its realism).

Different techniques were used to capture the different kinds of data. The consultants' verbalized thoughts were videotaped and transcribed *verbatim*. The consultants' data collection behaviour was logged automatically by the computer. The verbal protocols were also synchronized with the information on the consultants' information collection behaviour by linking each utterance to the information card the consultant looked at at the time. The consultants' proposal sketches were documented on the computer, as the consultants were asked to write these directly on a blank information card in the program.

In order to ensure that the chosen approach was realistic and generated data of a satisfactory quality, I carried out a test simulation. In these simulations, all the steps of data collection and analysis were gone through. The evaluation of the test led to some minor changes in the instructions, the information provided, and the formulation of the questions asked before and after the simulations.

### Recruiting participants

The recruitment of test persons was characterized by an effort to strike a balance between variety in central dimensions, sufficient similarities to enable comparisons, and what was deemed possible in terms of the consulting companies' willingness to devote time and effort to the research. This balancing turned out as follows. In total, six simulations were carried out with consultants from two organizations (local and international), three from one and four from the other (in the latter case, a simulation was carried out by two persons working together). The sample of consultants was controlled with respect to the consultants' experience. The consultants from each organization represented a spread from junior to experienced consultants. In the following account of the analysis, the test persons are denoted L1-L4 and I1-I3, respectively, with L/I indicating their belonging to the 'Local' or 'International' consultancy and the number 1–4 indicating their level of seniority (1 = least experienced, 4 = most experienced). These consultants were trained in three different methods – L1 and L2 applied the RBG methodology (Rummler and Brache 1990), L3/4 used xABC (a variant of activity-based costing) and I1-I3 followed a 'business integration model' (see Werr 1999 for a more thorough description of the methodology).

## Analyzing the data

The focus of the analysis of the obtained data was the comparison between the different consultants' approaches to the problem, as well as the consistency of these approaches with the method applied by the consultants. Given the richness of the data collected, the analysis was carried out in several steps, using different parts of the data. As a first step, the consultants' proposed approaches to solving the client organization's problem were analyzed. If methods were directly followed, the logic went, this should be reflected in similar designs from consultants using the same method. However, as a detailed consistency between the solutions proposed by consultants using the same method could not be found, a second step of the analysis focused more closely on the consultant's problem-solving process. The consultants' information acquisition behaviour was here compared through a cluster analysis based on the time spent by the consultants on different information categories. Finally, in a third step of the analysis, the results of the cluster analysis are complemented and elaborated on by a qualitative analysis of the consultants' reflections on the case data, using the verbal protocols, i.e. their reflections during the process.

### Proposal design

Comparing the different consultants' proposed approaches shows that, even if the consultants use the same method, they structure the suggested approach differently, using somewhat different labels for the different phases. Looking at L1 and L2's approaches, clear differences in the wording and sequencing of the process can be observed in spite of the existence of an underlying common method providing a detailed step-by-step model for the mapping phase. This indicates that the design of the approach is not directly and mechanically linked to the method. Instead of the design being a rational process of choosing activities from a larger menu, it would seem to be a largely intuitive activity, based on the consultants' accumulated experiences.

The intuitive and experience-based aspects of the problem-solving process are also highlighted by the consultants themselves in their reflections on the process:

> The design of a proposal is merely a question of experience. I believe the results between different consultants are relatively similar. When we talk about designing a solution in a case like this, it's very much a task for the experienced project leaders and the partners. In the Stockholm office, 20 to 30 people do these kinds of tasks. They make the adaptations for the respective companies. This limits the differences that can emerge between projects. Within this boundary, adaptations are made. The differences are not very large. People who have worked for 10, 15, 20 years, have a history that leads to similar results.
>
> (I3).

This indicates that the design process is to a large extent based on the individual consultant's personal experience and intuition, and lacks direct references to methods or other types of shared and formalized knowledge within the organization. This confirms the picture given in the literature. But does it mean that methods are completely decoupled from their users' practice? In order to further investigate this question, I turned to the consultants' problem-solving process. In a first step, I looked at the consultants' information collection behaviour and then at their reflections.

### Information acquisition

What data do the consultants focus on in their information acquisition, and what are the similarities and differences between different consultants in this respect? This was the second question asked of the simulation data in the quest for a deeper understanding of the link between consultants' methods and their practice. Although the project proposals of the consultants did not correlate directly with the method, I suspected that methods could still influence consultant practice, although more indirectly by shaping the way in which consultants perceived the problem and thus the kinds of solutions they proposed. This reasoning was inspired by Schön's (1983) discussion of the reflective practitioner, where problem setting was identified as a key activity influenced by the practitioner's media and language, appreciative systems, overarching theories and role frames, elements that showed some similarities with the methods of consultants. Again, in a first step, the analysis focused on identifying the similarities and differences between the different consultants. If consultants using the same method showed similar patterns in the way they collected information, this would be taken as an indication of the method influencing the consultants' approach.

In order to investigate this question, a hierarchical cluster analysis was carried out, analyzing the similarities between the consultants' relative time spent on different information categories (see Box 7.1 for a description of this analysis and its results). While the cluster analysis revealed some similarities in behaviour between consultants that use similar methods, the low number of participants in the simulation made it difficult to claim with any certainty that it is the methods that explain the similarities and differences. I therefore wanted to know more about the nature of the differences and similarities in order to be able to compare them to the respective methods. Are the approaches taken within the different clusters linked to characteristics of the method used? A first step in this direction was to take a closer look at the kind of information focused on in the clusters identified above (see Table 7.1). A second step went beyond information acquisition and looked at how the consultants dealt with the acquired information as reflected in their 'thinking aloud' (i.e. the verbal protocols). This will be discussed in more detail in the next section.

Table 7.1 lists the five most important information categories for each consultant, as reflected in the relative time spent on the category. The numbers represent rank orders, where 1 is the category on which the consultant spent the most time. This closer look at the similarities and differences in the information acquisition behaviour of consultants in the different clusters reveals that information on the background of the problem, and the organization, is central to most of the consultants. In the information

---

**Box 7.1**   *Comparing information acquisition behaviour by hierarchical cluster analysis*

The cluster analysis is aimed at identifying homogenous groups, clusters of consultants, that show similar patterns when it comes to the relative time spent working with different information categories in the case. I chose to use the relative time – rather than the absolute time – spent on each information category in order to control for differences in reading speed, thoroughness of the consultants, etc. The hierarchical cluster analysis applied establishes clusters based on the distance between different consultants' time spent on different information categories. In this process, consultants are grouped together in a step-by-step procedure. First, the two most similar consultants are combined into one cluster. Next, a new cluster (the second most similar pair) of two consultants is created, or a consultant similar to the first cluster is added to this cluster. In combining the consultants into clusters, the average linkage method is applied, which calculates the distance between two clusters as an average of the distances between all pairs of consultants in the two clusters.

This step-by-step clustering procedure is visualized in the dendrogram in Figure 7.2, which, read from left to right, shows the order clusters were formed in and the relative distance at which they were formed. The first cluster formed consists of I1 and L3/L4, who combine at a relative distance of 1, indicating large similarities between their behaviours. The second cluster formed is that of L1 and L2, which combine at a distance of 8. At a distance of 15, I3 is added to the first cluster, and at a distance of 24, I2 is added to the second cluster (L1 and L2). (For further information about cluster analysis, see Norusis 1994.)

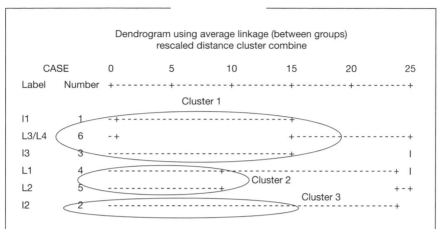

*Figure 7.2* Cluster analysis of the different consultants' approaches based on the relative time spent on different information categories.

*Note*: The cluster analysis was calculated with SPSS 8.0 using the 'average distance between groups' method for combining clusters and Euclidean distance for measuring distance.

Choosing a cut-off point at a relative distance of 15, three clusters may be identified (see Figure 7.2). The choice of cut-off point is a question of judgement, taking into account the structure of clusters and distances at which they were formed. Fifteen was deemed as a reasonable balance between the coherence of clusters and the number of clusters. The first cluster consists of I1, L3/L4 and I3, the second cluster of L1 and L2, and the third and final cluster is made up solely by I2. This reveals that two of the three consultants from each company show quite similar approaches – I1 and I3, as well as L1 and L2 – although the dendrogram shows that L1 and L2 are more similar than I1 and I3. One consultant in each company departs considerably from the pattern shown by his/her colleagues. In the case of L3/L4, who display a behaviour very similar to I1, the untypical behaviour correlates to the use of a different method – xABC – rather than the RBG method used by L1 and L2; I2's deviation from the other international consultants I1 and I3 is more difficult to explain.

category 'background', the surveyors' (i.e. the client's) own problem definition and goals for the project are presented. In the category 'organization', information about the central and local structure of the land-surveying authority is presented both verbally and graphically. The importance of this

*Table 7.1* Ranking of information categories according to proportion of time spent on gathering information for respective category

| | Cluster 1 | | | Cluster 2 | | Cluster 3 |
|---|---|---|---|---|---|---|
| | I1 | L3/L4 | I3 | L1 | L2 | I2 |
| Background | 1 | 1 | 3 | 1 | 1 | 1 |
| Organization | 2 | | 2 | 2 | 2 | 3 |
| Workflow | 4 | 2 | | | 4 | |
| Business | 3 | 3 | 1 | | | |
| Market | 5 | 5 | 4 | | | |
| Leadership style | | 4 | | 4 | 3 | |
| Personnel | | | | 3 | 5 | |
| Attitudes to change | | | | 5 | | 4 |
| History of change | | | | | | 5 |
| IT support | | | 5 | | | 2 |

information indicates that the client's own definition of the problem is an important point of departure when writing proposals. Even if the consultants to a greater or lesser extent question the client's problem definition, they all take it as their starting point.

Besides these similarities, Table 7.1 also reveals differences between the consultants, and especially between the clusters of consultants identified in the cluster analysis above. The comparison of the approaches between clusters 1 and 2 reveals one notable systematic difference. The consultants in cluster 1 seem to focus more on the external aspects of the organization (business, market), whereas the consultants in cluster 2 devote more time to the internal and people-oriented aspects of the organization (leadership style, personnel). Finally, I2 (cluster 3) differed from the others by focusing quite heavily on information about IT support and the organization's attitudes towards and history of change. In these areas, the overlap between the clusters is limited. In the case of method use, the three clusters overlap quite well, I2 being the exception, and the observed differences in the kind of information collected make sense in relation to the content of the method used, which I will come back to. This thus gave some support to an influence of methods on consultants' problem solving.

### Verbal protocols

The above investigation into what kind of information the different consultants spent time on gave some insights into the differences between the consultants' approaches. But what about their reasoning and their interpretation of the data? How did that differ and how did such differences relate to the content of their methods? Thus, in order to gain further insights, in a third step of the analysis, I turned to the consultants' verbal protocols, their verbalization of thinking during the simulation.

In this third step, the transcripts of the consultants' 'thinking aloud' were analyzed, again with a focus on similarities and differences between the consultants. The approach used may be described as an inductive content analysis (see Box 7.2). The analysis of the consultants' thinking aloud and the similarities and differences between their reflections pointed to three underlying dimensions that captured central differences between the consultants' ways of approaching the simulation problem. These dimensions represent differences in the consultants' organization theory (internal-external), their change theory (normative-rational) and their consulting theory (the degree of questioning of the client's view).

The *internal-external* dimension mainly indicates differences in the consultants' efforts to understand the organization and their identification of the organization's problems. Internally-oriented consultants focused more on information and problems related to issues such as culture and the mindsets of organizational members, reflecting a view of the organization as depending to a large extent on its employees for success. Consultants with a more external orientation, on the other hand, had a greater interest in the organization's link to its environment. Consequently, in their view, the organization was strongly interlinked with its environment and dependent on this for success.

The second dimension that emerged concerns the consultants' *change theory*. Barley and Kunda's (1992) distinction between a rational ideology and a normative ideology may be used to characterize the end points of this dimension. The differences along this continuum are reflected in the solution ideas, the proposed approach to change and the identified success factors. Towards the normative end of the scale, focus is on solutions in the realm of organization and competence, which may be contrasted to the solutions proposed by consultants on the rational end, where the focus is on control and reporting systems as the main vehicles for organizational change. When it comes to the approach to change and the barriers and enablers of change, the normative end implies a focus on the process rather than its content and the main barriers to change are described as cultural. At the rational end, focus is instead on the data to be collected in the consulting process and the barriers to change identified are of an economic and political nature.

Finally, the third dimension concerns the degree to which the consultants build on or question the client's analysis and are willing to accept the client's delimitation, indicating the use of different consulting theories. At the 'weak

**Box 7.2**   *Inductive content analysis of verbal protocols*

The consultants' thinking during the simulation, as reflected in the verbal protocols, took the form of comments on the data or questions asked of the data. The following is an example of a reflection made on the stated problem:

> Here we have a mix between cause and effect. But there is a root problem, which is stated as long lead times. But then the question is – what really causes this problem? But this is what they have identified as their root problem. . .
>
> (I1)

Comments and questions like this were numerous. In order to enable a comparison, the different consultants' comments and questions had to be sorted in some way. The choice was made to apply an inductive logic, thus sorting reflections into categories based on their similarity. The actual categorization of the consultants' reflections was carried out with the NUDIST computer analysis program, which supports the categorization of data and the easy retrieval of data stored in different categories or combinations thereof. The categorization in NUDIST was carried out in two consecutive stages. In the first stage, each consultant's verbal protocol was analyzed and all reflections categorized. New categories were created as they were needed, i.e. when the reflection to be categorized did not fit the existing categories. The second stage involved reading through the reflections assigned to each category in order to ensure that they described a common theme. At this stage, a number of errors in classification, as well as inconsistencies in the categories' content, were identified and corrected. Through this process 12 categories emerged, including: reflections on the client; the formal organization; the business; IT; the culture; the problems and change drivers; solution ideas; project organization, staffing and timing; approach to change; barriers to implementation; success factors; and delimitations.

Based on results from NUDIST, listing the reflections in each category, the reflections were summarized in short sentences and transferred to a table for the six consultants (see Table 7.2 for an example). These summaries constituted the basis for comparing the different consultants' reflections and thus for the formation of new sets of clusters of similar consultants for each of the themes. The actual comparison of different consultants' approaches was thus based on an aggregation of data, creating a risk of losing touch with the actual data behind the categories. However, I believe that this risk was partly avoided through the use of NUDIST, which made it possible to easily check the actual wording of a reflection, as well as trace it back to its source and context (see, for example, Fielding and Lee 1991; Richards and Richards 1994).

questioning' end of the scale, consultants to a large extent took the client's initial problem definition for granted and discussed delimitations within the client manager's area of authority. At the 'strong questioning' end, the questioning of the client's problem definition is instead in focus and reflections frequently concerned going beyond the authority of the client manager. The positions of the different consultants along the identified dimensions are shown in Figure 7.3.

This third step of the analysis, based on the consultants' thinking during the simulation, confirms to a large extent, although not entirely, the clustering of consultants produced in the analysis of the information acquisition behaviour (see Figure 7.2). It adds to this analysis, however, by providing a deeper understanding of the character of these differences. Given that consultants who use the same method seem to take similar positions along the identified dimensions, this elaborate analysis thus went one step further toward providing an understanding of the extent to which and how methods may influence the work of management consultants. Rather than providing a simple road map, it seems that methods may provide consultants with a theory of the organization, based on which it is analyzed, a theory of change, affecting the kinds of problems seen and solutions proposed, and a consulting theory, influencing the way in which the client is approached and the change process timed and delimited. However, this presupposes that the content of the method reflects the differences in the consultants' approaches observed. This called for a final step in the analysis to compare the observed differences along the identified dimensions with the content of the methods used.

## So – do methods influence consultants' work?

We are now approaching the end of this analytical journey, which aimed to establish the existence and character of a link between consultants' methods

Table 7.2 Summary of consultants' reflections on the client

| | L1 | L2 | L3/L4 | I1 | I2 | I3 |
|---|---|---|---|---|---|---|
| The client | Does Gustavsson (G) support the climate change? Gustavsson seems to be quite new. Is he accepted by the organization, or is he an outsider? | Reserved style, 'may not disturb the business'. Do they really want change? They talk about decentralization and wanting more initiative, but they send other signals. Who is the management for Västmanland? What expectations does the client have? | G is required by his managers to fix the handling times. Is G new or old in the organization? L3 and L4 are initially of different opinion, but conclude that he has a new style. G is conscious of cost being an important factor. | What does G expect – a mere process job or does he view it in a larger perspective? Time frame? It is important to understand what G sees. 'Why does he feel that change is necessary?' Who is the client? What does the procurement process look like, experience of consultants, change, etc? | Has G written the objectives himself? What is his view of BPR? Why has he invited me? | Important to understand G's situation (his boss, time pressure, pressure to change, etc.). G's mindset in relation to change. There are some indications in this case that he has the wrong mindset, which speaks for giving him a role as project manager. |

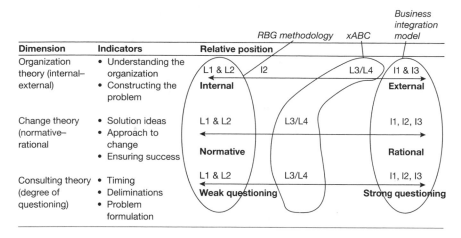

*Figure 7.3* The three basic dimensions summarizing differences in the consultants' reflections.

and their practice. The journey has taken us through a number of steps, looking at the different data generated by the simulations – first the proposals produced by the consultants, then the information acquisition behaviour and, finally, the consultants' reflections in the form of verbal protocols. The analysis has established groups of consultants acting in similar ways, and the analysis of the verbal protocols in particular has provided insights into the characteristic behaviours of the various different clusters of consultants.

Some evidence of the influence of methods on consultants' practice has been established through these processes of clustering since consultants using the same method generally followed similar approaches, as indicated by the analysis both of information acquisition behaviour and of the verbal protocols (with some exceptions however). However, a final step of the analysis still remains in order to establish a clear link between methods and consultants' practice. Do the methods the consultants claimed to use reflect the actual practice found, as reflected in the consultants' thinking? While space limitations prevent an in-depth account of this final step, it may be concluded that the differences in the consultants' organization, change and consulting theories were reflected in their method. The RGB methodology, users of which illustrated an internal organization theory, a normative change theory and a 'weak questioning' consulting theory, had a strong internal bias. The focus was on the organization's design and the capabilities of its members, and the role of the consultant was explicitly described as 'facilitator' rather than expert.

At the other extreme, users of the 'business integration model' demonstrated an externally-oriented organization theory, a rational change theory and a 'strong questioning' consulting theory. Again, these aspects were reflected in the methodology that clearly pointed out that an organization should be understood within its context, thus indicating the importance of external aspects. Implicit in this model was also a view of the consultant as an expert with the responsibility of the client's problem.

Finally, also the content of the xABC method matches the observed behaviour towards an externally-oriented change theory and change and consulting theories somewhere in the middle of the identified scales. This method explicitly focuses on the organization's links to its environment, and suggests a mixture of high client involvement in some steps and consultant expert analysis in other steps, which matches the observed intermediate position of the consultants for the change and consulting theories.

Against this background, we may thus not only conclude that methods influence the practice of consultants, but that the above analysis has also provided some insights into how this influence can take place. Throughout the analysis, it has become increasingly obvious that methods are not followed in detail. They do not provide the kind of 'road maps for change' that they are sometimes claimed to be. Instead, it seems that they influence consultants' actions through the consultants' organization theory, change theory and consulting theory. Based on Schön's (1983) conceptualization of the reflective practitioner, it may thus be argued that methods have an influence on consulting practice through their influence on the media and language through which practitioners understand the world, through the appreciative systems by which they judge it, through the overarching theories by which they make sense of it, and through the role frames by which they set their tasks. This influence, however, is to a large extent sub-conscious. The consultants seem to have internalized the main views and values underlying the method and act based on these internalized views and values. This indicates that methods do not exist 'outside' the individual and are 'applied' by the individual, such as is often described by consultants themselves as well as in the literature. Rather, methods are internalized, influencing the consultants' underlying theories concerning the organization, change and consulting.

## Reflections on the research practice

Above, I have described my efforts to understand the link between formal methods and consultants' thought processes through a simulation approach. In this final section of the chapter, I will critically reflect upon the data collection and analysis process in order to note some of the challenges involved in the simulation method and the use of verbal protocols when trying to capture problem-solving processes.

Firstly, the problem-solving process I studied above, by its character of simulation, was an artificial one, which raises the question of whether the observed process is representative of consultants' problem solving in 'real' situations. Secondly, the question of how the eliciting of verbal protocols affects the problem-solving process needs to be asked. Did the 'thinking aloud' of participants change their problem-solving behaviour in any significant way? Finally, the completeness of data given by verbal protocols needs to be discussed. To what extent were the consultants able to articulate their problem-solving processes?

The question of whether the simulations produced patterns of behaviour similar to what a real situation would is, of course, hard to answer with certainty without a study of the same process in a real situation. Such a study would, however, have been extremely difficult given the research questions in focus. However, there might be indicators of the realism of the simulations more readily available. One such indicator may be the test person's perceptions of the realism of the simulation. I identified two central aspects of such realism. The first concerned the problem and information presented in the case. The second aspect concerned the perception of the actual problem-solving situation (the simulation) and its coherence with a real-life situation.

The perceived realism of the case I discussed with the consultants involved in the simulation in the interview following the simulation. These interviews indicated that the test persons generally perceived the case as realistic. In some instances, they pointed out that the information was somewhat limited, but this was not viewed as a problem, as this was perceived as quite a usual situation in the proposal writing phase:

> I think the case felt quite realistic. You normally have a limited amount of information in the proposal phase . . .
>
> (I2)

The task as such, as well as the information provided to deal with it, was thus perceived as rather realistic. The problem-solving situation on the other hand, and especially the way in which the information was transmitted, the consultants perceived as more problematic. Here, they missed the interaction with the client, and the possibility to stroll around the organization in order to get a feel for it:

> What is difficult in relation to the way information is transmitted and the problem-solving situation in the simulation, is that you can't look at what is written and you can't see expressions on the faces. I miss the feeling of walking around in the organization, of seeing how people

scrutinize you, if they look frightened or expectant, things like that, which I think I register in a normal case. I can't get this here. But it was still quite richly described in the case, so you could get a bit of a feel for the organization, and its conservative, traditionalist character. This is naturally of importance, but I'm not sure whether it would have been very different if I had visited a client for about one and a half hours and sketched out something based on this meeting.

(L2)

This indicates that a first-hand impression of the client organization is an important source of information for the consultants. When writing the case, I made an effort to include information also of this more subtle kind. The effort was partly successful, as indicated by the citation above. On the other hand, this consultant also indicated that a certain lack of information did not actually change her approach to the problem as compared to a real situation. This is further confirmed later on in the same interview:

[Did you work differently now than in a real case?] No, I don't think so. Some of the things I've said here, I wouldn't say to the client, but this is the way I think.

(L2)

This indicates that, except for the way information was transmitted, the simulations were perceived as largely realistic. Some of the test persons also explicitly stated that how they worked in the simulation situation did not differ in any major way from a 'real' situation. This is congruent with the experiences with simulations of consultants' work reported by both Rhenman (1968) and Karlsson (1975).

A second issue, besides the perceived realism of the simulation situation, concerns the effects of verbalization on the problem-solving process. Verbal protocols have often been criticized based on the argument that the verbalization of a test person's thoughts influences the cognitive processes under study. The reports thus generated, it is argued, have little to do with the processes taking place in a real-life situation. Ericsson and Simon (1984) argue, however, based on both their own and others' empirical studies, that this criticism is unjustified in cases where the test persons are simply asked to verbalize what goes through their minds (think aloud). Alterations of the cognitive processes, they argue, are found only in situations where the test persons are asked for explanations during the process, or asked to make a selection of data to report in the process (see also Schweiger 1983; Patrick and James 2004). The instructions given to participants in the above simulation to 'think aloud', just say whatever crossed their mind, should thus not have altered the consultants' way of working and thinking.

A third issue that merits some concern in the study of problem-solving processes using verbal protocols relates to the subjects' ability to verbalize their thought processes. In their seminal work on verbal protocols, Ericsson and Simon (1984) take an information processing view of human thinking. Information is viewed as stored in different memories – the long-term memory and the short-term memory – that have different characteristics. The short-term memory contains the most recently applied information.

In order to be verbalized, Ericsson and Simon (1984) argue, information must be present in the short-term memory. They show, based on a large review of studies, that the information that passes the short-term memory during a mental process is accurately verbalized. Information that does not pass through the short-term memory, however, remains hidden. Certain aspects of the mental process are thus not accessible by verbalization. Examples include recognition, in which the results are transferred to the short-term memory but the actual process of recognition remains hidden. Also automated processes, which are no longer subject to cognitive control, are more difficult to verbalize. Such automation is the result of extended experience and might indicate that more experienced persons produce less complete verbal protocols than less experienced ones. Furthermore, the subjects' general ability to express their thoughts verbally may be an important criterion for the validity of simulations and verbal protocols. The test persons in this study, consultants, must be expected to have a good ability to express their thoughts verbally. As Brulin (1987) discusses, consultants must always be prepared to justify their thinking in front of both the client and their colleagues. Reflection is also an important aspect of and sometimes even a formalized part of the consultant's work. This can take place in discussion with colleagues, the evaluation of projects, the writing of reports for the client, etc. This recurring reflection should facilitate the consultant's verbalization of thoughts. The verbal protocols obtained were also rather detailed, as long as the consultants were reminded now and then to think aloud. However, as argued by Patrick and James (2004), the study of cognitive processes should, wherever possible, rely on a combination of methods, including both verbal protocols and some form of behavioural data, such as information acquisition data, as was the case in the above study.

# References

Barley, S.R. and Kunda, G. (1992) 'Design and Devotion: Surges of Rational and Normative Ideologies of Control in Managerial Discourse', *Administrative Science Quarterly*, 37: 363–599.

Brulin, G. (1987) *Konsulten – en kunskapsförmedlare?*, progress report, Department of Sociology, Uppsala University and Center for Working Life Studies.

Cooksey, R.W. (1996) *Judgment Analysis*, San Diego, CA: Academic Press.

Ericsson, K.A. and Simon, H.A. (1984) *Protocol Analysis: Verbal Reports as Data*, Cambridge, MA: MIT Press.

Fielding, N.G. and Lee, R.M. (eds) (1991) *Using Computers in Qualitative Research*, London: Sage.

Hansen, M.T., Nohria, N. and Tierney, T. (1999) 'What's Your Strategy for Managing Knowledge?' *Harvard Business Review* (March-April): 106–116.

Karlsson, C. (1975) *Komponenter i analys och värdering av förslag till organisationsstrukturer*, PhD thesis, Chalmers University of Technology.

Norusis, M.J. (1994) *SPSS Professional Statistics 6.1*, Chicago, IL: SPSS, Inc.

Patrick, J. and James, N. (2004) 'Process Tracing and Complex Cognitive Work Tasks', *Journal of Occupational and Organizational Psychology*, 77: 259–280.

Payne, J.W., Bettman, J. and Johnson, J.E. (1993) *The Adaptive Decision Maker*, Cambridge: Cambridge University Press.

Rhenman, E. (1968) *Organisationsplanering – En studie av organisationskonsulter*, Stockholm: Läromedelsförlagen.

Richards, T.J. and Richards, L. (1994) 'Using Computers in Qualitative Research', in N.K. Denzin and Y.S. Lincoln (eds) *Handbook of Qualitative Research*, Thousand Oaks, CA: Sage, 445–462.

Rummler, G.A. and Brache, A.P. (1990) *Improving Performance: How to Manage the White Space on the Organization Chart*, San Francisco, CA: Jossey-Bass.

Schön, D. (1983) *The Reflective Practitioner – How Professionals Think in Action*, Aldershot: Avebury.

Schweiger, D.M. (1983) 'Is the Simultaneous Verbal Protocol a Viable Method for Studying Managerial Problem Solving and Decision Making?', *Academy of Management Journal*, 26, 1: 185–192.

Weick, K.E. (1965) 'Laboratory Experimentation with Organizations', in J. March (ed.) *Handbook of Organizations*, Chicago: Rand McNally, 195–260.

Werr, A. (1999) *The Language of Change – The roles of methods in the work of management consultants*, PhD thesis, Stockholm School of Economics, Stockholm.

# Part III
# From data to theory

# 8 Interviews as a source of knowledge

*Torbjörn Stjernberg*

In this chapter, I will share my personal experiences of establishing interview relations, conducting interviews, and processing these interviews into something meaningful in relation to my area of study. The types of interviews that I will primarily focus on are related to my interest in understanding in depth how individuals experience life and work. At times, such interviews have also been carried out as a preparation for an intervention – such as when as consultant I have tried to help an organization deal with a combination of productivity problems, emotional stress and employee conflicts. However, it is important to remember that an interview is always an intervention to some extent, if not directly in the organizational processes then by its nature as a moment of reflection and verbalization of this reflection. The intervention may be the motive for the interview, such as when, as a consultant, I did an interview with a manager primarily because I wanted to add IT and work competence issues to his agenda. But mostly, the intended purpose of the interview is to obtain descriptions of actions, processes, attitudes, etc. and test my understanding of these by comparing my understanding with the understanding as described by the person interviewed.

There are situations where my interviews have had the purpose of learning about the life-world of the interviewee – such as when working on my thesis about organizational changes and changes in the quality of life of the organization's members during a four-year change process with the purpose of creating a more democratic work organization. That thesis is the primary source of the experiences that I share in this chapter – mainly because writing the thesis created a need to reflect on the process of interviewing. These interviews are experiences that have become the foundations on which many later interview studies have rested.

As mentioned by Kvale (1996), a good interview can be rewarding for the interviewee as well as for the interviewer. A colleague once mentioned that in the interviews he had with managing directors about their strategic work, a managing director would quite often ask his secretary to cancel the rest of the afternoon's appointments in order to take the rare opportunity to continue talking rather freely about strategies and personal aspects of work with an attentive and genuinely interested listener.

There may, however, be instances where one or the other (most often the interviewee) feels exploited or experiences anxiety about having shared feelings that should not have been shared. What is going to happen after the interview is one of the crucial questions that needs to be addressed when making the appointment or when starting or finishing the interview – or on all these occasions.

Whether the interviews are focused primarily on getting information about organizational facts, and the interviewees' thoughts about these facts, or on getting information about, for instance, the attitudes and emotions of the organization's employees, affects both the way the interview is conducted and the number of interviews. Interviews for different purposes will be discussed – and examples will be given in text boxes of some interview situations. I will also share some experiences about the preparation, as well as the documentation and analysis that comes after the interview.

## The interview as a relationship

> As Punch (1986) suggests, as field-workers we need to exercise common sense and moral responsibility, and, we would like to add, to our subjects first, to the study next, and ourselves last.
>
> (Fontana and Frey 2000: 373)

There are few common rules about how to do interviews, but the quote from Fontana and Frey above is probably valid in most research contexts – the exception may be research bordering on journalistic approaches of the kind made famous by Günter Wallraff (e.g. 1970, 1979). To 'wallraff' became a concept for sneaking into a situation and revealing unacceptable attitudes and behaviour of a person or an organization. In a number of famous books, Wallraff shared experiences such as how German employers, landlords, social workers, etc. treated him when he disguised himself pretending to be a Turkish guest worker.

Interviewing means that you, as an interviewer, enter into a relationship with the interviewee. As with any relationship, the interview situation is entered into with several already established biases. In motivating why the interviewer wants the interview, it is most certainly so that a message is also given about who the interviewer is, what type of answers are sought and what attitudes are expected. Asking someone to participate in the interview is a situation in which I generally feel that I lack power – it is really up to the individual to say yes or no. The answer I get is to a large extent based on some general goodwill that either I, my institution or the research community has – and this goodwill is a very precious capital to preserve.

Signals of power, as well as signals of acceptance and non-acceptance, are expressed in the interview situation. A balance in the relationship may be gained through a deliberate choice of the number of interviewers and inter-viewees to be present. A general rule is that there should not be too many interviewers facing a single interviewee. However, if the person being interviewed has a high power position, it is not likely that several interviewers coming to the interview will be a problem. On the other hand, I have also interviewed people that I have feared may perceive me as representing some degree of power (either due to my academic role or to my being a consultant). In such situations, I have often preferred to do the interview as a group interview. One reason for conducting group interviews has been ethical – in an attempt to prevent gossip about who may have given me sensitive infor-mation. In the group interview, whatever is said is witnessed by several peers. Sharing the 'burden' of providing inopportune information in this way may compensate for the fact that the individual is in a vulnerable situation.

When scheduling interviews, one important aspect, again for ethical reasons, is that you should not schedule your interviews so tightly as to be forced to end the interview abruptly at an emotional or sensitive point in the interview. A guideline is to start and end an interview on a positive or neutral note. This is especially crucial if the person you interview is vulnerable. On one occasion, when interviewing a person about her quality of life, I even felt that I had to skip some questions because I was afraid that, in her very depressed mode, these questions might have triggered suicidal thoughts. A basic rule I follow is to not bring up problems and issues that I do not have the resources and personal competence to deal with, either during the interview or afterwards.

Aspects such as the above have led me to schedule my interviews so that I have about the same amount of time between interviews, as I have for the interview itself. This means that a 1½-hour interview is scheduled so as to leave me about 1½ hours between interviews to work on my notes.

As interviewer I try to have and show empathy – which does not mean that I need to have and show sympathy. Empathy is more about making an honest effort to identify with the situation and emotions of the interviewee, to be genuinely interested in what is said. (See Box 8.1.)

## Studying attitudes in an aggregate of individuals

When studying an organization, the focus is often on the attitudes of its members. This means that some form of quantification is aimed at, and cross-tabulation of the different answers is usually necessary to make the

**Box 8.1**   *Notes from my interview diary before an interview about organizational change and quality of life (Stjernberg 1977: 27–29)*

In an hour and a half I shall be interviewing Rosa for the fourth time. I have already done an interview this morning: I talked to Selma for about two hours. She is one of those who are rather easy to talk to: I feel I have a good contact with her. It was nice to start this series of interviews with one of the people that are easy to talk to. I am a bit nervous about this interview. I feel it will be especially difficult to discuss the use of the material. When Rosa leaves I want her to feel that she can trust me to treat the material confidentially, and, at the same time, I hope she will say that this does not matter too much. I know that Rosa is rather sensitive about what comes out of the interviews, and what she has told me about earlier. The 'quality of life' changes I have traced, the increased anxiety between the first and the third interview, may be things one doesn't like to have discussed. It is also difficult to promise Rosa that one will not recognize what group she works in from the change descriptions. And if one recognizes the group it is also difficult to conceal what person is behind the pseudonym. . . .

I wonder whether she will allow me to use the tape-recorder? . . . Almost every person in the department has much more knowledge of each person interviewed than I have – at least, a different knowledge. What I get in my interviews is rather an understanding, a certain sympathy for the person: I reach somewhat behind the raw impressions you have of your fellow-men, and I may listen to the logic behind the attitudes, the logic behind the anxiety. I suppose this is why I so often feel that I like very much the person I am interviewing.

data meaningful. The data are given as means and/or medians and as standard deviations/variance, thus making it possible to express whether the differences over the years or between two departments are significant. In order to make general statements about relations between variables, based on attitude data, the number of interviews needs to be large enough to inform you about the distributions of attitudes in the population. Surveys, rather than oral interviews, are generally more effective for collecting such data. However, in order to interpret the surveys, complementary sources of information are most often needed. In the noted study of organizational change and quality of life, I used both interviews and data from the personnel records, such as average number of short- and long-term sick-leaves in different departments, thus complementing the analyses of the surveys.

In studying attitudes, there is a need for contrasts (see Box 8.2). It is the contrasts that create interesting 'puzzles' and analyses. You may also formulate similar research interests, for example 'what are the aspects of work that affect the satisfaction of workers?', and look for patterns in the answers. One such famous pattern-seeking approach is that of Herzberg *et al.* (1959), in which the researchers interviewed engineers and accountants about moments when they felt happy and unhappy in their work. The pattern that they found led them to believe that some factors, such as achievement, recognition, the content of the work itself, responsibility and advancement, are associated with satisfaction; whereas a different set of factors, such as company policy and administration, supervision, salary and working conditions, do not have the power to lead to satisfaction but, if not up to aspirations, will lead to dissatisfaction. Still, their interest focused not so much on individuals as single cases. The unit of analysis was not the individual, but the moments of happiness or unhappiness, and their results came from aggregating and analyzing the patterns of these moments (see also Box 8.7 below).

## Studying individuals as separate cases

The interviews may deal with each individual as a separate case. Herbst (1970) argues that we cannot establish behavioural laws on an aggregate level – but must instead look for generative patterns and concepts that help us understand each individual's behaviour. A different argument is that, when looking at patterns in a population, the exception may be of as much interest as the rule. What makes one person differ from the common behaviour (see Box 8.3.)?

When studying the individual case, the management researcher's goal is to generate knowledge that helps in understanding other cases. Yin calls this 'theoretical generalization' as opposed to 'statistical generalization' (1989: 21). We may also be interested in the individual case because it helps to understand organizational processes. One example may be interviewing a manager about his or her interpretations of facts, attitudes and his or her emotions in order to understand the organizational processes that this person has a strong influence on.

Trying to understand individuals as individual cases is challenging in the sense that the interview also becomes a simultaneous opportunity to analyze the data at hand and test this analysis in the conversation with the individual. But, if the interviews are focused on existential issues, doing the interviews may also be a very sensitive and emotional act, not only for the interviewee but also for the interviewer.

**Box 8.2** *Contrasts as 'puzzles'*

In our action research project (described also in the chapter by Docherty *et al.* in this volume), we used questionnaires with indexes of job satisfaction, organizational climate, perceived influence, etc. We analyzed changes in average scores over the years, and differences from the scores of other departments that did not undergo similar changes. We also analyzed individual survey questions such as, 'What influence do you think that the employees have on organizational issues in the department?' (scale of 1 = little, to 5 = very large). The results showed an interesting pattern. There was a marked increase when the project had started but no structural changes had yet been made, an even higher perceived influence after the changes towards shared power between management and employees in 1975, and back to almost the same values as in 1972 when the survey was administered again in 1984. Interestingly, in qualitative interviews in 1984, the interviewees said that the influence was the same as in 1975. I interpreted this as a result of changes in our use of language and our expectations of influence, i.e. a 4 = large influence in 1972 differed from the meaning given by the employees to a 4 = large influence in 1984.

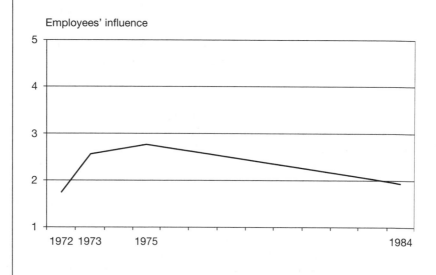

---

**Box 8.3**   *Embedded cases of quality of life changes during an organizational change process*

In my studies of organizational change and quality of life, the idea was to understand how organizational events affected the life situation of the members of the organization. Twenty-six individuals were chosen as cases, of whom 24 participated in at least two interviews, and 15 in the four scheduled interviews. A few were also interviewed in a follow-up ten years later. Each person was seen as an individual to understand as a single case, and less interest was given to the interviewees as one in a sample to learn about a population of employees. This means that I was looking for interesting patterns that could help me understand how individuals understood and were affected by the changes, and how the organizational changes and other aspects in their life affected their quality of life. Comparisons could be made with what was learned in previous interviews with the same individual, as well as with the interviews with other individuals. The prime interest focused on how the organizational change processes affected each individual's 'valences' in different parts of his or her 'life space', as well as how his or her resources to influence future life spaces were affected.

---

### Facts and thoughts

Every interview contains a mixture of questions about facts and feelings, attitudes and understandings of a situation. However, the character and the number of interviews are determined by the primary focus of the interview. Studying attitudes requires many interviews; determining facts requires just a few.

However, facts are seldom to be found and established by asking one insightful person. I have quite often been surprised when asking a second interviewee about the 'same facts'. There may be an objective situation to discover – such as the exact dates of certain events in the past, but the usual finding is that, unless the interview is also complemented by other sources of data, such as diaries, cross-checking against other events, etc., even such simple facts as when a certain event took place cannot be established in one interview alone. Most facts are socially constructed and reconstructed – memories and meaning influence what, in retrospect, seems to be important.

Rather than existing, facts – as you meet them in an interview – are always mediated by memories and understanding and thus interpreted and even constructed. This becomes even more true if these facts are linked to strongly held attitudes or to strong personal feelings. Denial of conflicts may be conscious, but it may also have the character of wishful thinking or even subconscious distortions.

I am seldom *only* interested in facts just to get a good description of a phenomenon. I also want to know the meaning of the facts in relation to a more general knowledge interest. I believe that interpreting facts means putting them in some meaningful context – as causing, or being caused by, something else, or as symbolizing something. When asking about facts, the opportunity also exists for getting data about the meaning that the interviewee gives to these facts.

Some years ago we studied the design and construction of a shopping mall (Hellgren and Stjernberg 1987, 1995). The physical existence of the mall is an obvious fact. The causal chain of decisions that lead to the existence of the shopping mall grew out of the interaction of several interests, and out of technical, economical and political considerations. When asking about those considerations, a mixture of historical and plausible future events are described. It is impossible for me as researcher to arrive at 'the truth and nothing but the truth' about all these possible answers to the motives and possible consequences as seen by all those involved in the decision-making processes. The interviews instead become entwined with my analysis of these decision processes – each successive interview giving me a chance to try my understanding so far. Thus, the interviews about facts are carried out not *only* to establish a set of events and motives, but also as an occasion to try to develop a richer meaning of these data in relation to my own understanding of the studied case in relation to other cases, and to theories and models. Asking 'why' questions helps me elicit the help of the interviewee, who is often a very knowledgeable and reflective practitioner. Interviewing several people, rather than a single person, also gives me the benefit of understanding the limits of any one person's story, and of doubting my own.

Such cross-checking of the interviewees' sense of the 'whys' becomes even more important when the purpose of the interviews is to facilitate organizational development, and especially when working with conflict resolution (see e.g. Walton 1969). The focus, then, is the interview as part of an intervention strategy (see Box 8.4). This means that it becomes important not only to know about a person's own feelings and frustrations and possible attributions – but also to get a feeling for how each interviewee sees others' feelings, frustrations and attributions, and is seen by each of the others. If the questions mirror an authentic sense of trying to understand the person being interviewed, and also elicit his or her help in understanding others, the interview in itself may be a step towards reconciliation.

---

**Box 8.4** *Interviews as interventions for conflict resolution*

In one particular case, we had, as consultants, been given the task of helping a department overcome conflicts that interfered with attempts to develop a new work organization based on self-managed teams. We interviewed every member of the organization and found a strong joint and shared wish for the new work organization to be successful. What seemed to be the basis for conflicts were worries about one's position, and worries about future wages. Knowing that this common positive feeling dominated, and that understandable worries rather than individual animosities were the dominating causes of conflicts, we arranged a feedback session with the entire department. We presented, in general terms, our impressions from the interviews. Then they were all asked to give a short summary of their views to the others. As the interviewers, we made a point of not revealing what had been said to us – but, by being present, every interviewee felt a pressure to give a fairly truthful picture of his or her feelings as they had been described to us. The result was, as anticipated, that the earlier conflicts were reinterpreted as caused by just concerns rather than by ill will, and a process started that addressed the concerns of the employees. Thus, interviews and the feedback from them may be powerful tools for intervening in an organization and for making different interests explicit and articulated.

---

*Thought processes*

As shown by Werr in his chapter in this volume, it may be interesting to follow thought processes in real time. Several years ago, Peter Docherty and I were interested in learning about how site agents on construction sites solved the many problems and contingencies they met in their daily work (Docherty and Stjernberg 1974). To study this, we used combinations of observations, interviews and surveys. One question concerned how the site agents' thought about how to solve a problem that they had just encountered. By asking them to 'think aloud' (see Ericsson and Simon 1993), we realized that the ideas we had developed, based on problem-solving literature, about how they saw the different steps were too simplified. Not only did the site agents describe steps as sequential, parallel and hierarchical, but also that these hierarchies of actions they planned overlapped. The site agents differed also in their 'verbal protocols' with regard to how early in the process they dismissed alternative solutions. Although thought processes are difficult to study, it is possible to obtain data through verbal protocols that may aid in the understanding and the problematization of previous understandings.

Other methods used by some of my colleagues have been to ask respondents to order cards with different information, or to draw relationships, e.g. between different actions (see also Philips 1988; Löwstedt 1989, 1993 for other examples). The most important thing to remember, regarding all these methods, however, is that you need to be very humble in your analysis of the data you get. The data can at best be seen as indicators of elements, and relations between some elements, in the thought processes. As cognitive maps, they are only very crude images of the cognitive realities – whatever they are!

## The questions

As mentioned above, the type of questions you ask depends on whether you view the interviewee as a source of data about an aggregate of individuals, or if you view him or her as an individual case – where the patterns and generalizations you want to make do not primarily follow statistical rules but a search for specificities in this particular person. Thus, the questions mirror your interests and the unit of analysis. They also reflect whether you see the interviewee as a source of 'objective facts', or whether you are primarily interested in attitudes or in the deeper feelings or thought processes of the interviewee. (See Box 8.5.)

---

**Box 8.5**    *Unstructured or semi-structured interviews in the study of organizational change and quality of life*

In my interviews about organizational change and quality of life, mentioned above, my interest was in understanding each individual as a complete person. The first round of interviews just had a few keywords. However, I found the analysis of these interviews quite complex, and since the study was longitudinal, I was also worried that I, in retrospect, would feel that there were sets of questions that I would have liked to ask everyone and that I would have liked to compare over the years. Therefore, I ended up making the next three rounds of interviews with a semi-structured schedule, where I had about thirty questions with follow up questions, that I made sure I asked every individual. Still, the interview process followed more the logic of a conversation, and my semi-structured questions were asked in the order and in the form that suited the conversation.

---

The structuring of the interview, at least for me, mirrors the degree to which I really have thought through the research questions and how to analyze these. In particular, this has been a problem in longitudinal studies. By their nature, such studies mean that your research focus may develop into areas that you were not aware of at the start of the project. On the other hand, if I am well prepared, I may much more easily adapt the interview to the information that I receive. Thus, paradoxically, the more questions formulated at a rather detailed level in advance, the more one may be able to adapt the interview to the information that is given by the interviewee. Preparing well, and formulating a semi-structured interview guide, may give the confidence to focus on listening rather than to focus on what questions to ask and how to formulate these.

Unless you actually want to make an orally-administered survey with predetermined categories of answers using, for example, a Likert scale of the type 'strongly agree' to 'strongly disagree', there is no reason to ask your questions in a predetermined order. Instead, the general recommendation is to listen carefully, using your listening ability, and to follow up any answers you do not fully understand. Your active listening will also yield a series of 'funnels', where you may ask more and more specific questions to deepen your understanding. You should usually also ask the interviewee about specific situations or incidents that illustrate what he or she is describing, thus attempting to move from a description of a general routine to a particular behaviour or critical incident that illustrates the routine as it is practised. (See Box 8.6.)

The researcher's motive for the interviews may be to establish a story that may be called 'the researcher's story' – in the sense that that story is a subjective account related to what makes the story meaningful from a more general theoretical perspective. The story may be focused on the individual case, in Kurt Lewin's words, 'analysis beginning with the situation as a whole' and 'seeing behaviour as a function of the field as it occurs' (1963: 62 and 63, respectively). In this field or life space, memories of the past as well as visions of the future are represented. Thus, the story, as communicated in an interview, communicates a current representation of 'facts' and feelings of the past – but it is not a true picture of the past as it was when it was the present. As illustrated in Figure 8.1, the steps from an event, interpretations of this event, and ultimately the reader's understanding, include many 'validity' losses. Furthermore, the validity is affected by the pre-understanding the interviewer brings to the situation; the chain of interpretations runs from the interviewer to the interviewee as well.

Describing and understanding the individual is not usually the aim of the management researcher. The story that the management researcher builds may be based on a search for patterns in several individuals' stories

– understood as wholes. Or the researcher's story may focus on particular parts of these stories – variables taken in isolation from the other parts of each person's story, as described above in my discussion of studies of attitudes.

---

**Box 8.6**   *Formulating and using questions in the study of organizational change and quality of life*

My formulations in my interview schedule worked as a kind of short-hand for my input in the conversation. In practice, it meant that I wrote down my question number in the notes I took of the interviewee's answers – and that I now and then stopped to check what questions were covered. This had the advantage of creating a legitimate moment of silence, often resulting in spontaneous additional explanations as the interviewee reflected on what he or she had just said. In this particular study, I did not use a tape-recorder and thus I did not make complete transcripts of the interviews. In later projects, I have tended to use a recorder in order to go back and check details when constructing the protocol. There has seldom been a need to check the exact wording, and I have tended to use the wording as captured in my detailed notes if I have felt a need for illustrating my texts with quotes from the interviews. Thus, I have not felt a need to transcribe the interviews, but instead used the time that would have been needed for transcription to analyze and group the data.

In retrospect, there was one occasion when I felt that I would have liked a transcribed version of the answers. I asked the interviewees to describe happy moments in life, and also happy moments at work. During my analysis I discovered a pattern in the answers – the happy moments in life in general were in most cases described in the progressive tense ('when I am working in my garden'), whereas the happy moments at work mostly were described in the perfect tense ('when I have finished a task').

---

## The analysis before, during and after the interview

In most of the interviews I do, the process of analyzing the data is strongly interlinked with the interview itself. It is a process that to some extent starts during the interview, and in a sense already before the interview when my expectations and 'pre-understandings' are formulated while preparing the interview schedule. During the interview, the active listening may be seen

*'True' information:*

| An event, change, etc. |
| --- |
| Partly recognized by the interviewee and interpreted from earlier experiences |
| Partly conscious feelings and reactions |

*Data that might be of interest to analyze if the focus is more on the deeper psychological reactions to change:*

| Some of these are remembered at the time of the interview |
| --- |
| Some are mentioned, other information is 'filtered', i.e. none of the interviewer's business, or distorted |

*'Errors', of which some may be interpretations guided by an explicit frame of reference. Thus, not only is information lost, but new information is added:*

| The interviewer hears and understands a part of what is said, interpreting with reference to earlier experiences, etc. |
| --- |
| Part of this is written down and loses, for example, tone of voice, body language |
| From the notes and memory, interview minutes are dictated and later typed out |
| Minutes are read: some aspects are seen as important when analyzing |
| Some of this is interpreted and written down |
| From these words the reader gets an impression of the events, changes and interviewee's reactions |

*Figure 8.1* The chain of data transformation.

as a sense-making process and thus as a way of making an immediate analysis, providing an impetus to search for more information and a deeper understanding. Often much of this happens at a tacit level. Checking the interview notes during the interview may bring uncertainties to the surface.

In general, I nowadays use a recorder of some kind during interviews, always after asking for consent. However, using a recorder does not mean that taking notes during the interview is unnecessary. As mentioned above, taking notes makes it possible to stop now and then and check that you have the information that you were seeking.

Taking notes facilitates the first and immediate steps in the analysis. Immediately after an interview, I try to use the energy that was created by the interview. The time that I schedule between interviews has the purpose of enabling me to go through my notes and formulate my first impressions. This is the first step in the analysis – and perhaps the most important. It is the best opportunity to formulate the impressions of the 'whole', i.e. of finding anomalies and inconsistencies and using the feelings created in me during the interview as a guide for what to focus on. Similarly, after a day of interviews, it is also important to capture the impressions and gestalt of not only what was said in the interviews, but also of what happened 'around' the interviews. (See Box 8.7.)

---

**Box 8.7**   *The immediate analysis*

Directly after each interview, I made an interview protocol, using a dictaphone. I found that if I had to wait with this work for some reason, my protocol became 'just' the notes, whereas if the protocol was prepared directly, it contained more data, building on my memory of the conversation. Also, the analysis I made of the interview in a commentary that ended every protocol was much richer. The commentary, usually only half a page, was the most important part of the protocol. In it, I captured what stood out to me as my most important immediate impressions from the particular interview, i.e. the 'gestalt'.

An example from a study of viability and diffusion of organizational innovations is the gestalt created by the impressions from two interviews. In the morning, when doing a group interview with five women from the pre-assembly line of Volvo Cars, the interviewees entered the interview room seething with anger. In the hallway on the way to the room, they had met one of the young time-and-motion engineers that had been responsible for the re-structuring of their work cycles a few months earlier.

The same afternoon, Åke Philips and I met an engineer and some workers on the new automated press-line. They mentioned that they had spent the morning working together to make the press-line more effective.

This triggered a process of theorizing about the importance for the work organization of the relations between who does the task (the worker or the machine) and how this process is supervised (by a supervisor or a worker) – relating this to rationalization strategies and to patterns in the 13 cases we analyzed (Stjernberg 1993; Stjernberg and Philips 1993).

---

During the interview, your attempts to make sense of what you hear means that you constantly compare this ongoing interview with your entire pre-understanding, based not only on theories and other studies but also on all previous interviews that you have done. This is a truly creative process that is difficult to describe. Your conceptual schemes and theories are used to make sense, and energy and interest are created when you run into difficulties in this sense-making.

The process may be quite crude and creative, even when using content analysis methods, such as described by Anell and by Werr in their respective chapters. Having established a coding scheme, which may be revised during the coding process, I prefer to put the statements concerning a particular aspect I am interested in side by side. When looking at the statement, trying to get a feeling for what are similarities and differences and nuances, comparing with other 'piles' of statements, a pattern gradually emerges. These patterns need to be checked by a close reading of the statements in their context, and by counting the number of statements, checking to see whether the pattern can be explained by chance. This truly inductive process (compare Brytting's chapter) may be seen as constantly alternating between being very close to the data and taking a step back to check and question the impressions and patterns.

## Conclusion

This chapter about interviewing has intended to illustrate a creative knowledge production process – a process that is strongly integrated with using and reformulating theories and concepts and with comparisons with other empirical material. Interviewing is a relationship, in which trust based on empathy and genuine interest is an important ingredient. The focus of the chapter has been on semi-structured interviews. The questions are open in the sense that the interviewer follows up aspects that are of interest in relation to the study, although these may not have been part of the preconceived ideas about what to ask. This means using both pre-formulated 'funnels' to delve deeper and deeper into the understanding of a phenomenon, but also spontaneous 'funnels' – following up paradoxes and making sure that the interviewee is understood. Specific examples or 'critical incidents' illustrate, and sometimes problematize, the descriptions of attitudes and routines. Descriptions of routines otherwise tend to be descriptions of how something should be rather than how it is. The interview itself, not only the interview as a protocol, is an important part of the theorizing and analyzing. The analysis is based on understanding the interviewee as a single case – not as a source of data on specific variables.

I have not said much in this chapter about interviews that aim to collect data for statistical analysis (although statistics may be used also in open interviews). Similarly to surveys, such data collection sets other important demands in order to guarantee that each interviewee has understood the questions and the alternative answers (the reliability issue) and that this understanding corresponds to what the study aims to address (the validity issue). Issues of validity and reliability also exist in semi-structured and open interviews, but are dealt with more as an integrated part of the sense-making that takes place during the interview. As shown in Figure 8.1 above, there are a number of validity problems on the path from an event or an idea to an understanding of that event by the reader.

# References

Docherty, P. and Stjernberg, T. (1974) *Decision-making in Contingencies*, Stockholm: Stockholm School of Economics.

Ericsson, K.A. and Simon, H.A. (1993) *Protocol Analysis: Verbal Reports as Data*, Cambridge, MA: MIT Press.

Fontana, A. and Frey, J.H. (2000) in N.K. Denzin and Y.S. Lincoln (eds), *Handbook of Qualitative Research*, Thousand Oaks, CA: Sage, 361–376.

Hellgren, B. and Stjernberg, T. (1987) 'Networks: An Analytical Tool for Understanding Complex Decision Processes', *International Studies of Management & Organization*, 17: 88–102.

Hellgren, B. and Stjernberg, T. (1995) 'Design and Implementation in Major investments – a Project Network Approach', *Scandinavian Journal of Management*, 11: 377–394.

Herbst, P.H. (1970) *Behavioural Worlds – The Study of Individual Cases*, London: Tavistock.

Herzberg, F., Mausner, B. and Snyderman, B.B. (1959) *The Motivation to Work*, New York: Wiley.

Kvale, S. (1996) *InterViews: An Introduction to Qualitative Research Interviewing*, Thousand Oaks, CA: Sage.

Lewin, K. (1963) 'Field Theory and Learning', in D. Cartwright (ed.) *Field Theory in Social Science – Selected Theoretical Papers*, London: Associated Publishers and Tavistock. (First published in 1951.)

Löwstedt, J. (1989) *Föreställningar, ny teknik och förändring. Tre organiserings-processer ur ett kognitivt aktörsperspektiv* (Organizing Frameworks, New Technology and Change, in Swedish with summary in English), Lund: Doxa.

Löwstedt, J. (1993) 'Organizing Frameworks in Emerging Organizations: A Cognitive Approach to the Analysis of Change', *Human Relations*, 46, 4: 501–526.

Philips, Å. (1988) *Eldsjälar* (Souls-of-Fire, in Swedish with summary in English), Stockholm: Stockholm School of Economics.

Punch, M. (1986) *The Politics and Ethics of Fieldwork*, Newbury Park, CA: Sage.

Stjernberg, T. (1977) *Organizational Change and Quality of Life*, Stockholm: Stockholm School of Economics.

Stjernberg, T. (1993) *Organisationsideal – livskraft och spridning. Ett tjugoårigt perspektiv* (see Stjernberg and Philips (1993), based on the same study), Stockholm: Norstedts Juridik.

Stjernberg, T. and Philips, Å. (1993) 'Organizational Innovations in a Long-term Perspective: Legitimacy and Souls-of-Fire as Critical Factors of Change and Viability', *Human Relations*, 46: 10, 1193–1219.

Wallraff, G. (1970) *13 unerwünschte Reportagen*, Köln: Rowohlt.

Wallraff, G. (1979) *The Undesirable Journalist*, New York: Overlook Press.

Walton, R.E. (1969) *Interpersonal Peacemaking: Confrontations and Third-party Consultation*, Reading, MA: Addison-Wesley.

Yin, R.K. (1989) *Case Study Research: Design and Methods*, second edition, Newbury Park, CA: Sage.

# 9  Listening to executives

## Content analysis of life stories

*Barbro Anell*

> When we conceive the same things differently, we can hardly avoid different naming of them. For though the nature of what we conceive be the same, yet the diversity of our reception of it, in respect of different constitutions of the body, and prejudice of opinions, gives everything a tincture of our different passions. And therefore in reasoning a man must take heed of words; which beside the signification of what we imagine their nature, have significance also of the nature, disposition and interests of the speaker.
>
> (Hobbes 1996)

How do you analyze life stories? This research project concerning life stories of executives was started in the 1970s. Since then the interest in narratives and narrative analysis has become more widespread. Still, however, content analysis plays an important role as a flexible and useful analytic research tool.

Content analysis is easy to apply if you want to use it mechanistically for counting words or for statistical semantics in general. Data programs to do this have been developed. Using content analysis grows more problematic in other contexts, for instance when qualitatively analyzing the symbolic meanings in texts and images. In such a case, the researcher must draw on theoretical schemes for interpretation, something that is difficult to translate into a data program.

This is the story of the hard-learned lessons about using content analysis, drawn from an ambitious project, 'Norms and Values of Big Business Leaders in Sweden'. The project aimed at uncovering how big business leaders made sense of their world, and how this was related to their backgrounds, career patterns and personalities.

## The study

In a world of organizations, could it be said that the influence of an executive officer increases with the size of the company he or she leads? The way the company conducts its business affects not only the employees but a number of other groups in its immediate environment, such as customers and suppliers and, in the end, society at large. Listening to and analyzing how big business leaders see their world and their actions might provide important insight into how a certain industry works and why. The basic assumption of the project was that leaders of big business may be seen as an elite group in society and that their thoughts and actions have an impact on society. Their values and norms may support or hinder socially desirable development of, for instance, equality between individuals in society and the creation of meaningful jobs. The underlying premise said that big business leaders possess some freedom of action and that their actions have an impact on the company and the surrounding environment. (For a different opinion, see for example Alchian 1986.)

Twenty-one leaders/owners of large enterprises in the building industry in Sweden were chosen for participation in the study. They were interviewed by the project leader and the interviews, which took between three and six hours to conduct, were taped. The tapes were then transcribed verbatim to protocols of about 40 pages or more. The number of pages of course varied from interview to interview.

The executives were asked to relate their thoughts about their social background, career, their roles today and their views about relationships with different stakeholders of the company. The study explored perceptions of the relationship with owners, the capital market, to the employees and the labour market, customers, the government and with competitors. The executives' views about how to run a large firm and about short- and long-range problems and opportunities were also elicited.

It was possible to create a relaxed and open atmosphere during the interviews and many of the busy, work-driven executives seemed to enjoy the opportunity to 'think through' their careers and current situation aloud. (See Cyert and March 1963.)

The study concerned several aspects of the world of big business leaders – their early years, their careers, their psychological orientation, and their ways of running their business in an industry with tough competition. Information from several sources was combined in the study, such as autobiographies and company documents. The most important data, however, were culled from the written protocols of semi-structured in-depth interviews.

This chapter addresses the methodological problems encountered in the project and exemplifies the findings with results from the analysis of social backgrounds and career patterns. As the data were so rich, it was decided that a systematic analysis of different aspects of the executives' life stories should be carried out. Content analysis seemed to be the most suitable tool for this analysis.

## Content analysis history

The use of primarily quantitatively oriented content analysis of mass communications grew in the US during the 1930s and the 1940s. (See, for example, Lasswell *et al.* 1952.) Conclusions were drawn not only about the text generators, the sources, but also about the effects of the texts on the readers, the receivers, which is rather daring as long as validation studies of readers' reactions are not made.

After the Second World War, the use of content analysis started to move away from the purely quantitative approach into a more qualitatively-oriented mode, and journalism and political science were not the only fields where content analysis was applied. For example, it was also used in psychiatry and psychology to study cognitive traits such as authoritarianism (Adorno *et al.* 1950) and dogmatism (Rokeach 1968). Small group research used content analysis with coding schemes based on Bales' development of categories for the analysis of interactions in small groups (Bales 1950). History and anthropology also made use of content analysis. (See, for example, Merton 1957; Lévi-Strauss 1964.) Not only texts, but also images have been the target of content analyses.

New ways of conducting content analyses were added to the old ones, such as analyzing co-occurrences between words or themes or analyzing networks of connections between themes in texts. (See, for example, 'Letters from Jenny', in Stone *et al.* 1966.)

Studies of the embraced values of different groups using content analysis have been fairly common. General categories for the coding of values have been developed, for instance by Lasswell and Kaplan (1950). Cochran (1953) analyzed business values in letters from railroad presidents.

In the 1960s, special data programs were developed for analyzing text, such as 'The General Enquirer' (GE) (Stone *et al.* 1966). GE has since been updated and is now available on the Internet (www.wjh.harvard.edu/~ inquirer/) and new programs are continually being launched. (See, for example, www. google.com, search phrase: 'computer content analysis programs'.) These programs allowed the study of extensive texts and are very helpful when it comes to sorting and storing large amounts of data. The interpretation, however, still resides with the researcher.

### Basics of content analysis

Definitions of content analysis of course vary from author to author. One definition used might be: 'content analysis is a research method that uses a set of categorization procedures for making valid and reliable inferences from texts or images to their context.' Another is: '. . . in general terms, content analysis is the application of scientific methods to documentary evidence' (Holsti 1969: 5). The preparatory steps to carrying out content analysis, such as generating or identifying texts, are left out in this context.

Applying content to a text involves a number of steps, viz.:

- *Coding*, that is, determining the basic unit of analysis – a word, sentence or longer segment of a text – and assigning a 'tag' to it. For instance, 'judge' might be tagged 'job, legal'. The emotional loading of words or themes might also be coded, for instance, from 'strongly negative' to 'strongly positive'. A 'glossary' of words with their respective tags might be developed to help the coder. What tags to use depends on the semantic universe to be explored. In a text of European origin, for instance, 'dragon' might be tagged as 'evil', while in a text of Chinese origin it might be tagged as 'good'.
- *Counting* the tags in different texts. It is usually assumed that the (relative) frequency of tags is related to the theme's importance in the text, and in the text-producer's mind.
- *Categorizing*, that is, creating theory-relevant categories to group the tagged units of analysis. When studying a person's psychological traits, for example, this could involve deciding which units should be placed in the category 'need for achievement' and which in the category 'need for power'. The categories should be mutually exclusive and exhaustive.
- *Classifying*, that is, ensuring and checking that the tagged units can be unambiguously assigned to the appropriate categories. Usually some measure of inter-coder reliability is used.
- *Comparing* the results across different texts. For example, comparing one person with another, one group of business leaders with another, or how the content in texts from one source changes over time. Looking for differences between self-made business leaders and business leaders who followed in their fathers' footsteps is one example of the comparisons that were made in our project.
- *Concluding*, that is, interpreting the results and relating them back to the theories of the study or developing these theories further.

The steps in the content analysis process might not always follow this pattern and some steps might even be left out. There are, however, some steps that might need further discussion. It is assumed, for instance, that the actual study is based on some theory or theories, and that these guide the development of categories. In some instances, categories are not determined from theory beforehand by the researcher; ad hoc categories are instead supposed to pop up from the text. As the text itself has sometimes been generated 'through' the researcher, for instance when conducting unstructured interviews, it is a bit doubtful what the findings reflect – the subject's or the researcher's ideas. The problem of objectivity has to be approached in this context. If no checks of reliability and validity are made, one might ask if this procedure can be called content analysis or not.

To count or not to count, that is the question. In some definitions of content analysis, the method is singled out for statistical use only. As early as 1943, however, Kaplan argued for going beyond statistical semantics of political discourse to include also qualitative analysis of the symbolic meanings of texts. Statistical semantics are, of course, totally dependent on counting. What about more qualitative approaches? Frequencies are often used as indicators of a theme's importance to the source of the text. This is probably due to the basic assumption that people tend to talk about the things that occupy their mind. The importance of a theme might be inferred in other ways, of course, such as in the intensity of expressed positive or negative feelings about the subject. If the text was generated in an interview, other indicators such as body language, intonation, flushing or tears might also be noted as expressions of strong feelings. A more delicate question concerns what is *not* said in the text. Swedes, at least, prefer not to show emotion and to avoid talking about unpleasant or embarrassing themes, so these themes might not crop up in an interview. When the text generator is ironic or sarcastic, this has to be inferred from the context. For instance, if, during an interview, somebody says 'I have the most fantastic job', after a long discourse on all the trials and tribulations he or she meets in the job, it might be concluded that irony is intended.

Words are also 'ground down' and diminished by frequent use. The statement 'I hate porridge' might be used to convey that porridge is not high on the list of the subject's preferred dishes. 'Providing optimal conditions for . . .' might just mean good conditions.

It is usually recommended that the researcher use both quantitative and qualitative data to supplement each other (Holsti 1969).

## Categories and coding

As mentioned earlier, several aspects of the executive's life were covered in the interview. A number of separate supra-categories were therefore developed to sort overarching themes in the protocols. One such category was 'Childhood', another was 'Career', a third 'Personality' and a fourth, naturally, 'Values'. Each of these supra-categories then contained sub-categories, that is, special categorization schemes. For instance, the supra-category: 'Childhood' contained six sub-categories, each containing three sub-sub-categories. The six sub-categories concerned, among other things, codes for the interviewee's perceptions of the roles of his or her father and mother, and of other important persons, such as teachers and friends. It might be added that this coding of the narrative was relatively unambiguous in comparison with the coding of other supra-categories, such as 'Personality'. Yet, it implied that the coder had to make a number of choices – first, about how to delimit a certain part of the text, and then about whether this 'lump' of text belonged to the supra-category in question or not. In cases where it did, it must then be decided in which of the six sub-categories it should be coded and, finally, in which of the three sub-sub-categories. Still, it was possible to reach an acceptable level of inter-coder agreement – even if it required some effort.

The development of the categories in the supra-category 'Personality' was based on McClelland's theory of motivational needs ('need for achievement, need for affiliation and need for power'; McClelland *et al.* 1953). It was hypothesized that the executives studied would show a great need for achievement and that those who had founded their own companies would show a higher need for achievement than those who had taken over the company after their father. According to theory, the parents, especially the father, have a very important role in instilling the achievement motive in their children.

## Preparing for analysis

It was not decided on beforehand how long the 'lumps' of text to be coded should be, only that a lump should be long enough to make the speaker's intention clear. Tags were not used; the lumps of text were instead coded directly into the sub-categories and sub-sub-categories of each supra-category.

The coded items were cut out from the protocols' texts, placed on separate cards and properly identified so that they could always be tracked back to their context in the interviews. The cards for each supra-category were then sorted into the respective sub-categories. As there were 21 extensive protocols and several supra-categories, each consisting of several sub-categories with sub-sub-categories, the cards soon filled several boxes. This part of the work could really be described as content analysis by hand. Today, much of this work would be done with the help of computer programs.

A lump of text could be coded into more than one supra-category. For instance, one lump could be coded as belonging both to the category 'Childhood' and to the category 'Personality'. The text would then have to be duplicated so the lump in question could be placed in the right categories. This means that the supra-categories could have common items. Both the sub-categories and the sub-sub categories were, however, mutually exclusive. This multiple use of a lump of text did not clash with the rule that categories should be mutually exclusive, as the supra-categories reflected various perspectives on the executives' lives.

Difficulties arose rather quickly. It was difficult for one coder to be consistent across all interviews, and even more difficult to reach a decent level of inter-coder consensus, particularly when coding the 'Personality' items. The border between what was actually said and our interpretation of its meaning had to be drawn again and again. What not to code was also debated. Did we miss anything of importance? Was there some subtle under-text we could not read?

The problem of inter-coder reliability was solved by letting one person do all the coding. The coding of especially problematic items was discussed in the group.

Analyzing so much material and using such a wealth of different categorizations was extremely resource-consuming. Stone, one of the men behind the GE, is quoted as having said: 'Doing content analysis by hand will reduce even the most fanatical post-modernist to plead for a computer.'

## Analysis: co-occurrences

The content analysis carried out on a series of letters written by Jenny Masterson (a pseudonym) to her son's former room-mate and his wife inspired us (Stone *et al.* 1966). The letters, written by 'Jenny' in the last 11 years of her life, were analyzed to show her feelings, first and foremost about her son and, secondly, about the changes in her life during that period.

The focus on a single individual and the complex coding might be an example of the level of sophistication that could be reached in content analysis.

The letters were first published by Allport, who used them to illustrate his personality theories (Allport 1964). Besides being analyzed with the help of the GE, the letters have been the target of analyses by hand and from several psychological traditions. Jenny showed a high need for affiliation in her letters. In the positive-pole letters, Jenny told about needing the room-mate and his wife, and praised them and their home. In the negative-pole letters, Jenny told about her personal miseries in an attempt to call forth their sympathy.

The GE analysis made it possible to 'provide a stable, quantified picture of her personality in terms of her own verbal behaviour' (Paige 1966: 451). Furthermore, the analysis showed how Jenny's life changed over time and what she thought about it. It was also possible to corroborate the content analysis by analyzing Jenny's behaviour. Her letters showed an aggressive trait, expressed as physical violence later in her old age when she stayed in a nursing home.

The GE (Stone *et al.* 1966) also inspired us by frequent discussions of contingency analysis or co-occurrence analysis. How are themes connected in the text? The assumption is that it is possible to uncover how the subject constructs his or her world-view to make sense. In our case, it was possible to see if 'competition' was connected with specific other themes, such as 'threat' or 'opportunity', or with the behaviour of other firms.

## Drawing conclusions

The analytical step after the coding of contents of all the protocols into all the different categories embraced by the supra-categories concerned fusing the material into a picture of each business leader and comparing them so that a typology could be created. To our surprise, this was relatively easy when analyzing the 'Childhood' categories. The descriptions of the home, the parents, and the general conditions of youth could easily be grouped into two extremes. One group of executives had an upper class background (coded 'affluence'), while the other group came from poorer families (coded 'scarcity'). An in-between group also existed, with a middle class background (coded 'middle'). Interestingly enough, these three types of backgrounds were reflected in the types of career patterns. According to theory, personality is formed in a person's early life. We were nevertheless surprised to find such a close match between childhood conditions and career patterns. Three career patterns were identified and labelled, viz. the 'bourgeois', the 'revolutionary' and the 'plodder'.

The 'bourgeois' executive came from a privileged background and took over his father's company. The 'revolutionary' broke away from jobs and companies that did not suit him, just as he had broken away from his home and its tradition of scarcity. The 'plodder' came from a middle class family and typically stayed with the company. Members of this group were promoted for their hard work and tenacity until eventually reaching the top as chief executive. The subject's mother was almost always described in positive terms, as a warm, supportive person. In most of the interviews, however, the mother's role was not discussed at length. Concerning the description of the father and the subject's attitude towards him, an interesting bipolarity was demonstrated. Either the father was seen as a positive role model, someone to emulate, or he was seen as a negative role model. In the latter case, the executive in question had decided early on never to be like his father. The executives in this group were typically 'revolutionaries'; their careers showed a pattern of quitting non-satisfying jobs, to finally starting their own company. The 'bourgeois' type, on the other hand, had his father as a role model and often inherited the company leadership when the father retired. Hence, the idea that our personality and orientation in life is formed early was supported in our study.

## Interpretation

How much can the results of our analysis be trusted? The question of objectivity has already been touched upon, as has the question of reliability. An acceptable level of inter-coder agreement was reached concerning most supra-categories and their under categories, but after much practice. The category 'Personality' was the most troublesome, however. As the single final coder, I could test myself by recoding an interview or by coding two halves of an interview and comparing the results. The latter method did not work well, as the interview proceeded from a description of events in the early years of the executive's life to his perception of the current situation, which made comparison difficult. Recoding an interview yielded better results, but if this can be ascribed to good memory or to consistency in the coding remains an open question.

The highly consistent patterns of relations and careers that were found indicate that the coding was valid. The validity of the results might also be tested against other narratives or accounts of the executives' careers. The factual information showed great consistency between sources. We had, of course, limited opportunity to correlate our personality analyses and our analyses of the executives' views of good business practices with actual personal or firm behaviour.

The ambition to generalize conclusions from our study to other business leaders in Sweden or abroad was not foremost among the intentions of the study.

Drawing conclusions from the manifest content, i.e. the surface level of the text, to the latent content, i.e. the deeper layers of meaning embedded in the text, has been controversial. Holsti has resolved this by recommending that the coding be restricted to the manifest content, though, when interpreting the results, 'the investigator is free to use all of his powers of imagination and intuition to draw meaningful conclusions from the data' (Holsti, 1969:13).

## Conclusions

Much water has run under the bridge since the study of the 21 executives in the Swedish building industry was conducted. The study showed that it was possible to achieve good results without the aid of computers and sophisticated coding programs. The coding instructions were developed especially for this study, albeit based on established theories and earlier research, and they have not been used in other studies.

Content analysis as a method has developed in analyzed formats, e.g. from texts to images, and in embraced content, e.g. from political texts to TV soap opera scripts, and in the sources used, e.g. from mass media to the single individual, and, last but not least, in user friendliness. Several data programs are now available, but the researcher must still choose the theories to draw on and, in most cases, develop the categories to use. If our study were carried out today, the methods would certainly be different. I will, however, indulge myself by saying that we did not do too badly. The perfect fit between childhood patterns and career patterns was an unexpected highlight.

## References

Adorno, T.W. (1950) *The Authoritarian Personality*, New York: Harper.

Alchian, A. (1986) 'Uncertainty, Evolution, and Economic Theory', in J.B. Barney and W.G. Ouchi (eds) *Organizational Economics*, San Francisco, CA: Jossey-Bass.

Allport, G.W. (ed.) (1964) *Letters from Jenny*, New York: Harcourt, Brace & World.

Bales, R.F. (1950) *Interaction Process Analysis: A Method for the Study of Small Groups*, Cambridge, MA: Addison-Wesley.

Cochran, T.C. (1953) *Railroad Leaders, 1845–1890: The Business Mind in Action*, Cambridge, MA: Harvard University Press.

Cyert, R.M. and March, J.G. (1963) *A Behavioral Theory of the Firm*, Englewood Cliffs, NJ: Prentice Hall.

Hobbes, T. (1996) *Leviathan*, Cambridge: Cambridge University Press. (First published in 1660.)

Holsti, O.R. (1969) *Content Analysis for the Social Sciences and Humanities*, Reading, MA: Addison-Wesley.

Lasswell, H.D. and Kaplan, A. (1950) *Power and Society: A Framework for Political Inquiry*, New Haven, CT: Yale University Press.

Lasswell, H.D., Lerner, D. and de Sola Pool, I. (1952) *The Comparative Study of Symbols*, Stanford, CA: Stanford University Press.

Lévi-Strauss, C. (1964) *Le cru et le cuit*, Paris: Plon.

McClelland, D.C. *et al.* (1953) *The Achievement Motive*, New York: Appleton Century Crofts.

Merton, R.K. (1957) 'Science and Economy of 17th Century England', in R.K. Merton (ed.) *Social Theory and Social Structure*, Glencoe, IL: Free Press.

Paige, J.M. (1966) 'Letters from Jenny: An Approach to the Clinical Analysis of Personality Structure by Computer', in Stone *et al.* (eds) *The General Enquirer*, Cambridge, MA: MIT Press.

Rokeach, M.R. (1968) *Beliefs, Values and Attitudes*, San Francisco, CA: Jossey-Bass.

Stone, P.J. *et al.* (1966) *The General Enquirer: A Computer Approach to Content Analysis*, Cambridge, MA: MIT Press.

# 10 Building theory about small firms

## A grounded theory approach

*Tomas Brytting*

I had just finished my PhD thesis about organizing processes in small firms when someone from SIDA (the Swedish International Development Cooperation Agency) phoned me and arranged for an appointment. They had been asked to participate in a programme set up by the World Bank. The purpose was to design support systems for entrepreneurs in Sub-Saharan Africa. Could I look into the project, meet with the researchers involved and give my general impression?

At the meeting, two professors in economics from Harvard drew up the deductive research design. Based on the traditional rational economic man theory, the problem was defined as one of less than perfect local markets for information. By training 2000 interviewers and sending them with well-defined questionnaires out into the African countryside, asking entrepreneurs about their knowledge of and need for some predefined services and support, the researchers thought they would get a clear picture of how the entrepreneurial climate could be improved in the future.

I suggested humbly, being junior in rank, that the design should be more open-ended. Was it possible to include some open questions, or even historical case studies in order that we could learn more about the actual entrepreneurial process in Sub-Saharan Africa? Organization research in general, and entrepreneurial research in particular, had shown that managers do not always behave according to the rational, profit-maximizing stereotype. Maybe the typical African entrepreneur followed a logic that we, coming from the USA and Europe, did not fully understand? One of the professors then interrupted me with an irritated voice saying: 'Oh, so you mean they are loss-seekers?'

I was astonished to see the difference between deductive and inductive research being demonstrated so clearly, and I was sad to see the incapability of my senior colleague to see any relevance in an inductive approach.

This chapter will argue for inductive approaches to knowledge production by presenting, in detail, how it was done in my thesis (Brytting 1991). My ambition is to follow a grounded theory approach – in as rigorous a manner as I can.

## Small firms – a field to explore

Generally speaking, the importance of, and interest in, small firms is, in my opinion, not matched by adequate theoretical concepts and models. The received view has serious weaknesses connected to its rationalistic, objectivistic and structuralistic bias. Concepts taken from traditional management theory and organization theory (not to mention macro or micro economics!) are rejected by small firm managers, and our models do not make proper predictions.[1]

Without meaningful concepts and theories, small firms stand out as irrational, complex and difficult to understand. It is therefore worthwhile to design and carry out an explorative study, i.e. a research project designed for the purpose of constructing conceptual categories, and a theory that could help us identify and discuss organizational processes in small firms from a management perspective.

Small firms are organized both by formal and cognitive structures. Cognitive structures are especially important to study. The function of these structures is to make sense of the organizational reality. Therefore, I studied situations where people actually were trying to make sense of their own company history, first in a retrospective case study, and then in longitudinal direct observation.

The ambition was to explore the issue concerning organizational processes in the small firm – not necessarily giving it a firm answer. Like all explorers, I believe this work should be grounded on empirical observations. Theories should be firmly rooted in empirical data. With these ambitions, the use of a grounded theory approach seemed reasonable.

## Ontological and epistemological assumptions

One way or the other, knowledge is based on an interplay between systems of conceptual categories – theories – and empirical data; in the end sensory perceptions. In the past, 'scientists' have emphasized various aspects of this interplay. The ancient Greeks seldom concerned themselves with any empirical tests of their hypotheses. Their main criterion of quality was logical consistency among presumptions and conclusions. In positivism, on the other hand, to withstand an empirical test is the only acceptable way of getting a new hypothesis accepted.

So far, most researchers have been occupied with theoretical testing – verification or falsification. However, the generation of theory as such has also been put forward as a legitimate and important area of research. The choice of such an approach, however, can be based on a number of assumptions. To understand the explorative research carried out in this study, these assumptions must be discussed. In some theory-generating research, one finds a constructivist ontology paired with a constructivist epistemology. According to these assumptions, there is no objective reality. What we normally call 'reality' is instead sensations raised, particularly from our use of language. Language characteristics and certain characteristic ways in which the brain processes information produce regularities and patterns that we call, in a slightly misleading way, 'knowledge of reality'. We cannot know anything about the 'raw material' processed. It can either be plain noise or emptiness. Reality, as we know it, consists of subjective, individual and social constructions.

From constructivist assumptions, the following demands can be placed on new theories. They shall:

- Help those involved to understand the phenomena differently.
- Facilitate changes of the subjective and social constructions within which humans exist.
- Increase exchange and interplay of ideas.

One point of critique that can be raised is that assumptions of constructivism, if they are taken seriously, ultimately lead to a degradation of reason. The production of knowledge becomes romantic, a development that could, and historically has, become fascist (Lindholm 1979). A further difficulty with radical constructivism is the apparent contradiction between its relativism, on the one hand, and its own claims of general validity, on the other.

Popper (1934, cited in Miller 1983) regards society as a social construction, but in another way than do 'pure' constructivists. He argues that social cause-effect relations have a real existence and can be studied scientifically. However, he also treats social science theories as objective phenomena in themselves. When a theory is formulated, it starts to live a life of its own. It can affect the actions of individuals, and through this also add to the changes in society. The existence of social 'laws', therefore, does not imply that society is static.

Even though Popper did not explicitly formulate quality criteria for explorative research, the following could be derived from his thoughts:

- The theory should be possible to falsify through empirical testing.
- The theory should be formulated in such a way that an empirical test of the theory implies a test of the largest possible part of existing theory.

- *Ad hoc* hypotheses should be allowed only if they broaden the empirical domain of the theory, or *if* they increase the possibility of falsification.

Such a critical attitude towards one's own work and that of others will be a guarantee against elitist dogmatism as well as destructive romanticism. My thesis was designed to generate conceptual categories for describing and analyzing organization in small firms. These categories were to be firmly based on empirical data. When integrated and elaborated on, the concepts were intended to be used to formulate fragments of theory, hypotheses and models that should be possible to falsify through an empirical test. Falsification or acceptance of these theories, etc. should ideally affect present theory.

The use of a grounded theory approach facilitates the formulation of theories that should meet these ambitions.

## The grounded theory approach

'Grounded theory' is strictly speaking not *a* method but a labelling of a class of methods aimed at generating theory from empirical data through an inductive analytical process. The approach is based on a parallel development of theory and collection of data. The classical presentation is found in Glaser and Strauss (1967).[2]

According to Glaser and Strauss (1967: 3), the interrelated tasks of theory in sociology are:

(1) To enable prediction and explanation of behaviour.
(2) To be useful in theoretical advance in sociology.
(3) To be usable in practical applications – prediction and explanation should be able to give the practitioner understanding and some control of situations.
(4) To provide a perspective on behaviour – a stance to be taken toward data.
(5) To guide and provide a style for research on particular areas of behaviour.

They continue:

> Theory that can meet these requirements must fit the situation being researched, and work when put into use. By 'fit' we mean that the categories must be readily (not forcibly) applicable to and indicated by the data under study; by 'work' we mean that they must be meaningfully relevant to and able to explain the behaviour under study.

Glaser and Strauss claim that when using the grounded theory approach, which has the following general characteristics, theories of this type can be developed.

Conceptual categories are initially generated by a comparison between data observations. The formulation of a *category* is an attempt to find a concept that is on a slightly higher level of abstraction than the data itself. The category labels a set of observations that describe the same phenomenon. A category is a separate element of a theory – a concept. The categories must be *analytical* – and must convey some important characteristics of a phenomenon, not just the phenomenon as such. Categories must also be '*sensitizing*' or meaningful, i.e. they should make us interested in, and help us understand what we are studying. An example of a category that was developed in my study is the *Natural Organization* (A9) (see below).

Such categories and their *properties*, while indicated by the data, are not the data themselves. (The properties of the category Natural Organization (A9), for example, have to do with the way in which the structure of the firm is considered to be self-evident as well as organically developed, not deliberately designed.) The generation of categories and properties is therefore a creative process that adds something to the data observations. This process cannot be automated. It demands some acquaintance with both present theory and empirical research.

Empirical observations illustrate and give meaning to categories. These empirical observations are also used to generate the properties of the categories (e.g. when an interviewee says about his work tasks: 'Given my background, it was natural that I took responsibility for xx,' this quotation can be used to specify the properties of Natural Organization (A9)). The properties can therefore be regarded as the elements of the categories.

Whether or not a category is appropriate cannot be judged solely from the correctness of the underlying data (traditional reliability and validity demands). Rather, the usefulness of a category must be decided from its ability to contribute to the emerging theory. The categories must 'fit' and 'work' (see above). Consequently, the collection of data is guided by a theoretical relevance criterion. According to this criterion, the researcher should look for data that can help him or her develop:

- More categories.
- More properties in already developed categories.
- More relations between categories.

The collection of data continues until no further properties can be found or added to the categories. Glaser and Strauss call this stage *theoretical saturation*.

By first comparing data, and then comparing data with evolving categories, properties and new categories can be generated. Comparisons between categories generate *hypotheses*, which are defined as categories related to one another. Hypotheses, even contradictory ones, can also be developed further through new data collection and comparisons.

Some critical voices have been raised against Glaser and Strauss. One valid point of critique is that their 1967 book lacks practical descriptions of how the research can actually be carried out.[3] Categories and theories are said to 'emerge' in the mind of the researcher. A description of how this process occurs and how it can be designed and supported is neglected. Only vague and sweeping descriptions are given:

> Lower level categories emerge rather quickly during the early phases of data collection. Higher level, overriding and integrating, conceptualizations – and the properties that elaborate them – tend to come later during the joint collection, coding and analysis of the data.
>
> (Glaser and Strauss 1967)

No further details are given in their book. In this chapter, I illustrate how grounded theory may be used to understand organizing in small firms.

## How data was collected

The first empirical source (Case One) was a mid-sized manufacturing firm with 90 employees, which had already experienced a period of growth and recently reorganized. Data were gathered through 11 semi-structured interviews. All managers, including first-line supervisors, were asked to give their own description of the firm's organizational structure (responsibilities, coordination, and information channels) and how it had emerged. My notes from these interviews were later redistributed to the interviewees for comments.

As a result, Case One is an *ex post* description of a firm and its history. In a sense, this description is 'shared', meaning that it is a version based only on what the respondents have told me. On the other hand, no respondent has given me the whole picture. As will be explained below, the coding of the data also partly includes my own understanding of what the respondents have described. It should be noted that individual differences may have been present, although they were not found (or looked for) in the interviews.

After the first case study had been completed, a study based on direct observation was undertaken (Case Two). A very small firm was followed during a growth process of three years. The aim was to elaborate the experiences from Case One by investigating more deeply the reasoning of a small business leader as he or she experienced a significant process of change.

Data was collected through tape-recorded interviews every second or third month, interviews that I then had typed out. At these interviews, the owner/manager was encouraged to talk freely about his firm as it was at that particular time; what had happened since our last meeting, how he felt about the present situation, and what he would do next. This meant minimizing my own influence on what should be considered important and relevant subjects.

All in all, I conducted 25 formal interviews in Case Two and met with the entire staff on three occasions, but the case builds mainly on the interviews conducted with the owner/manager. The data is therefore not 'the firm's' shared understanding of the process, but primarily a description of the owner/manager's understanding, agony and joy.

The collected material consisted of roughly 300 pages of interview protocols.

## How data was coded

Data from Case One, i.e. my notes from the interviews, were divided into conceptual categories. These categories could be described as recurrent themes on a micro-level.[4]

A form was filled in for each category and a name for the category was chosen. The form also contained all data (citations or observations) that made up the category. Generation of categories did not stop until all interviews were coded. A total of 162 citations or observations from Case One were organized in this way.

Each category's relations to the other categories were also coded. These relations were found by comparing all categories two by two. Three types of relations were coded: *similarity*, *opposition* and *influence*. *Similarity* and *opposition* were the result of the comparative approach and helped clarify each category as much as possible. The coding of *influence* was necessary in order to establish causal chains for the conceptual categories. In essence, these causal chains formed descriptions of organizational processes. It should be stressed that the direction of this 'influence' and thus the directions of the arrows in the figures, such as the example in Figure 10.2, are empirically based. For example, the influence of Formalization (A8) on Enthusiasm (A14) stems from interviewees who described situations where a formalization, e.g. of responsibilities, had released energy.

Each category was given an identification code consisting of a letter – A, B and C – and a number. The letter indicated the theoretical level, i.e. the level of abstraction of the category, from A – the lowest level of abstraction, to C – the highest. The material from Case One was divided into 25 A-categories.

On the back of each form, I continuously noted properties of each category and any ideas or theoretical associations that might come to mind.

One category was named *Natural Organization* (A9). This category was grounded in data with the citations and observations noted in Box 10.1. This category was found to be related (in this particular case through similarity) with two other categories: Coincidences (A15) and Formalization (A8).

Natural Organization (A9) has two different properties, both grounded in data:

- The organization is natural, meaning 'self-evident' in the eyes of the respondent.
- The category also depicts a dynamic process; work roles emerge and change little by little.

A-categories were generated directly from Case One data. An interpretation of relations between these A-categories resulted in 23 B-categories and five C-categories. These categories formed elements in the emerging theory and guided the analysis of Case Two.

---

**Box 10.1** *Natural Organization (A9)*

- NN saw the reorganization as a formalization of the organization in practice . . .
- . . . slowly I moved over to selling . . . became involved in the reorganization and that's the way it is . . .
- The present organization is characterized by NN as 'the natural' . . .
- NN is interested in language and images and it is therefore natural that he has taken care of marketing issues . . .
- His present position did not exist when he entered the firm but has emerged little by little . . .
- Export was automatically taken over by NN . . .
- Hospitals were a natural thing for NN to handle . . . plus what was left . . .
- Everything sticks together (about the formal organization) . . . you can't separate – although there are 'clusters' . . .
- Personal contacts with Norway made NN take responsibility for that export . . .

Data from Case Two were coded and analyzed in a similar way. The 300 pages of interview protocols were coded in the form of almost 700 citations. These citations were organized using 23 of the 25 A-categories from Case One, plus an additional 15 A-categories.

## How data was analyzed

The properties of a category are most easily found in relation to other categories. For this reason, all A-categories were compared two by two. This exercise showed that some categories were vague or inconsistent. Three alternative procedures were then used:

- Change of name of category.
- Division of the category.
- Collection of more data.

For instance, I changed a category named *Lack of Information* to *Lack of Communication* (A7). A re-reading of the data showed that this change made the category 'fit' the data better.

An early category named *Increased Flexibility* covered inconsistent pieces of underlying data. This category (and the data behind it) was therefore divided into three: *Internal Flexibility* (A23), *Adaptation to Customers* (A24) and *Service to Customers* (A25).

I found some categories of special interest. They were either connected to cognitive processes or difficult to relate to traditional organization theory:

- Natural Organization (A9)
- Sufficient Size (All)
- Think Alike (A12)
- Coincidences (Al5)
- Create an Overview (A21)

I found these categories worth elaborating further through the collection of more data. Longitudinal studies were considered necessary to follow how the small firm is organized. This led to the collection of additional data from a second firm, Case Two.

When all A-categories had been compared and their relations had been established, a visual display of relations was drawn. This relations schema was the raw material used in the continued analysis. (Figure 10.1 shows all relations from Case One only.) The total complexities in the relations schema were then reduced through four different techniques (described below) with increasing levels of 'objectivity'. The aim was to identify meaningful clusters of A-categories that could be used as theoretical building blocks. These clusters were called B-categories and were interpreted as descriptions of organizational processes in small firms. Groups of B-categories and a discussion of some general characteristics of these categories led to a small number of C-categories.

## Moving from A- to B-level categories

The analysis developed into a cumulative reasoning about the observed data and about A-categories. B-level categories were formulated as they 'emerged'. The generation of new B-categories continued as long as available B-categories did not cover new aspects of the relations schema. The guiding logic was 'theoretical saturation' (Glaser and Strauss 1967: 61), i.e. new B-level categories were formed until all the important clusters of A-level categories (found using the different search techniques described below) had been made sense of.

Four alternative methods were used to cluster A-level categories into B-level categories. The four methods were: (1) unrestricted search, (2) framework-guided search, (3) cause-map sub-cluster identification, and (4) centrality-based search.

### Unrestricted search

The first method used to organize the total complexity in the relations schema into meaningful clusters was a search for clusters of A-categories that either described important empirical phenomena (found during the interviews), or suggested some theoretical issue (treated in the literature). This search for relevant or sense-making B-level categories was conducted in a fairly open-minded and unsystematic way, and therefore called 'unrestricted search'. In practice, it meant a careful and playful combinatory search from one A-category to the next, translating labels and relations into meaningful fragments of theory.

The unrestricted search resulted in ten B-level categories. *Spontaneous Coordination* (B2), for example, was made up of the relations between A3, A10, A12 and A16, at the right-hand side of Figure 10.1. The corresponding theoretical fragment could be described in the following way: *A shared view of the firms activities (A12) can be achieved by solving priorities together (A16). This will in turn facilitate future problem solving. As long as this shared view is maintained, participants can act autonomously (A3). However, this autonomy will be withdrawn as soon as conflicts arise (A10).*

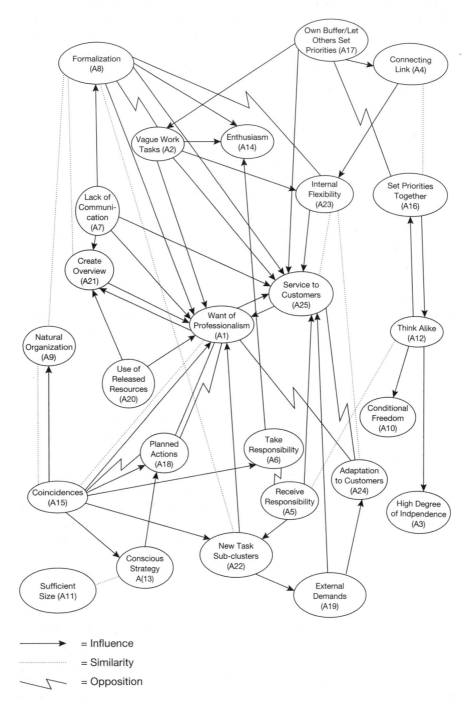

*Figure 10.1* Relations between A-level categories from Case One.

*Framework-guided search.*

The second technique used to find sense-making B-categories was deliberately guided by what I then considered to be the established or received view of organization theory. I was particularly interested in how it described the functions of organizational structures. In summary, I claimed that the received view identified four functions of organizational structure: division of labour, coordination, motivation and institutionalization. In the framework-guided search in the relations schema, the A-categories were therefore used in a straightforward attempt to elaborate these four central concepts. This was accomplished in four steps. First, by eliminating all relations coded as *similarity* or *opposition*, the relations schema was transformed into a cause map. The resulting cause map is shown in Figure 10.2.

One reason behind this reduction was that the relations called 'similarity' and 'opposition' were primarily used to clarify the properties of the category. After this clarification was made, 'influence' was considered more interesting in order to formulate ideas about the mechanisms that drive small firm organizing.

Second, for each of the four central concepts, those A-categories that were thought to be relevant in the elaboration of that particular concept were selected. In other words, I selected those A-categories that I intuitively thought could describe the structural mechanisms behind *division of labour, coordination, motivation* and *institutionalization* in small firms. Third, cause maps of the selected A-categories were drawn for each of those central concepts. Finally, independent sub-clusters – i.e. clusters with no relations to categories outside the cluster – were identified and interpreted.

For example, the following A-categories were tentatively selected as reasonably relevant for a discussion about mechanisms that support 'coordination' in small firms': Want of Professionalism (A1), High Degree of Independence (A3), Connecting Link (A4), Receive Responsibility (A5), Formalization (A8), Conditional Freedom (A10), Think Alike (A12), Set Priorities Together (A16), Planned Actions (A18), Create an Overview (A21) and New Task Sub-Clusters (A22).

One sub-cluster that emerged from this exercise was *Goal Setting* (B13), which was described in the following way: *The head of the firm coordinates activities by deliberately (A18) reinforcing the goal of professionalism (A1). The fact that this ideal is well-circulated and accepted in the firm has a coordinating effect in itself. For the manager, it is also a way to reach an understanding of the firm, which, for him, is an important goal per se (A21). Organizational measures, such as formalization (A8) and the creation of new areas of responsibility (A22), are also used for coordination, which aims for professional appearance (A1).*

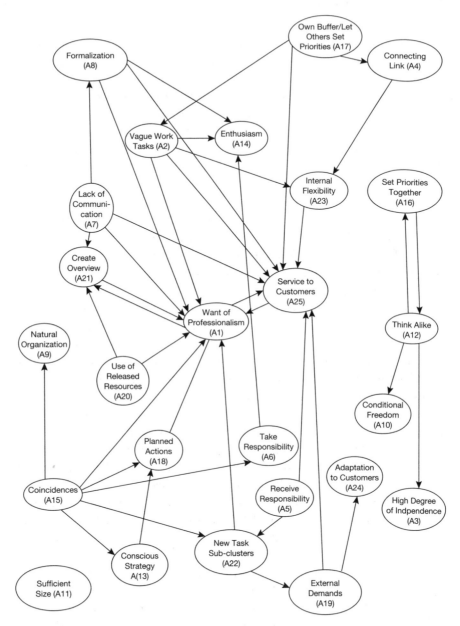

*Figure 10.2* Cause map from two case studies of small, growing firms.

The framework-guided search confirmed some B-categories already identified, and added six new ones.

### Cause-map sub-cluster identification

The third method of simplifying the complexity in the relations schema was designed to reduce influences from any prejudices (which might have reproduced themselves in the unrestricted search) or influences from the structure present in pre-formulated theories. The 'cause-map sub-cluster identification' was carried out in three steps. First, just as in the frame-work-guided search, the total relations schema was transformed into a cause map. Second, I decided to merge the two A-categories *Want of Professionalism* (A1) and *Service to Customer* (A25) into the B-category *Professionalism* (B1), already identified during the unrestricted search. The reason for this was that the similarity between these categories guaranteed that no information would be lost. At the same time, the number of relations, and thus complexity, could be substantially reduced.

The third step was to identify isolated, or semi-isolated, clusters in this reduced cause map. Semi-isolated clusters were defined as clusters of A-categories with only one causal relation to other clusters with the exception of Professionalism (B1) (since this category was included in all sub-clusters and thus considered as the main goal of the firm). In this way, some B-categories already identified were confirmed and an additional two new ones were identified.

### Centrality-based search

The fourth method that was used to reduce complexity in the relations schema, and generate more B-categories, focused on central A-categories in the complete cause map. 'Central' was defined as categories having three or more causal relations. Through this design, only two pre-defined clusters were elaborated. A-categories that were influenced by many other A-categories were named '*goals*', for example *Professionalism* (A1), which is clearly a primary goal in growing small firms. A-categories that influence many other A-categories were named '*causes*', for example *Coincidences* (A15), i.e. sudden unforeseen incidents that start significant processes in the small firm.

## Moving from B- to C-level categories

After each of these four types of analyses of the relations schema from Case One, I conducted an integration of the results, i.e. a summary of the organizational processes (B-categories) suggested by the analyses. When doing this, certain themes, or common characteristics among these organizational processes, became apparent. These themes were given illustrative labels and together made up the so-called C-level categories of this study. These C-categories thus form a kind of typology of organizational processes in growing small firms.

The step from B- to C-level categories was not guided by any rigorous technique. However, the ambition was to sustain a grounded approach, i.e. to let lower-level concepts guide the development of higher-level concepts. The search for C-categories also followed a cumulative process. A new C-category was introduced only if already available C-categories could not cover the specific aspect in question. In retrospect, I realize that these five C-level categories fall into a dualistic pattern, although this was not used as a conscious 'technique' for analyzing B-level categories. When a certain theme was found, e.g. Spontaneity (C1), its opposite, Systematic Planning (C2), was easy to recognize. Similarly, once Sensemaking (C3) was identified, Confusion (C5) came out as a complementary category. Adaptation (C4) described maybe the most abstract of all categories, a summary of all mechanisms that drive the organizing of the small firm.

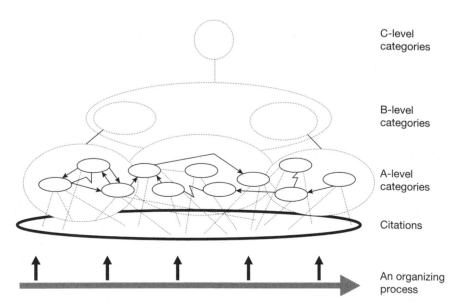

*Figure 10.3* A schematic representation of the different analytical steps from an actual organizational process to C-level categories.

## Some thoughts on small firm organizing

Before I end this chapter with some further epistemological comments, let me just hint at some of the 'conclusions' coming out of this study.

First of all, I would hypothesize that intentional organizing processes, summarized in what I called Systematic Planning (C2), do not differ between large and small firms. Building of hierarchies and routinization of information, etc. take place through similar processes in small and large firms. However, there are aspects that seem to be particularly important for small firms, e.g. *Hitchhiking* (B29), which depicts a conscious effort of negotiating with potential collaborators in order to make profitable use of others' resources without direct control or ownership. I would also hypothesize that fate, coincidences and blind chance to a very large degree determine the design of the small firm. However, these coincidences can, to some extent, also be influenced. By maintaining a large personal network, and being prepared to grasp sudden opportunities, the owner/manager can increase the probability of a favourable 'coincidence' and remain in control psychologically.

Second, many of the characteristics of small firms might be inefficient from an economical point of view but are effective means of self-expression. Thus, there exist certain small-scale advantages that are difficult to preserve during growth, however profitable. The complementarity of small and large firms should therefore be stressed. They play different roles in the economy and in social life. Economic advantages for small firms might be reproduced in decentralized hierarchies, but the existential importance of small firms demands full autonomy.

## Some epistemological comments on the method

The analysis carried out in this research project treats protocols from interviews with individual actors as empirical data. These individual perceptions, feelings and associations are regarded as relevant data in the process of identifying organizational processes in small firms.

It should be noted that the relation analysis is not simply a mechanical counting of relations and forming of clusters. A quantitative analysis can only work with the labels of categories, connecting these with their number of relations and number of data. The analysis will easily lose the original empirical content behind them. A quantitative analysis can select clusters with many data or many relations, but not clusters with theoretically significant data and significant relations.

The material used in the relation analysis is the empirical content of the categories and its properties, not the immediate associations that might grow out simply from their labels.

In the case of my study, it is important to take along the empirical content during the analysis, but even more important, perhaps, is the necessity of leaving room for some kind of stepwise value-adding process, i.e. a successive theoretical interpretation of categories and their relations. The method described therefore uses the researcher and his or her intellect, as instruments – in much the same way as Glaser and Strauss envisioned.

To understand the method used in this study, it is crucial to distinguish between the *extension* of a conceptual category and its *intention* (see Figure 10.4). *Extension* refers to the empirical observations that form the category, i.e. the empirical data (quotations from interviews) on which the category is grounded. The *intention* of a category, on the other hand, is the theoretical meaning of that particular category, and is described in the properties or attributes of the category – properties developed through the comparative analysis described. This leap, from extension to intention, which is exactly what happens during the construction of A-, B- and C-categories, is the researcher's main contribution to inductive research. I believe that this leap cannot be made without prior theoretical knowledge and training; it cannot be made by computers or by the layperson. Moreover, the fact that the researcher interferes 'subjectively' in the analysis might prove not only necessary but also feasible.

The act of (subjective) interpretation is in fact an act of choosing meaning (or conceptual intention). My opinion is that the researcher should choose meaning that 'fits' data and 'works', i.e. conveys relevant meaning to other researchers involved in the area studied. The objection that this subjective act limits the applicability of the categories is admittedly relevant. This

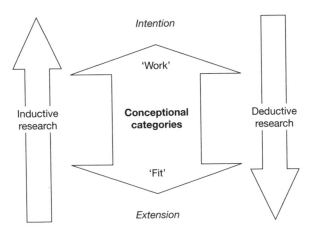

*Figure 10.4* Some principle differences between inductive and deductive research.

subjective choice of meaning implies that the ability to make proper predictions (generalizable models) may be reduced. However, it does not follow that interpretation should be abandoned. In fact, I believe it is inevitable. Rather, a balance between meaning and generality is required. On the one hand, meaning without generality hampers the scientific dialogue and the accumulation of knowledge. On the other, generality without meaning is, in the real sense, meaningless (Miller 1983).[5]

The method used in this study shares many similarities with content analysis. However, content analysis is often presented as an objective method used to *discover* a deeper meaning or pattern in written, verbal or 'social' texts. It is, for example, often used in studies of cognitive mapping (Laukkanen 1989).[6] Usually it uses a pre-set selection of conceptual categories. The grounded theory approach, as applied here, *generates* one of several possible subjective interpretations. It involves an iterative change between data and theory, between extension and intention. Accordingly, the method used here could be described as: a *content analysis of the researcher's own cognitive map after empirical exposure.*

A theory is therefore similar to a cognitive map, or an interpretive schema, with some qualifications. A non-scientific, what psychologists call 'naive', cognitive map might contain contradictions and be highly 'private' and idiosyncratic. What is presented as a scientific theory is a cognitive map deliberately aimed at consistency and public acceptance (primarily) within the scientific community. It is also incorrect to say that generation of theory through a grounded theory approach is equivalent to a mapping of the researcher's prior knowledge and understanding of certain empirical phenomena, a reification of so-called 'pet theories'. It should not be forgotten that the theory is deliberately and actually generated, changed and put together as part of a specific research project.

For instance, the fact that the use of four different techniques for finding B-categories gave rise to four different sets of B-categories makes it apparent that the researcher's choice between different alternative theoretical fragments is influenced by his or her method of analysis. The B-categories are thus more than projections of the researcher's theoretical prejudices. On the other hand, the way a certain cluster of A-categories is interpreted into a meaningful B-category may differ depending on who is doing the interpretation. In this sense, the grounded theory approach, as it has been adopted in this study, allows for creative input during the analysis.

The title of Glaser and Strauss' book – *The Discovery of Grounded Theory* – is therefore, in my opinion, slightly misleading in this regard. Theory does not exist 'out there', (not even 'in there') waiting to be discovered. It is – in this case – constructed by the researcher through conscious rigorous empirical work and theoretical training. The trick is to make this theory-building – or even theory-choosing process – open to constructive criticism. The method developed here is an attempt to move in that direction.

Finally, the method used here admittedly involves subjective interpretation of data. The careful recording and coding of data, on the other hand, acts against an uncontrolled selective perception that sometimes plagues traditional case study methods. Here, a deliberate decision must be taken to avoid or disregard a piece of data, and omitted data can be analyzed in order to see any systematic patterns.

## Notes

1   For instance, Plaschka (1987) compared 62 successful and 63 unsuccessful entrepreneurs and concluded that 'schoolish and job oriented education has no significant influence on entrepreneurial success'.
2   An attempt to present a more detailed description of how this is done can also be found in Glaser (1978, 1995).
3   Turner (1981:226). Note however, that on the whole, Turner is sympathetic towards the grounded theory approach and makes a valuable contribution to it in his article.
4   After this study was completed, I became aware of Turner's (1981) article. Our methods of coding data have much in common, but our analysis and interpretation techniques differ. Late in my research process, Laukkanen (1989) published his method for cognitive mapping, which also has many parallels with the one presented here. My method of coding data was developed in discussions with Chris Steyaert at the Catholic University of Leuven.
5   This is in a sense a paraphrasing of Popper's statement that 'with increasing content, probability decreases, and vice versa' (Popper, in Miller 1983:174).
6   For a review of these studies see Laukkanen (1989: 22–33).

## References

Brytting, T. (1991) *Organizing in the Small Growing Firm: A Grounded Theory Approach*, Stockholm: Stockholm School of Economics.

Glaser, B. (1978) *Theoretical Sensitivity*, San Francisco, CA: Sociology Press.

Glaser, B. (1995) (ed.) *Grounded Theory, 1984–1994*, Mill Valley, CA: Sociology Press.

Glaser, B. and Strauss, A. (1967) *The Discovery of Grounded Theory – Strategies for Qualitative Research*, Chicago, IL: Aldine.

Laukkanen, M. (1989) Understanding the Formation of Managers' Cognitive Maps – A Comparative Case Study of Context in Two Business Firm Clusters, Helsinki: Helsinki School of Economics and Business Administration, dissertation.

Lindholm, S. (1979) *Vetenskap, verklighet och paradigm* (Science, Reality and Paradigm), Stockholm: AWE/Gebers.

Miller, D. (1983) (ed.) *A Pocket Popper*, Glasgow: Fontana Press.

Plaschka, G. (1987) Characteristics of Successful and Unsuccessful Entrepreneurs – A Theoretical Guided Empirical Investigation of Person-related and Micro-social Factors, papers presented at the 'Workshop on Recent Research on Entrepreneurship in Europe', EIASM, Brussels, May 14–15.

Popper, K. (1934) 'Scientific Method', in Miller, D. (1983) *A Pocket Popper*, Glasgow: Fontana Press.

Turner, B.A. (1981) 'Some Practical Aspects of Qualitative Data Analysis – One Way of Organising the Cognitive Processes Associated with the Generation of Grounded Theory', *Quality and Quantity*, 15, 225–247.

# 11 The making of a metaphor
## Developing a theoretical framework

*Thomas Durand*

## Introduction

My intent in this chapter is twofold: (1) to illustrate and discuss how I conduct my own research in management, from a not-so-common combined academic and consulting standpoint; and (2) to present a representation of management knowledge resulting from this research activity.

More specifically, I try to discuss research about management as a practice, taking here the example of a specific research question: What is knowledge in organizations? The result of this discussion leads in turn to a representation of *knowledge* via a metaphor, which may hopefully be seen as an element of knowledge about management, thus providing an insight into both the process and the output of management research.

This piece about organizational knowledge thus offers a concrete case to discuss my own stance as a researcher who is also actively involved in consulting. It offers a description of how I go about trying to contribute to management knowledge in my own way.

For me, this question of organizational knowledge stems from three different lines of activities that I developed at various points in time, all of which ended up converging towards the same issue of grasping competence in organizations. First, I had been working as a researcher on the strategic consequences of technological change and came to the conclusion that the best way of thinking about change was to look at the set of competences that the focal actors would either reinforce or lose through the change (Durand and Gonard, 1986; Durand and Stymne, 1988). But that led me to a difficult question: What is competence exactly? This was before Prahalad and Hamel's (1990) piece on core competencies, and I must admit that I had missed Wernerfelt's earlier article (1984) in the *Strategic Management Journal*.

Second, at about the same period, I had, as a consultant, also been developing a 'Who's Who in Technology' in a multinational company. We were trying to find ways of systematically listing the portfolio of technologies in a large organization. I came up with the idea of identifying technologies through the people who bear the technical competence. We thus decided to build a database (which took the form of a book), with one page per technical staff (engineer, researcher, technician) who could claim some technological knowledge of any form. Each page would describe the technological expertise of a given member of the organization. In a way, we were collecting 'technological resumes', with a specific format, to compile into a book – hence the wording, 'who's who in technology within the firm' (Durand 1988). We were obviously trying to grasp the technological capabilities of the company via its human resources. Yet, as we were collecting the information, asking about 3000 technology staff in the firm to fill out a written questionnaire, one executive asked why we did not do the same analysis for managerial competencies. He was hinting at competence beyond the purely technological. The point struck me; it was a small signal stemming from a 'user' (à la von Hippel 1976), generated through my consulting activities, that ticked away in my head for several years.

Third, both as a researcher and consultant, I came up with the idea of building visual representations of technological options to fulfil market needs. That led to the concept of 'dual technology trees' (Durand 1992a). In a way, this was also an attempt to represent Clark's (1985) hierarchies. I later had the opportunity to use this tool in my consulting practice, thus trying to capture knowledge in a visual map. Practitioners loved it. This, in turn, led me to cognitive map research. However, together with Eleonore Mounoud and Bernard Ramanantsoa, we eventually came to the conclusion that we wanted to stay away from cognitive maps, preferring the concept of 'social representation' (Durand et al. 1996). We would ask the following questions: Where does strategy come from? How does an organization build a capability to scan its environment, identify market opportunities, position its offering against the competition? How does it build a representation of its environment? How does a firm become competent in such difficult and crucial domains that are key to shaping its future?

Our trio then expanded into a larger group of researchers, named Drisse,[1] who launched a research programme around the theme of representations in strategic management (Drisse 2001). More specifically, we viewed strategy as the activity aimed at designing and shaping the future of the organization. In this sense, we chose to view strategy as organizational knowledge, i.e. which emerges through organizational learning. But that brought us back to the same old question: What is knowledge? And we added a few more: Can knowledge in companies really be managed? What is the real nature of organizational knowledge? How can management researchers find ways to grasp knowledge not only from a theoretical point of view but also through relevant empirical investigations?

This is how it all started for me on this theme, stemming from both research and consulting, with a set of questions and ideas periodically ticking in my head over a period of several years. My research activity can thus be described as a patient hunt to understand management.

The present chapter aims to show how a combined stance (academic and consulting) can contribute to building from two streams of input:

- Existing theoretical contributions from prominent scholars of social science, who have already worked on these issues of organizational knowledge.
- Empirical work conducted over the years either directly as research activities and/or reflective rethinking of consulting assignments, providing useful material for interpretation, somewhat adapted from the grounded theory approach.

In turn, the output of this specific research agenda on strategy and organizational knowledge (which I will call 'organizational competence') led to a representation of knowledge and competence, aiming at contributing to management knowledge.

## The making of a metaphor

The focus of the chapter addresses how I ended up presenting, discussing and using the concept of 'competence leaves' and 'knowledge as foliage'. I argue that this is a metaphor that can be used to grasp and describe some of the characteristics of the texture of the competence tissues that compose this hybrid and fuzzy object of analysis known in the literature as 'organizational knowledge'.

As is often the case, my overall theoretical framework essentially came from a purely theoretically-oriented research perspective. Note, however, that any theoretical model I use must 'fit' (meaning that it fits with, i.e. does not contradict, in a Popperian sense, the material and experience that I, both as an empirical researcher and a consultant working in many organizations, have had over the years). In this sense, the theoretical frameworks used in most of my research stem from the literature. But I tend to sift the literature according to both my own research data, as most researchers do, and the 'overall interpretation of my field experience' that comes from consulting. I scan the literature with not only internal validity criteria (is this logical?) but also, if not primarily, with external validity criteria in mind (does this fit what I have seen/experienced before? Does it make sense to me, given what I have observed in companies and organizations over the years?).

This is typical of a research practice where experience shapes intuition – here the filtering device – which may be seen as part of knowledge. Experience contributes to building the sieving device, helping to recognize when a theory may be useful or not to look at organizations. In mathematical terms, my sieving capability, as a researcher, may be seen as the inversely discounted integral of past experience.

From this perspective, my practice of research in management is made up of four components. My field experience accounts for the first two:

- Empirical research.
- Consulting.

In research, I know what I am looking for, or at least I think I do. Conversely, if my consulting activities generate ideas, examples and counter examples, this usually occurs in unexpected ways. The third and fourth components are made up of:

- My attempts to read and understand the literature.
- My classroom activities (both with students and executives).

Through teaching, I test my thinking, and find illustrations and examples. I confront my research outputs with an audience. This often leads me to revisit the concepts and the way I present them.

These four components obviously interact with one another continuously in my 'practice'.

Among other difficulties I face in conducting research in management, are that I often run into the problems of what to call things. Should I use the word 'knowledge' to name what I was after? Following some of my former work (Durand 1996, 1998, 2001; Durand and Guerra Viera 1997), I decided to use the generic word 'competence' to describe the firm's capabilities to combine, bundle and integrate resources into products and services. And I will do so in most of the rest of this chapter.

As I struggled with ways to look at organizational competence, I had two enlightening discussions with researcher colleagues. One took place in a taxi on the way to catch a plane after a conference (when an Italian colleague sharing the cab with me offered a categorization of competence which I found very helpful, if perhaps not comprehensive enough), and the second with a Swedish colleague attending a seminar I gave at the Stockholm School of Economics. This colleague suggested that I borrow the three dimensions of learning from research on education: knowledge, practice and attitudes. (He actually spoke about 'the historian' (knowledge), 'the mechanic' (know-how) and 'the politician' (attitudes).) I subsequently found out that this followed Pestalozzi (1797), who referred to these as 'head, hand and heart'.

For young researchers should note in passing the importance of opportunities like conferences, informal discussions with colleagues and presenting work in progress at seminars to get feedback. This is crucial. One may then revisit the material to rethink the framework, which is still emerging. The way I do this is twofold: first, I write drafts to put my ideas into words; second, I draw diagrams, tables and other representations to offer a visual version of my thinking. In Microsoft terms, this is PowerPoint complementing Word, and vice versa, and represents two very different modes of formalization. Some would argue that the two are even divergent. Personally, I find it useful to crystallize my thinking using both forms, precisely because they usually do not yield the same type of output. Hence, by confronting the results of verbalization and schematization, I try to gain a wider, richer and deeper form of research output. A text is much richer, more detailed and nuanced, but can be too flexible in a way. A diagram, or some other form of visual representation, is often limiting, 'sketchy' or too square, but imposes a structure, a sense of meaning that can be lost in the labyrinth of a wordy text. Although I know that many colleagues from the social sciences tend to dislike the latter, essentially valuing writing, I find the confrontation of both very helpful. I should add that this is often a painful process, but extremely rewarding when it is over.

In this instance, I wrote several pieces attempting to offer taxonomies and classifications of competence (Durand 1996, 1998, 2001; Durand and Guerra Viera 1997). Tables 11.1 and 11.2 illustrate some of these attempts. None of these attempts were satisfactory, however; they were incomplete, heterogeneous, fit poorly with existing concepts in the literature, insufficiently self-contained, etc.

In other words, I could relate these classifications to practice, but not to theoretical frameworks. This was a source of frustration for me, which, I believe, is often the engine that drives researchers. That is, frustration often drives my research hunt. I thus continued my search for more satisfactory representations of what I sought to grasp and describe.

I finally came to use the knowledge/know-how/attitudes trilogy from Pestalozzi, which I presented formally as follows below:

*Knowledge* corresponds to the structured sets of assimilated information that make it possible to understand the world, obviously with partial and somewhat contradictory interpretations. Knowledge thus encompasses the access to data, the ability to enact them into acceptable information and to integrate them into pre-existing schemes, which naturally evolve along the way. In this sense, knowledge is now seen only as one dimension of competence. (This last point justifies the shift in wording from *knowledge* to *competence*.)

*Table 11.1* Competence

| Competence | |
| --- | --- |
| ↗ Stand-alone assets<br>*Tangible and intangible* | Equipment, buildings, products, software, brandnames, etc. |
| ↗ Cognitive capabilities<br>*Individual and collective, explicit and tacit* | Knowledge, know-how skills, technologies, patents, etc. |
| ↗ Organizational processes and routines | Coordinating mechanisms in the organization, combining individual actions into collective functioning. |
| ↗ Organizational structure<br>*May facilitate or hinder the ability of a firm to adapt to certain changes* | The structural design of the organization and its linkages to the environment (suppliers, clients, etc.) |
| ↗ Identity<br>*May facilitate or hinder the ability of a firm to adapt to certain changes* | Behavioural and cultural characteristics of the firm. Shared values, beliefs, rites and taboos are symptoms of the identity |

*Table 11.2* Competence (degree of)

| Competence (degree of) | |
| --- | --- |
| ↗ *Data* | ↘ *I have access to external pieces of information* |
| ↗ *Information* | ↘ *I know, I have learnt, I found out* |
| ↗ *Knowledge* | ↘ *I have an integrated framework of information that I can explain to someone else* |
| ↗ *Skill* | ↘ *I can do it* |
| ↗ *Know-how* | ↘ *I know how to do it, I can do it, and I can show someone else how to do it* |
| ↗ *Competence* | ↘ *I am more able than others to explain what to do and how to do it (knowledge), as well as to do it (know-how)* |
| ↗ *Expertise* | ↘ *I am an expert at doing it, as well as understanding what to do and explaining how to do it* |

*Know-how* refers to the ability to act in a concrete way according to predefined objectives or processes. Know-how does not exclude knowledge but does not necessitate a full understanding of why the skills and capabilities, when put into operation, actually work. Know-how thus relates, in part, to empiricism and tacitness.

*Attitudes* refer to behaviours, commitment and culture. Attitudes are too often neglected in the resource-based view, as well as in the competence-based theory of the firm. Behaviour, and even more so identity and will (determination), are an essential part of the capability of an organization to achieve anything. Including, as I suggest, an element of attitude into the concept of competence is a matter of choice in defining concepts. I argue that an active, dedicated organization, eager to succeed, is more competent than a demoralized, passive one with exactly the same knowledge and know-how.

I argue that these three basic dimensions constitute a useful referential to describe the competence of an organization.

However, this did not fully fit my practical experience: management, through classical managerial levers (strategizing, organizing, motivating), is not necessarily capable of acting directly upon the dimensions of knowledge – know-how – attitudes. Attitudes, for example, are not fully directed by management, but stem from conformance, as members of the organization tacitly (and sometimes explicitly) adopt the same posture and behaviours, conforming to a norm that may or may not have been set by managerial hierarchies. I knew how difficult it was for management to shape cultures. However, I had also seen how great leaders were able to motivate their staff. This meant that I had to recognize the difference between a descriptive framework and a normative tool. The three dimensions I was using were essentially descriptive.

More importantly, it led me to take stock of the importance of the 'attitudes' dimension as something that the literature on knowledge and competence did not seem to address. I have learnt from Henry Mintzberg to always look carefully at special cases, misfits and exceptions. This is what I felt here; the 'attitudes' category was a new piece in the jigsaw. This in turn led to the idea that the heart of the concept of competence, the 'organizational alchemy of competence' as I called it, which, according to the literature, essentially has to do with the coordinated deployment of resources and assets, should be enlarged to encompass more than management processes. I argued that identity (the shared values, rites, taboos and beliefs) operates as a cement, holding the organizational pieces together at least as efficiently as any other coordinating and integrating mechanism.

For the sake of being systematic, I then continued to scan the other dimensions of the framework. Looking at *knowledge*, I further argued that a shared vision also contributes to the coordinated deployment of strategy, channelling people's energy, motivation and commitment. Finally, I suggested that organizational structure is also a key element of the same coordinated deployment of assets and capabilities.

All in all, I thus suggested reviewing and enlarging the content of the 'coordinated deployment' concept in order to encompass four elements:

management processes, identity, strategic vision and structure. In other words, organizations learn, and thus build competence, in several ways, not just 'cognitively' and not just through management processes.

Note that such a proposal for three key dimensions of organizational competence, plus four components of the organizational cement, stemmed from an empirical interpretive 'feel' for what competence may cover. This relates to the 'intuition' generated by an 'overall interpretation of field experience'. The input from Pestalozzi was a trigger for a theorizing process that cannot be directly related to any specific fieldwork of mine. However, I would claim that this meta-theorizing happened to be fed by the totality of both my field experience and readings.

For example, many different consulting assignments – not just one – had convinced me of the importance of culture and identity in the ability of an organization to deliver. It was thus a normal step for me to think of integrating some form of culture, in this case 'attitudes', as a component of organizational competence. That had appeared in my preliminary attempts to build classifications, before receiving the input from Pestalozzi's model. When that input came in, it could naturally fit into my own thinking.

I would argue that, in a way, intuition is the result of the totality of experience gained through practice, reading, discussions, observation, etc. In other words, the practice of research both builds and exploits intuition.

## Introducing learning and 'competence leaves' into the model

The intermediate classifications I had generated along the way included the idea that competence was a stock resulting from a flux, namely, learning: competence develops through learning, which reinforces and enlarges the 'competence base' of the organization along the three dimensions of the referential model. In addition, the intermediary classifications I had built (see above) had suggested some form of a dynamic accumulation process with stages: external information, as data, being accepted (or not) as pieces of relevant information, and in turn integrated into pieces of knowledge. This led to wording of the following type: knowledge builds up as information is integrated and assimilated into Goffman's (1991) interpretive frames, which ensure coherence and structure of the organizational knowledge. Yet, information is not just data. Information is data that were acknowledged, sieved, transformed and adapted to fit into the pre-existing structure of knowledge, i.e. to the existing frames.

I also sought support from the social sciences: the psychology literature suggests that individuals tend to reject data that do not fit their previous knowledge, while they overemphasize data that reinforce their existing understanding and beliefs (Schwenk 1984; Barnes 1984, 1988; Stubbart 1989).

At that point, I tested my idea in a workshop and got interesting feedback. This in turn led to a synthetic formalization of the argument: one may thus consider that data need to be accepted before they reach the status of information, which can then be integrated as an element of knowledge. At the other end of the spectrum, expertise should be regarded as much higher a step than knowledge. Not only does expertise relate to a significantly more advanced level of capability, it also requires an integrated combination of knowledge, know-how and attitudes, thus assuming a 'state-of-the-art' ability to understand, explain and even act within the domain of competence. In a way, expertise 'transcends' competence, through both (a) a quantum jump in the level of competence, and (b) a recombination and merging of various elements of competence (i.e. knowledge, know-how and attitudes).

In other words, as I suggested (Durand 1992b), there is a sequence of stages from data and information, to knowledge and expertise, as shown in Figure 11.1. That being done on one dimension of the framework (knowledge), it was thus natural to think of a similar dynamic process for the other two dimensions (know-how and attitudes). This was done for the sake of pure analogy but the extension proved useful. It led to the following formalization, as illustrated in Table 11.3.

Table 11.3 illustrates the parallelism that prevails in the way learning mechanisms operate for each dimension of the referential. Know-how is built through action that shapes skills and techniques. Similarly, attitudes are shaped through interaction when individuals conform to group or organizational behaviour, adopt the same cultural values and share the same basic commitments. Expertise requires one step further, as it needs some form of quantum jump in competence together with a merging of the three generic dimensions of competence. Putting the pieces together thus led to an overall framework by which to view the dynamics of organizational competence.

*Figure 11.1* Sequence of stages from data and information to knowledge and expertise.

*Table 11.3* Parallel learning processes and stages

| Knowledge | Know-how | Attitudes |
|---|---|---|
| Data reception | Action | Interaction |
| Information | Skills and capabilities | Behaviour, culture, will |
| Knowledge | Know-how | Attitudes |
| Expertise | Expertise | Expertise |

Figure 11.2 illustrates the proposed framework graphically, detailing the learning processes at hand. The categories of knowledge, know-how and attitudes in Figure 11.2 make it possible to describe the building of competence: the upper arrows represent knowledge building through *data reception*, which generates information to be assimilated. External data flow in through ongoing activities of the organization (providing learning by 'learning to' listen to the environment, interact with other members of the organization, etc.). Additional flows of data also come from formal training. All these data are filtered by and confronted with the prevailing knowledge base in the organization. The data are thus either rejected or retained, completely or in part, as credible and relevant pieces of information. The resulting pieces of information are in turn integrated into aggregates of knowledge.

A similar learning process takes place for the know-how (represented by the arrows in the lower-left corner), where *action* generates skills and capabilities through practice (companionship supporting a learning-by-doing process, filtered and constrained by the pre-existing skills). The bits and pieces of capabilities are integrated into aggregates of know-how.

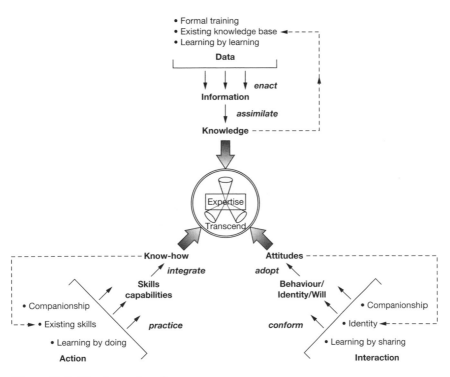

*Figure 11.2* The dynamics of competence.

Finally, a similar process takes place for the attitudes (arrows in lower-right corner), where *interaction* shapes the identity and the culture of the groups of individuals who conform to collective values, norms and beliefs. These lead to aggregates of attitudes that are adopted in the organizations, thus forming elements of the collective culture.

At that point, I had what I saw as a promising framework. Yet, my consulting experience, plus several attempts to discuss this framework in front of a class of executives, hinted at my needing something to reformat the framework in order to make it accessible.

Around this time, three very distinct inputs appeared to help me out. First, I felt that I needed to rename the 'interpretive frames', thus departing from Goffman, which I suggested enlarging. Second, I was increasingly convinced by my consulting activities that knowledge was a 'loose, complex tissue' that could not be reduced entirely to codifiable/storable/retrievable information to be managed in computer systems. I increasingly felt (I viewed, I sensed) that organizational knowledge was fuzzy by nature. Third, because I often combine writing and drawing in my research practice, I drew a representation of a piece of competence as a page with the three dimensions of the framework on it. These looked like ribs on a leaf. Thus the leaf metaphor. This in turn led me to think of the overall set of pieces of competence as foliage. And I found that the metaphor worked well. From there, I could follow with my idea, introducing the notion of interrelatedness between the three dimensions of the framework, the loose overlap between leaves, the complex texture of foliage, the filtering role of pre-existing competence, etc.

The written formalization could follow: competence 'leaves' incorporate the result of these parallel interrelated learning processes, operating through data reception, action and interaction. In this sense, 'competence leaves' constitute the essence of organizational knowledge. They both structure and filter new learning, while representing the stabilized form of organizational competence. They may operate as a booster to build up competence fast. They may also become a source of bias and inertia, hindering any real new learning. History indeed matters. The 'installed base' counts. This is shown graphically in Figure 11.2: for each axis, the dotted arrows loop back to the pre-existing combination of 'competence leaves', which in turn influences new learning. The result of learning is not just a function of the learning process. It is also dependent upon the pre-existing competence leaves.

It should be stressed that the three generic dimensions of competence are interdependent. Building upon Piaget's work (see, for example, Piaget 1959), we first have to follow Senge (1990): there is little real learning and knowledge building without action. In fact, as learning requires action, knowledge and know-how are built at the same time. This idea can be extrapolated and extended. Learning actually takes place in organizations simultaneously for the three generic dimensions of our referential. This happens in parallel but in an interrelated mode. In other words, reception of data, action and interaction are three parallel and interrelated modes of learning, building up competence simultaneously.

### Specifying competence leaves

At this point, I needed to specify more closely what the three dimensions of my referential meant in practical terms. I needed to touch ground. I needed this to help executives understand what the model exactly meant. I also needed to find ways of conducting empirical investigations based on the model.

This is where I bridged the gap between my early classifications and the emergent framework. I systematically scanned through the categories I had identified earlier to see how they could fit into the framework. That led to the following: we suggest that the *knowledge* elements are made up of explicit *rules*, *sayings* and *stories* told over and over throughout the organization, e.g. 'never change the leader of a project' or 'when you are invited for a performance review just before your holiday, that's bad news', etc. Some of these rules are self-explanatory and contain their own rationale. Others have no apparent logic and are simply known, used in practice and related to newcomers as company experience. Most of the knowledge ingredients of the leaves are explicit, if not formalized.

*Know-how* encompasses *skills* and *routinized processes*, e.g. operating a complex and sensitive piece of equipment, treating an incoming order from a client, hiring new staff, etc. Most of this may be tacit. It may have been codified as a process, at least in part, at some stage, but this know-how is now largely routinized and embedded in everyday practice. The initial intent or recommended way of doing something may have been distorted and forgotten over the years, what counts now is what remains in the reality of the activities of the organization today. Such know-how elements of the leaves are thus not easily observed or copied.

*Elements of attitudes* correspond to *rites, symbols, beliefs, taboos and values* which norm and shape attitudes. Working late hours and claiming it, showing respect or disrespect to hierarchy, avoiding certain topics, worshipping the memory of the company founder, etc. are typical elements of behavioural components of the leaves that exist in organizations. Some may be explicit but most are actually tacit and rooted deep in the 'unconscious part' of the organization. In fact, some authors (Larçon and Reitter 1979) draw the line of divide between culture and identity there. Culture is visible and corresponds to the symptoms, while identity is hidden and tacit.

I continued to draw leaves and foliage, which led to Figure 7.3. (I always hesitate to include such naive representations in a paper because visual representations are often poorly regarded. Yet, as mentioned, writing and drawing are two components of formalization in my thinking process.)

This helped to enrich the metaphor: the three sub-units of competence leaves should be seen as interdependent dimensions of the same organizational competence. See Figure 11.3. Should one consider eating fish on Fridays, eating kosher or forbidding pork as a rule (knowledge) designed to guarantee food quality against diseases existing in given contexts, as a practice (know-how) that became routine over the centuries, or as a religious rite (cultural attitudes)? Could we not consider the annual planning process in large multinational corporations as a ritual? (A management process that has become a rite?) These 'competence leaves' actually combine, overlap, interfere with and contradict one another. They are not neatly organized building blocks, but look more like the leafy and fuzzy foliage that gives the volume, texture and shape to the tree.

To build elements of explanation about the role of the competence leaves, i.e. the role of these pieces of competence, I partly borrowed from a colleague from Drisse. We see the competence leaves as having four major roles:

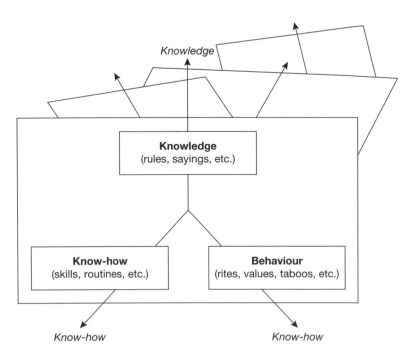

*Figure 11.3* Competence leaves.

- Competence leaves provide a way to *save time and resources* by defining what to do, how to do it and how to behave, without having to justify it. Rules are applied as a way to make things simple. It has worked on other occasions; no one will be blamed if a rule, routine or social code is unsuccessful, as long as it was used.
- Competence leaves *structure learning*. This leads to the idea of bifurcations when early atypical experience (small events à la David or Arthur) may lead to a variety of outcomes.
- Competence leaves help interpret and *give meaning* to contexts and situations (Goffman's 'interpretive frames'). They help to define which rule or code should be selected and applied.
- Competence leaves interact with one another and *shape a strange and intriguing overall foliage* that constitutes organizational competence: partly tacit, partly explicit; partly knowledge, know-how and attitudes; always moving and developing; and difficult to grasp.

I then took the metaphor one step further, reaching a disturbing but interesting conclusion: What can be done with foliage? Can a carpenter put it to use? Can knowledge-foliage be managed? One way to go may be to water the tree, prune the branches, feed the soil – as a gardener. But we suggest that it is as difficult to monitor the overall foliage as it is difficult, if not meaningless, to try to manage competence. The overall foliage can be shaped, the context can be gardened. In other words, conditions for building and leveraging competence can be organized and managed, but the intangible competence itself cannot be directly managed. In other words, the representation of organizational knowledge that we propose here strongly questions classical knowledge management (KM) approaches.

To rephrase, I had been searching for ways to grasp what organizational competence was all about, and ended up with a conclusion that organizational competence is of a nature that makes it difficult, if not impossible, to manage. This was a paradoxical result. It was also puzzling in a management research context. On one hand, it meant that the result of this research process led to no direct application in practice and, in particular, in my own consulting. On the other, it led to an interesting perspective on existing practices in so-called 'knowledge management', backed by fancy IT systems.

And this is how I actually made use of this piece of research in my consulting practice and in executive education: since I finalized the research, I have been systematically questioning the attempts made by many companies to implant IT tools to manage knowledge and competence. (And the empirical evidence of failure of such attempts tends to support my stance on this.) Instead, I have been exploring the social dimensions of organizational competence, looking at how management could deal with such things as 'communities of practice' with relevant and subtle approaches (seed, water, prune) as these are not fully manageable social objects (they tend to be spontaneous, self-organized, informal, inter-organizational, somewhat rebellious, etc.). From a consulting point of view, I do not see this result as disappointing. In fact, although not directly applicable, I find it to be useful.

My research helped me stay away from KM in consulting. I now regard KM as a dead end. Instead, I encourage companies to look at the softer, social side of organizational competence, that dealing with people, processes and shared vision in communities.

## *Accessing competence empirically*

Finally, from a research standpoint, I still needed to clarify how to go about conducting empirical work on the framework. This is where the contributions of my researcher colleagues from DRISSE (2001, 2004) were the most useful.

Based on Mounoud (1997) and de la Ville (2001), I suggest the observation of and listening to conversations in situ as a way to generate empirical data about competence leaves. Conversation (von Krogh and Roos 1995) and 'languaging' are key to accessing elements of what I call 'competence', i.e. the 'competence leaves'. However, I also suggest following Rouleau (2001), who recommends engaging in participative observation of routines and processes. I further follow Colas (2001), who in turn suggests writing portraits of actors and organizations as a way to identify and grasp rites, taboos and symbols, i.e. the visible cultural aspects of organizational identity.

When looking for specific fields in which to investigate competence leaves, I suggest a focus on situations of formation and evolution, i.e. reformation. Piaget focused his attention on child learning; de la Ville conducts a longitudinal study of a start-up that slowly builds its strategic competence over time; and Mounoud studies a still-emerging industry, the sector believed to be developing around the so-called 'green technologies'. This is clearly because the astrophysicist can learn more from watching a star form than looking at an old one. Sedimented situations tend to hide their secrets, while the researcher acting as a detective is more likely to find clues in evolving contexts, where the action is. Rouleau studies turnaround strategies when companies need to reform their representations and competence. Colas looks at municipalities where established procedures and rituals are suddenly faced with a new management paradigm from the private sector. Start-ups, emerging sectors, restructuring and radical changes are, I suggest, relevant fields in which to investigate competence empirically. In other words, knowledge about how and where to conduct research about management, here about organizational competence, could not be sought in consulting or executive education but had to come from both the literature and the practice of empirical research. However, my consulting and teaching activities helped to shape the thinking and thus the model along the way.

## Conclusion

This discussion of organizational knowledge is intended to illustrate my personal attempts to generate a contribution to knowledge in management. The discussion has presented an intermediate model of knowledge (competence) in organizations. The model is not directly empirically grounded but is derived from elements of theory filtered by my field experience (acquired through the dual practice of management research and consulting). This field experience operates as a sieve when reading the literature and a guide to support intuition and theory building for the model. As in the grounded theory approach, interpretation, analogy and pattern recognition are key mechanisms at work in this process.

The model presents a dynamic framework to describe how organizational competence grows up and evolves. It leads to a metaphor suggesting that – as with the unruly foliage of a tree – organizational competence is a loose, diffuse object that cannot really be managed. This finding is not easy to apply in practice, except for the questions it raises about the IT-based approaches to what is known as Knowledge Management. The model also illustrates how metaphor building may contribute to knowledge about management.

Could this model of competence in organizations be extrapolated to the case of management knowledge? This is yet to be investigated. Let me simply observe that the model may help to suggest that management knowledge should not merely be about knowledge (the first dimension of the model), but also about knowing how to generate new knowledge (the research process – where I have added consulting activities as well) and to some extent also about the attitudes in conducting the research and conveying the research results.

I personally conduct research to learn about management, hoping to contribute to generating some form of knowledge in management. I also do it because it reflects on my activity in the classroom as well as consulting. I have learnt that reflexive thinking is essential. This is not easy, nor straightforward. It implies constantly changing mindset and wavelength, going from (a) hands-on activity intended to help organizations and/or audiences, to (b) theoretical thinking about the status and nature of knowledge in management, including an ontology to view the world, an epistemic stance to relate to the world, and a methodology to generate knowledge about the world. Let me also add that I conduct research activities because it is fun and I love it.

# Note

1   From the French 'Discours, représentations et intéractions sociales en stratégie d'entreprise' (Speeches, Representation and Social Interactions in Business Strategy). Drisse is a group of nine researchers from various universities, eight from France and one from Québec, who decided to look at strategy as a social representation. The group claims that it is useful to view the building of strategy as the result of a process of social interaction. Hence the suggestion to investigate social representations, including through analysis of discourse. Drisse has published two books (2001, 2004).

# References

Barnes, J. (1984) 'Cognitive Biases and their Impact on Strategic Planning', *Strategic Management Journal*, 5: 129–137.

Clark, K.B. (1985) 'The Interaction of Design Hierarchies and Market Concepts in Technological Evolution', *Research Policy*, 4: 235–251.

Colas, H. (2001) 'Les portraits en sciences de gestion et l'interprétation partici-pante', in Drisse, *Le management stratégique en représentations*, Paris: Ellipses.

Drisse (2001) *Le management stratégique en représentations*, Paris: Ellipses.

Drisse (2004) *La stratégie et son double*, Paris: L'Harmattan.

Durand, T. (1988) 'Programs Competencies Matrix: Analyzing R&D Expertise within the Firm', *R&D Management*, 16, 2.

Durand, T. (1992a) 'Dual Technological Trees: Assessing the Intensity and Strategic Significance of Technological Change', *Research Policy*, 21, 4: 361–380.

Durand, T. (1992b) 'The Dynamics of Cognitive Technological Maps', in P. Lorange, J. Roos, B. Chakravarty and A. Van de Ven (eds) *Strategic Processes*, Oxford: Blackwell Business.

Durand, T. (1996) 'Strategizing Innovation: Competence Analysis in Assessing Strategic Change', in A. Heene and R. Sanchez (eds) *Competence-based Strategic Management*, Chichester: Wiley.

Durand, T. (1998) 'The Alchemy of Competence', in G. Hamel, C.K. Prahalad, H. Thomas and D. O'Neal (eds) *Strategic Flexibility: Managing in a Turbulent Environment*, Chichester: Wiley.

Durand, T. (2001) 'La compétence organisationnelle au macroscope :Accéder aux 'cadres de compétence' pour explorer la formation de la stratégie', in Drisse, *Le management stratégique en représentations*, Paris: Ellipses.

Durand, T. and Gonard, T. (1986) 'Stratégies Technologiques: le Cas de l'Insuline', *Revue Française de Gestion*, 60: 86.

Durand, T. and Guerra Viera, S. (1997) 'Competence-Based Strategies When Facing Innovation: But What is Competence?', in H. Thomas and D. O'Neal (eds) *Strategic Discovery: Competing in New Arenas*, Chichester: Wiley.

Durand, T. and Stymne, B. (1988) '*Lessons from the Public Switching Past Technological Evolution in the Telecoms*', proceedings of the Prince Bertil Symposium, Stockholm, November 9–11.

Durand, T., Mounoud, E. and Ramanantsoa, B. (1996) 'Uncovering Strategic Assumptions: Understanding Managers' Ability to Build Representations', *European Management Journal*, 14, 4: 389–398.

Goffman, E. (1991) *Les cadres d'expérience (originally in English, (1974)* An Essay on The Organization of Experience, New York: Harper & Row), Paris: Les Ed. de minuit.

Hippel, E. von, (1976) 'The Dominant Role of Users in the Scientific Instrument Innovation Process', *Research Policy*, 5, 3: 212–239.

Krogh, G. von and Roos, J. (1995) 'Conversation Management', *European Management Journal*, 13, 4: 390–394.

La Ville, de, V. (2001) 'L'actualisation collective des pratiques stratégiques', in Drisse *Le management stratégique en représentations*, Paris: Ellipses.

Larçon, J.P. and Reitter, R. (1979) *Structures de pouvoir et identité de l'entreprise*, Paris: Nathan.

Mounoud, E. (1997) 'L'Inscription Sociale des Discours et des Représentations Stratégiques dans l'Industrie de l'Environnement', doctoral dissertation, HEC-Ecole Centrale Paris.

Pestalozzi, J.H. (1797) *Mes recherches sur la marche de la nature dans l'évolution du genre humain*, Lausanne: Ed Payot.

Prahalad, C.K. and Hamel, G. (1990) 'The Core Competence of the Corporation', *Harvard Business Review*, 68, 3: 79–91.

Rouleau, L. (2001) 'La structuration sociale des stratégies d'entreprise', in Drisse, *Le management stratégique en représentations*, Paris: Ellipses.

Schwenk, C. (1984) 'Cognitive Simplification Processes in Strategic Decision-making', *Strategic Management Review*, 5: 111–128.

Schwenk, C. (1988) 'The Cognitive Perspective on Strategic Decision-making', *Journal of Management Studies*, 25: 41–55.

Senge (1990) *The Fifth Discipline*, New York: Doubleday.

Stubbart, C. (1989) 'Cognitive Science: A Missing Link in Strategic Management Research', *Journal of Management Review*, 10: 724–736.

Wernerfelt, B. (1984) 'A Resource-based View of the Firm', *Strategic Management Journal*, 5: 171–180.

# Part IV

# Co-producing management

# 12 Researching organization design

## Comparative vs collaborative approaches

*Harvey Kolodny and A. B. (Rami) Shani*

## Organization design as a research topic

Research on organization design tends to utilize a variety of research approaches and methodologies. For the most part, this seems to have generated a static body of knowledge that is not always particularly relevant to the organizations studied (Stebbins and Shani 2002). We take a narrower focus in this chapter. We examine two research approaches to organization design that we have used to enhance our understanding of the topic. The two approaches are 'comparative analysis' and 'collaborative'. The *comparative analysis* approach is a systematic comparative investigation of two or more organizations with a focus, in this case, on organization design research issues. In other comparative research studies, investigators may draw on a wide variety of both macro and micro organizational variables as the basis of comparison. In our approach, we have drawn on a data base that was developed from a study of organizational arrangements in a number of different countries (Stymne and the ORGNOVATION International Research Team 1996). The organizational arrangements all focused on a specific set of managerial innovations (which we have also called our 'research themes'). We then compared organization design practices for these specific managerial innovations across different countries. For example, in one study, we compared and contrasted how the research theme of continuous quality improvement systems was designed in six different countries (Lillrank *et al.* 1998). In another study, we compared and contrasted the research theme of how government organizations in eight different countries designed organizations to support their chosen strategies of helping their small and medium-sized enterprises to succeed (Kolodny *et al.* 2001).

The *collaborative* approach to understanding organization design is embedded in a systematic collaborative research process that centres on a scientific and collaborative investigation of organization design issues. Collaborative research is defined as an *emergent and systematic inquiry* associated with this type of research constrains the generalizability and the research tends to focus on developing hypotheses rather than proving them. Since the context of the organizations within the data set can vary so much, the research also concentrates on a small number of variables so that some common statements can be made across organizations. Despite the caveats, this relatively incremental process is the building block for knowledge advancement in, in this case, organization design knowledge for continuous improvement organizations.

Collaborative research aims at creating new knowledge as well as actionable knowledge. For example, the success of knowledge-intensive organizations is dependent on their ability to link in a meaningful way the micro communities that exist within them. The ultimate success of product development depends on how these micro communities and other organizational members relate throughout the knowledge-creation process (von Krogh *et al.* 2000). A collaborative research methodology is viewed as an enabler of knowledge creation since it provides a platform, the mechanisms and processes for the interactions between the micro communities and others in and around the organization (Adler and Shani 2001).

### Research outcomes for organizational action

The long time periods for comparative analysis research and the even longer horizons for publishing results suggest that actions that might result from the findings will seldom take place within the studied set of organizations. However, the findings will add to the data base of knowledge in the field and may contribute significantly to organizational action in future organizational situations.

Collaborative research by its very nature leads to organizational action, as one of its objectives is to create actionable knowledge. Being centred in the one organization and being embedded in a co-inquiry process creates the context of actionability. The topic that was identified and viewed as a 'red and hot topic' – is viewed as mission critical. One of the challenges for those that facilitate collaborative research is that the very nature of the orientation and its true partnership creates pressure for fast implementation even before the study is complete or has been systematically reflected on.

## Discussion

Is research in organization design better served through a comparative analysis approach or through a collaborative approach? Is knowledge about organization design better advanced through one approach or the other or by some combination of the two? If both approaches are used to both carry out *process*, embedded in a true *partnership* between researchers and members of a living system, in which behavioural, social, organizational and management scientific knowledge is *integrated* with existing organizational knowledge for the purpose of generating actionable knowledge (Adler *et al.* 2004). At the most basic level, collaborative research brings about the challenge of balance and interdependence between actors, between academic research and actual applications, between knowledge creation and problem solving and between inquiry from the inside and inquiry from the outside. It is a partnership among a variety of individuals forming a 'community of inquiry' and is viewed as an emergent inquiry process that differs from the notion of scientific research as a closed, linear and planned activity. For example, in one study we have focused on continuous improvement in a healthcare organization (Stebbins and Shani 2002), while in another we investigated the role that learning mechanisms played in improving organizational effectiveness and performance in a paper mill organization (Mitki and Shani 2003).

We will use a set of research 'components' to explore the essence of these two approaches. These research components are typical research topics or research areas that describe the context and content of organizational research that researchers normally encounter when they attempt to learn more about organizations and how they are designed. We will examine each research component by drawing up a table that describes that component when it is used in a comparative analysis approach to research and when it is used in a collaborative approach (see Table 12.2).

Before we explore these research components, we will briefly describe two case studies, one drawn from a comparative analysis research approach and one drawn from a collaborative research approach. Our descriptions of each case have been prepared in the format of Table 12.2 (i.e. using the research components of Table 12.2 as an organizing framework) as a way of illustrating the different research components before we elaborate upon them. Table 12.1 summarizes our discussion of these two cases.

We will follow these case descriptions with a more elaborate discussion of each of the research components. In doing so, we will develop some conceptual statements about each research component for each of the two approaches. And we will speculate about how generalizable we believe some of these conceptual statements could be. We will also speculate about when to apply one approach to organization design and when the other approach might be more appropriate. We will conclude with some thoughts about how research into organization design could be enhanced by calling on both approaches at the same time to further our understanding of how to improve the design of organizations as well as how to design improved organizations.

## Organization design: an examination of two studies

### *Continuous improvement – a comparative analysis study[1]*

The direction of our international comparative analysis study (Stymne *et al.* 1996) was largely informed by the shared values and interests of the team of researchers who assembled to conduct this research. We had all previously worked together and had encountered managerial innovations in our respective countries that were both salient to the respective countries and of research interest to us as individuals and as a team. We had focused on organizational design issues in our previous collaborations and this again was the orientation we took to the research themes we had identified (Liu *et al.* 1990). We wanted to continue working together but faced several challenges.

One obvious challenge was resources and this was largely solved through grant applications to research programmes at the European Commission as well as to different research-focused institutions in our respective home countries. An equally challenging task for us was to find a methodology that would be comfortable for all of us, given our different institutional backgrounds, yet would give us a high level of confidence that the methodology would yield findings that would contribute to generalizable knowledge. This was a longer-run goal and our primary objective. We also hoped, in the shorter run, to develop specific organizational design advice that could be applied to the research theme under study. This led us to develop a methodology around using a lead case that illustrated best practice for that particular research theme as the forerunner for developing our research instruments and then comparing the organizations in the other countries to that lead case. In this way we could generate generalizable knowledge from the comparisons. It also allowed us to take the best practices from the lead case and from the comparative cases back to the organizations that provided us with research access as suggestions for how they might change their organization design to improve their operations, if they were open to (a) receiving such advice and (b) acting on it.

For the comparative analysis study described in the paragraphs that follow, the research theme was the organization design of continuous improvement programmes that was beginning to occur in many countries around the world as the quest for higher quality in products and services was becoming more widespread. Our description of this case follows as an illustration of the research components framework we have developed (see Table 12.2).

*Table 12.1* A comparison of two approaches to organization design analysis

| | CI Study – a comparative study | Product development organization redesign – a collaborative study |
|---|---|---|
| Background | A study of the continuous improvement programmes in eight organizations, each in a different country | This study involved the renewal of Volvo Car Corporation's (VCC) product development organization |
| Study focus | How different organization design requirements led to different structural arrangements for carrying out continuous improvement | The design of a product development organization that integrates a design-oriented and process-oriented design |
| Essence of study orientation | A traditional comparative analysis approach with a focus on using organization design to explain the differences between study sites | A hybrid between action research, action learning, reflective inquiry and qualitative methodologies |
| Research process/phases/ steps/activities/methods and tools | Sites were selected based on national origin and the existence of a continuous improvement programme that was well regarded. Archival data was then collected and interviews were conducted at different levels within the organization. The research team met at intervals to compare findings and occasionally re-orient the data collection. In several sessions the research team analyzed the data to establish a set of design requirements and then compared and contrasted the design dimensions that each site used as a response to the design requirement | A three-phased collaborative research process: 1 Systematic analysis and mapping of strengths and weaknesses of the current design via initial analysis of company documents about the way the system works and interviews and interactive dialogue sessions that have occurred at three levels: top managers, support teams and modular teams 2 The collaborative crafting of the alternative design based on the knowledge gained through the systematic reflection and collaborative sense-making process 3 The implementation of the new design |

| | | |
|---|---|---|
| The researchers' role | The researchers served as outside investigators at each site but since each selected a site from their own nation, each brought intrinsic economic, historical, social and cultural context to the analysis | The research team included two insiders and three outsiders. The researchers' role shifted as the study progressed from initiators, to educators about research methods and tools, to facilitators of systematic reflective inquiry, and data sense-making, to active participants in the exploration of alternative designs |
| Organization members' involvement | The organizations studied provided access to the site and interviewees, archival data and occasionally some members from management participated in a session that fed back some of the findings, although usually well after the study was completed | Wide and varied level of participation occurred at different stages of the inquiry process. For example, during the in-depth study of the 'module team' concept, 800 people that are directly engaged in parallel development participated in large group data collection and data sense-making activities |
| Research outcomes: (a) Knowledge creation (b) Organizational action | (a) One book chapter was published describing the study (Lillrank et al. 1998) and all the sites were published as a set of case studies together with an extensive set of working papers describing the larger study of which this particular study was one component (Stymne et al. 1996) (b) Unknown | (a) Two doctoral dissertations and nine journal manuscripts were generated during the five-year collaboration (b) Top management used the inquiry process and the studies results as inputs into the decision-making process about the implementation of alternative designs and organization change |

*Background*

This study was part of an international comparative study of four organization design research themes in eight different countries using a team of researchers drawn from each country. This particular research theme was the organization design of continuous improvement organizations in each of these countries. The objective of the comparative aspect was to find common organizational design concepts that would hold across themes and across countries and would lead to improved organizational designs.

*Focus*

This study was designed to unearth common organization design features in each of the different continuous improvement programmes in each country. This was accomplished by discovering design requirements that were common for each continuous improvement programme even though each was set in a different context; namely, the economic, historical, social and cultural situations of each different country as well as the different strategies, policies, businesses and managerial actions of the organizations studied. The design dimensions that responded to the design requirements varied according to these national and company variables and the analysis focused on explaining how these variables affected the different design dimensions such that similar and different organizational design approaches to continuous improvement resulted.

*The essence of the study orientation*

This was a traditional comparative analysis study that was designed to produce generalizable knowledge about organization design; knowledge that could be generalized to other continuous improvement change programmes and, hopefully, beyond that to organization design issues in still other change situations.

*Research process*

Members of the research team selected sites in their respective country that were deemed to be good research challenges for each of the themes. The team met frequently and chose Komatsu in Japan as the lead organization for the continuous improvement theme. As the lead organization, Komatsu exemplified continuous improvement organization design practice and the organizations in the other countries were compared to their practices. Data collection was traditional: access was obtained, archival data was collected and interviews were conducted. A case study was written up for each study site and the cases were shared amongst the research team members. Face-to-face meetings, once or twice a year, were the primary vehicle for analyzing, comparing and contrasting the data from each of the study sites. From the meetings and analyses, contextual similarities and differences, common design requirements, and different design dimensions were established. Researchers associated with the lead case initiated the writing of the results and the rest of the team contributed to its evolution.

### The researchers' role

The researchers were all academics and carried out their research roles, their efforts at finding grant support and their approaches to writing in traditional scholarly fashion. A primary research grant from the European Foundation covered the research costs for administration and for some of the international meeting costs, but individual researchers secured their own support for the work within their own countries.

### Organizational member involvement

Organizational members from the eight companies whose sites were studied were not involved in the research in any way, other than to provide access to the site and some archival material and to help set up the interviews that were conducted.

### Research outcomes

A significant set of working papers, including all the cases that were written, were prepared for the European Foundation, who were the primary funders for the research. Several academic articles were also published in both journals and books, including this particular continuous improvement study (Lillrank *et al.* 1998). In a few of the sites, the findings were presented back to the managers who had originally provided access, although the duration of the study was long and interest in the study sites had largely waned.

### Product development organization redesign – a collaborative study[2]

The direction of our collaborative study was largely informed by the shared values and interests of the research team that was composed of two insiders and three outsider action researchers (Mikaelsson 2002) who conducted this research. The research was conducted as part of the FENIX research programme, which represents a collaborative partnership between two Swedish academic institutions (at Chalmers University of Technology and Stockholm School of Economics) and four large Swedish companies (Astra-Zeneca, Ericsson, Telia-Sonera and Volvo Cars). The overall objective of the FENIX programme has been to create knowledge that can be used in both develop-ment and practice of management and advance scientific knowledge. The setting – the context and practice of management at the specific workplace – has affected both the focus of the research and the choices of the research methodology.

The two insiders were executive doctoral students that moved between scientific and practical perspectives on managerial challenges. Prior to join-ing the doctoral studies, both were involved with managing strategic changes and implementing new organizational structures, work procedures and policies in the R&D organization. The three outsiders were researchers that were a part of the FENIX faculty team that co-led the programme. The research focus for this project emerged as a result of ongoing dialogue that occurred at multiple levels between the members of the research team and their respective communities.

### Background

This study involved the renewal of Volvo Car Corporation's (VCC) product development organization. The study has been regarded within Volvo as successful in terms of contributing to increased effectiveness – developing more car models faster and with relatively less resources.

### Focus

The study centred on the design of a product development organization. The notion of building alternatives to the functional organization as well as using different ways of organizing projects is continuously being explored and reported in the literature (Mikaelsson 2002). Recent research suggests that the use of groups and teams as entities for producing knowledge and processing information in the context of product development seems to be on the rise (von Krogh *et al.* 2000). Yet, as the pressures for more efficient product development and more innovative products increases, the focus of the study was on the integration of design-oriented and change-oriented processes.

### The essence of the study orientation

A collaborative research orientation that is embedded in a hybrid between action research, action learning, reflective inquiry and qualitative method-ologies was developed and utilized.

## Research process

The research process – based on an iterative and collaborative interaction cycle – was used in order to capture and jointly interpret people's perceptions of key elements in the change effort. A steering committee was established to lead the study. A three-phased collaborative research process was developed and utilized. The essence of collaborative reflective inquiry processes included systematic analysis and mapping of strengths and weakness of the current design via initial analysis of company documents about the way the system works and interviews and interactive dialogue sessions that have occurred at three levels: top managers, support teams and modular teams; the collaborative crafting of the alternative design based on the knowledge gained through the systematic reflection and collaborative sense-making process; and the implementation of the changes. The study mechanism included the steering committee and a number of study teams that were established for the purpose of creating relevant knowledge about the different aspects of design, as the need for them was identified. For example a 'pilot study engineering team' was created and charged with creating the knowledge-based definition of new working methods and ways of organizing, as well as a 'support study team' that focused on creating knowledge about the modular team design.

## The researchers' role

As mentioned earlier, the research team included two insiders and three outsiders. The researchers' role shifted as the study progressed from initiators, to educators about research methods and tools, to facilitators of systematic data collection, to facilitators of systematic reflective inquiry and data sense-making, to active participants in the exploration of alternative designs.

## Organizational member involvement

The study mechanism that was established included the steering committee and a number of study teams that focused on the investigation of a specific design-related topic. While participation was wide and across levels and organizational boundaries, as the study progressed at different stages of the inquiry process participation seemed to vary. For example, during the in-depth study of the 'module team' concept about 800 people that were directly engaged in parallel development participated in large group data collection, data sense-making activities and the exploration of alternative ways of organizing.

*Research outcomes*

The success of knowledge-intensive organizations is dependent on their ability to link in a meaningful way the micro communities that exist within them. The ultimate success of product development depends on how these micro communities and other organizational members relate throughout the knowledge-creation process (von Krogh *et al.* 2000). The collaborative research methodology that was employed in this study acted as an enabler of knowledge creation since it provided the platform, the mechanisms and processes for the interactions between the micro communities and others in and around the organization. As far as measurable outcomes, two doctoral dissertations and nine journal manuscripts were generated during the five-year collaboration and top management used the inquiry process and the study's results as inputs into the decision-making process about the implementation of alternative designs and organization change.

## Some research components of organization design

### Organizational unit of analysis

In our approach to comparative analysis research, the unit of analysis is at the level of the organization (see Table 12.2). Some researchers carry out comparative analysis research on particular organizational variables such as communication systems or reward systems or decision-making systems rather than entire organizations. However, since our context for comparison was international, when we examined similar managerial innovations in different countries, the entire unit where the research theme was centred became the unit of analysis. For example, where the technology extension services of different countries were compared, it was usually the particular government agency that was tasked with helping small and medium-sized enterprise with technology that was the unit of analysis for the research. Government policy on how they were to go about helping (one country might choose to add financial assistance to technical assistance while another may restrict help to providing technological information) might come from a higher level than the particular agency. And other government units or universities might partner in the help, but the primary agency tasked with the technology extension delivery was the organizational unit that was compared to similar units in all the countries in the study. So the set of such organizations was the data base for carrying out comparative research.

The unit of analysis in a collaborative research approach is a single organization. The researchers in a co-inquiry process sharpen the problem definition or issue to be studied, its scope and the relevant organization unit.

As such the unit of analysis can be individual, team, department, interdepartmental, organizational or network level. When the focus is on organization design, most of the time the unit of analysis is the total organization. For example, where the issue was how to reconfigure the product development organization, it was the collaborative process that articulated both the problem scope and the level of analysis that had to be conducted.

## The essence of the research orientation

Comparative analysis research can be conducted on a wide variety of components. However, most such analyses focus on just one or two main themes (e.g. organization structure, human resource practices, quality management approaches) as the basis for comparison. It is difficult to compare and contrast even a single component or theme when they are embedded in complex contexts. For example, the international data base we are calling upon draws on nine different countries with different histories, cultures, social systems and economic systems that all impact on whatever common theme or variable is the focus of the research. While the context cannot be held constant, there is still much new knowledge to be gained from the comparison of similarities and differences along a single study component.

Collaborative research takes one unit of an organization or the organization as a whole and examines how organizational understanding can be improved by the collaboration of actors inside and outside that unit. Usually this entails analysis at multiple levels within that unit, e.g. at the level of the individual, the work group and the larger unit itself. The essence of the research orientation in collaborative research is based on the refinement of the relationship between academic researchers and organizational actors from research 'on' or 'for' to research 'with'. In doing so, it attempts to integrate knowledge creation with problem solving and 'inquiry from the inside' with 'inquiry from the outside'. As such, collaborative research is viewed as a partnership among a variety of individuals forming a 'community of inquiry' within communities of practice for the purpose of gaining new knowledge about organization design.

## Research process/phases/steps/activities/methods/tools

Comparative analysis research tends to use traditional techniques to collect and analyze data. Archival data and questionnaires are used to build the data base and individual interviews augment these. Even with common questionnaires and interview formats, it is often difficult to compare findings. For example, different countries have different cut-off points for what they consider the size of a small versus a medium-sized company so that their data

Table 12.2 Researching organization design through comparative and collaborative analyses

| Item | Comparative analysis | | Collaborative analysis | |
|---|---|---|---|---|
| | Description | Comments | Description | Comments |
| Essence of research orientation | Focuses on a relatively narrow organization topic, e.g. technology extension; continuous quality; study conducted on organization(s) | Complex context, e.g. different countries *with* different histories, culture, social systems, economics; high level analysis | Focuses on one organizational area, e.g. R&D; study conducted *with* an organization | Multiple levels of analysis within an organization |
| Organizational unit of analysis | Two or more comparable organizations | Small sample sizes; difficult to hold contexts constant | Single organization | Multiple levels to consider |
| Research process/phases/ steps/activities/methods and tools | Interviews, archival data, questionnaires | Constrained by access to study sites; difficult to compare some data | Interviews, observations, questionnaires, participative action research, archival data | Constrained by proprietary information |

| | | |
|---|---|---|
| | Orientation towards generalizable knowledge | Orientation towards firm-specific knowledge |
| | Focus on small number of variables; integrate policy and design issues | Comprehensive in nature; strive towards holistic understanding; creating actionable knowledge |
| The researchers' role | Outsiders, detached scientists, academics only, multinational team | Combined outsider/s and insider/s research team; involved, educational, academics and practitioners; joint research teams |
| Organization members' involvement | Passive involvement in providing data requested by the research team | Active involvement in the development of the research focus, research methodology, data collection, data sense-making, etc. |
| Research outcomes: (a) Knowledge creation (b) Organizational action | (a) Generalizable organizational concepts constrained by small sample size; long publishing horizon constrains learning (b) None | (a) Generalizable around processes; concepts constrained by single case context (b) Immediate organizational action |

on how they help smaller organizations is not comparable. Sample sizes are small in comparative analysis research so traditional statistical analysis is seldom relevant. Pattern recognition is more dominant than statistical signi-ficance to identify trends and relationships and as a consequence hypothesis generation tends to dominate comparative analysis rather than do attempts at statistical proof. Comparative analysis research at the whole organization level is more about asking better questions than finding answers.

Access to study sites is sometimes difficult and in some domains of research there are no alternative organizations to substitute when access to the desired site is denied.

Collaborative research tends to utilize a combination of traditional and non-traditional methods to collect, analyze and interpret data. The emergent nature of the inquiry process coupled with the true partnership between the different actors with varied experiences and insight tends to generate a unique inquiry process, data collection techniques and data interpretation. Collaborative research cannot be classified as one single methodology, rather it includes a wide range and levels of inquiry approaches, activities and methods (Reason and Bradbury 2001). Common to the variety of approaches are the complex dynamics of the inquiry process that are triggered by the design orientation of the collaborative effort. The collaborative research framework, at the most basic level, includes four key features: context, inquiry mechanism (design requirements and design dimensions), inquiry cycle and outcomes. The context refers to environmental, organizational and individual characteristics, interpersonal dynamics and the strategic purpose that result in the decision to pursue research. The inquiry mechanism refers to the formal and informal configuration – structures, processes, procedures, rules, tools, methods and physical configurations – created within the organization for the purpose of developing and enhancing human and organizational performance (Shani and Docherty 2003). The inquiry cycle refers to the four main phases of diagnosing, planning action, taking action and evaluating action (Coghlan and Brannick 2005). Outcome refers to the actionable knowledge that was created as a result of the effort. Thus, a systematic collaborative perspective brings to the forefront the issues of context, roles, power dynamics and ethics that are embedded in the research process and influence its emergent process, quality and outcomes.

As we will see later in this manuscript, the study of the R&D unit design and change emphasized action learning and reflective inquiry and resulted in increased knowledge and actionable knowledge about the complexities of the unit design. This approach – based on an iterative and collaborative interaction cycle – was used in order to capture and jointly interpret people's perceptions of key elements in the redesign effort.

## The researcher's role

The researcher in a comparative analysis approach is an outsider to the organizations under study. He or she is an academic independent of the organizations in the study and functions as a detached observer and scientist. When the study is large, involving many countries in the study set, there is usually a team of researchers, but they are all still outsiders to the organizations under study.

In the collaborative approach the researcher has multiple roles that shift as the research process progresses, from educator, to researcher, to reflective scholar. Since the research is *with* people, rather than *on* people, developing mutual trusting relationships is critical. Members of the system being studied are co-inquirers with the outsider/s researcher/s, as ultimately it is their system and they will live with the future created through the research process when the project is completed. For example, at the front end of the inquiry process the basic research skills need to be acquired by the organizational members. In many instances in this phase of the process the researcher plays a critical role of educator.

## Organization members' involvement

In a comparative analysis, the organization's members are not involved with the research. They may answer questionnaires and they may respond to interviews but this involvement is passive. With no direct involvement in the analysis, they have no ownership in the results that are fed back. Since the analysis time is often long, organization members may find that the results of the analyses, when they are fed back to them, are irrelevant because events have changed the situation since data was first collected.

The collaborative process is embedded in the involvement of organizational members as active participants and co-inquirers. As we have seen earlier, organizational members are involved in the identification of the research focus, defining its scope, developing the data collection methods, participating in collecting the data, conducting the data analysis and participating in the data interpretation process. Collaborative research assumes that the higher the quality of ownership of the issues, the higher the quality of collaboration between members and the outside researchers and the joint enactment of the research process, the more successful will the outcomes be.

## Research outcomes for knowledge creation

Comparative analysis research aims to produce knowledge that can be generalized to other similar situations. However, the small sample sizes

organization design and to build knowledge about researching organization design, are there some points of intersection between the two approaches or are the two approaches the proverbial 'ships passing in the night'?

As can be seen in Table 12.2, comparative analysis research falls into the camp of traditional academic research: the goal is to produce generalizable knowledge about how best to, in this case, investigate and understand the subject of organization design. The units of analysis being compared are at the total organizational level. However, the uniqueness of each organization forces the research methodology to focus on relatively narrow organizational components in order to find truly comparable conditions. This is a slow process requiring many comparative studies to build up the body of knowledge about organization theory. However, it is an acceptable way to advance organization theory knowledge because the foundation that is built is solid.

There is still the challenge of translating organization theory into organization design practice. For although organization theory is not organization design, organization theory does inform organization design. On occasion, organization theory and organization design are tightly coupled. At other times the relationship is a tenuous one and this piece of the knowledge generation puzzle for organization design is still in its early days.

Table 12.1 provides an illustration of the above discussion. In each country, the economic, historical, social and cultural context had its greatest impact on the overall structure and design of each organization studied because these contextual variables were closest to the structural variables. As such, organization structure comparisons at this level were not really possible because of the large differences between country contexts. The continuous improvement programmes in each country, however, were one step removed from the organization structure so that they were somewhat buffered from the country context differences. Furthermore, there were some common generalizations about how to conduct continuous improvement programmes that were widely shared because there were relatively few 'gurus' of the total quality management movement (Demming 1982; Ishikawa 1985). Therefore a basis for comparative analysis at the level of the continuous improvement programme and its processes did exist and the continuous improvement organizations in the different countries could be compared (Lillrank *et al.* 1998).

Comparative analysis research could be focused on organizational processes rather than structural components of organizations, for example comparing how two different organizations go about involving their employees in decisions that affect their work. However, establishing comparable conditions is even more of a challenge for researchers when organizational processes are the objects of study because processes are more fluid than structural components. In addition, there is no widely accepted way to design organizational processes in the way that the total quality management movement provides guidance for designing continuous improvement programmes. The results of a comparative analysis research study of organizational processes would appear, then, to be even more challenging for organization designers than a comparative analysis study of organizational structural components.

Is there a short cut whereby comparative analysis research can directly inform the organization designer without passing through the filter of organization theory? There could be if there was a way to disseminate the research findings more quickly, for example by publishing them in practitioner journals rather than more traditional academic journals. However, comparative analysis research tends to be carried out by academics and not practitioners and academics are rewarded more for publications that advance organization theory than for publications that improve the skill of organization designers, i.e. by publishing in traditional academic journals.

Collaborative research falls into the traditional camp of 'action research', a more participative research approach, the goal of which is to produce generalizable and actionable knowledge about how best to research and impact the subject of organization design. As such, it aims at generating knowledge that satisfies both the scientific community and organizational needs. Since the unit of analysis is the single organization, the uniqueness of each organization forces the research methodology to focus on a holistic understanding of organizational components within its environmental context in order to gain insight into alternative designs that will yield desired outcomes. As a contribution to knowledge, this is acceptable because the participative inquiry process synthesizes the bits and pieces of knowledge that reside within and outside the organizational boundaries to generate new knowledge. The single organization unit of analysis presents a continuous challenge of translating the new organization design practice into organization theory. At the same time, the new holistic insight is of utmost value to organization designers.

As can be seen in Table 12.2, collaborative research in contrast to comparative analysis research focuses on both organizational processes and structural components of organizations. Using the example above, studying how the organization goes about involving the employees in decisions and how the involvement affects the employees' work, while involving the employees in the design and implementation of the study, is likely to generate new insights as well as lead to some actions based on the study. However, not establishing comparable conditions, as would be created in a comparative-base study, is likely to limit the degree of generalizability of the study. Thus, the challenge for researchers is both in making sure that the scientific discovery process is upheld and that the study is carried out within the context of the existing body of scientific knowledge. As such, collaborative research methodology for studying both organizational processes and structures would appear to offer significant relevance to organization designers, but at the same time require extra effort on the part of the researcher when compared to comparative analysis research.

Collaborative research, in comparison with comparative analysis research, brings about the challenge of balance and interdependence between actors, between academic research and actual applications, between knowledge creation and problem solving, and between inquiry from the inside and inquiry from the outside. The partnership among a variety of individuals forming a 'community of inquiry' represents a challenge to the management of the scientific discovery process. The emergent inquiry process that differs from the notion of scientific research as a closed, linear and planned activity that is at the foundation of comparative analysis research adds to the complexity of managing such a process. As such, no short cuts can be taken, which also means that the process of data collection and data sense-making can be lengthy. The ultimate success of knowledge creation about organization design depends on how the different knowledge actor groups or micro communities relate through the knowledge-creation process. Collaborative research is viewed as an enabler for the understanding of organization design since it provides the methods, mechanisms and processes for interactions between the micro communities of knowledge and other relevant individuals inside and outside the organization for the purpose of creating new knowledge that can be acted upon.

A careful examination of Tables 12.1 and 12.2 reveals that one of the distinct difference between the two orientations centres on organizational learning mechanisms. Collaborative research is about the development of a community of inquiry that utilizes organizational learning mechanisms as a way to facilitate continuous learning and action about design and redesign of the firm. Recent research suggests that, in practice, organizational learning mechanisms could be designed and managed in various ways. These 'various ways' have been described as a set of learning design dimensions, each of which fulfills a necessary learning requirement for achieving learning and performance. As such, the learning design dimensions are a basic set of alternative solutions managers can choose from in order to meet the learning design requirements. The range of alternatives needs to be investigated by every organization and could integrate some alternative solutions from the literature as well as by benchmarking existing solutions (Shani and Docherty 2003).

The set of necessary but not sufficient learning requirements for achieving learning is referred to as learning design requirements. Some examples of learning design requirements might include the following: a legitimate forum for exchange of ideas must be created; a specific set of processes that facilitate ongoing participation, dialogue and conversations must be developed; a specific set of tools need to be developed and/or adopted that facilitate learning; the design forum and processes must reflect and incorporate the totality of the organization and not just parts; goals and objectives that define the direction of the learning efforts must be formulated. Some examples of learning design dimensions might include the following: Is learning an integral part of ordinary work or not? Is learning work performed at a permanent working group or in a specially formed task force? Are group members from one or several functions? Are the group members from the same or different levels? Is goal setting made centrally or in the group(s)? Is it process guided or free?

The learning design dimensions represent different possible ways to respond to the learning design requirements. Along each learning design dimension there is a range of choices an organizational designer can make. The conscious choices could be functionally equivalent ways to achieve the same objectives in a different context. An integral part of the rational decision-making process is to identify the external and internal conditions requiring improvements in the existing learning mechanisms or the decision to create a new one, identify the specific learning design requirements that fit the business situation and business dynamics and investigate and explore the alternative most appropriate learning design dimensions for the firm. Learning mechanisms provide a platform for both ongoing organizational learning, reflection, and action as well as a way to advance the theoretical understanding of work and organization design and organization redesign processes.

## Conclusion

In this manuscript we have compared and contrasted two research approaches, namely collaborative and comparative analysis approaches. As Tables 12.1 and 12.2 illustrate, there are very few areas of commonality between the approaches. There is some commonality around the issue of small sample size. Collaborative research focuses on a single organization and the sample size for comparative analysis research is usually small (pairs of organizations or small sets of organizations). For both research approaches, then, the findings will lie in the direction of hypothesis generation research rather than hypothesis testing research. There is some common methodology in data collection as both approaches use archival data, observations, questionnaires and interviews. However, collaborative research goes on to use action research methodology that is not used in comparative analysis research and we have not seen very much discussion on the nature of knowledge and actionable knowledge creation in the field. In effect, the differences between the approaches stand out more starkly than do the similarities.

Nevertheless, these differences, rather than being seen as a liability of different methodological approaches, present an opportunity for the field of organization design. The combination of comparative analysis and collaborative research approaches could speed the development of organizational design knowledge if the outcomes can be synthesized. For example, in a comparative study of eight continuous improvement efforts in different countries that we have conducted, seven design requirements were identified, one of which was 'a legitimate forum for exchange of ideas must be created' (Lillrank *et al.* 1998). This design requirement was further investigated and specific design configurations of the legitimate forum for dialogue were developed in a set of collaborative studies that were conducted with different companies (Shani and Docherty 2003). The integration of different research orientations could be invaluable as each approach seems to contribute supplementary insights about the field. The cumulative experience and the knowledge created via two different research approaches to organization design provides the foundation for an enriched discovery process and knowledge creation as we embark on the challenges of designing and managing sustainable organizations in the new millennium.

## Notes

1   Lillrank, P. *et al.* (1998: 47–71).
2   For a comprehensive account of the study, see Mikaelsson and Shani 2004; Mikaelsson 2002.

## References

Adler, N. and Shani, A.B. (2001) 'In Search of an Alternative Framework for the Creation of Actionable Knowledge, in W. Pasmore and R. Woodman (eds) *Research in Organization Change and Development*, Vol. 13, Greenwich, CT: JAI Press, 43–79.

Adler, N., Shani, A.B and Styhre, A. (eds) (2004) *Collaborative Research in Organizations: Foundations for Learning, Change, and Theoretical Development*, Thousand Oaks, CA: Sage.

Coghlan, D. and Brannick, T. (2005) *Doing Action Research in Your Own Organization*, second edition, London: Sage.

Demming, W.E. (1982) *Quality, Productivity and Competitive Position*, Cambridge, MA: MIT Press.

Ishikawa, K. (1985) *What is Total Quality Control? The Japanese Way* (translated by David Wu), Englewood Cliffs, NJ: Prentice Hall.

Kolodny, H., Stymne, B., Shani, A.B., Figuera, J.R. and Lillrank, P. (2001) 'Design and Policy Choices for Technology Extension Organizations', *Journal of Research Policy*, 30, 1: 201–225.

Krogh, G. von, Ichijo, K. and Nonaka, I. (2000) *Enabling Knowledge Creation*, Oxford: Oxford University Press.

Lillrank, P., Shani, A.B., Kolodny, H., Stymne, B., Figuera, J.R. and Liu, M. (1998) 'Learning from the Success of Continuous Improvement Programs: An International Comparative Study', in W. Pasmore and R. Woodman (eds) *Research in Organization Change and Development*, Vol. 11, Greenwich, CT: JAI Press, 47–71.

Liu, M., Denis, H., Kolodny, H. and Stymne, B. (1990) 'Organization Design for Technological Change', *Human Relations*, 43, 1: 7–22.

Mikaelsson, J. (2002) 'Managing Change in Product Development Organizations: Learning from Volvo Car Corporation', *Leadership and Organizational Development Journal*, 23, 6: 301–313.

Mikaelsson, J. and Shani, A.B. (2004) 'Rethinking and Transforming Product Development', in N. Adler, A.B. Shani and A. Styhre (eds) *Collaborative Research in Organizations: Foundations for Learning, Change, & Theoretical Development*, Thousand Oaks, CA: Sage, 181–196.

Mitki, Y. and Shani, A.B. (2003) 'Development Processes, Learning and Competitiveness', in A.B. Shani and P. Docherty (eds) *Learning by Design: Building Sustainable Organizations*, Oxford: Blackwell, 106–126.

Reason, P. and Bradbury, H. (2001) (eds) *Handbook of Action Research*, London: Sage.

Shani, A.B. and Docherty, P. (2003) *Learning by Design*, Oxford: Blackwell.

Stebbins, M. and Shani, A.B. (2002) 'Eclectic Design for Change', in P. Docherty, J. Forslin and A.B. Shani (eds) *Creating Sustainable Work Systems*, London: Routledge, 201–212.

Stymne, B. and the ORGNOVATION International Research Team (Canada: Harvey Kolodny; Germany: Erik. Latniak and Ulrick Pekruhl; France: Michel Liu; Italy: Franko Malerba; Giovanni Gavetti and Laura Campanini; Japan: Paul Lillrank; Spain: Juan Ramon Figuera and Rafael Ramos; Sweden: Bengt Stymne, Torild Carlsson and Peter Hägglund; United Kingdom: Peter Clark, Frank Muller and Fred Seward; USA: A.B. Shani) (1996) *International Transfer of Organizational Innovation*, Stockholm: Institute for Management of Innovation and Technology. (Research under contract EIMS 94/106 with Directorate General XIII of the European Commission.)

# 13 The changing practice of action research

*Peter Docherty, Anders Ljung and Torbjörn Stjernberg*

In the late 1960s our experiences of research were, on the whole, of a more traditional character. The people we met in working life could be classified in two broad categories: those who commissioned or sanctioned the research and those who were subjected to it. In many cases those who had provided the data received feedback on the results of the studies, either via formal presentations or written reports. In some cases, the feedback was provided with the explicit purpose of discussing the researchers' analyses and inter-pretations in order to check and deepen our understanding of the work processes and situations being studied. In this traditional research people are regarded as subjects of study rather than partners with whom research is conducted.

This chapter describes our involvement in research characterized by working *with* people. In the early 1970s this took the form of *action research*, in which the democratic participation of the workforce and their unions was formalized. We give an extensive example of this in an insurance company. Changes have occurred since then in the priorities given to the needs and ambitions of different stakeholders when researchers work with practitioners. Collaborative research gives more attention to management's and customers' needs, while recent experiences in the health and educational sectors with sustainable development processes address all the major stakeholder needs in efforts to achieve a 'win-win-win' solution.

## An offer to pursue 'action research' in Skandia Insurance Co.

In Scandinavia, the development of action research in the late 1960s and early 1970s took place through a cooperation between researchers from the Tavistock Institute in London, such as Fred Emery and Phil Herbst, and researchers at the Work Research Institute in Norway, led by Einar Thorsrud. This work combined action research with socio-technical systems theory.[1] The developments were politically anchored with the Norwegian social partners, i.e. the employers' and the unions' confederations (see, for example, Thorsrud and Emery 1969).

The Norwegian ideas spread to Sweden in the late 1960s, both to companies owned by the Swedish state and to the employers and unions in the private sector. The Swedish employers were eager to maintain developments in working life within the framework of the Saltsjöbaden Agreement from 1938. This stated that work life and labour market issues should be settled by the social partners in specific agreements without the intervention of government. Considerable experimentation took place in the 1960s and early 1970s in Sweden in the spirit of socio-technical systems theory, with semi-autonomous working groups and different models for worker participation.

Two of this chapter's authors participated in an action research project in Skandia that may be seen as typical of its time. The Skandia project is a useful example to capture some of the essence of the approach to action research of the early 1970s. In many respects, the approach is still, in principle, valid, although the issue of developing more democratic and humanistic work forms in industry, on the workplace level, were very much part of the Swedish zeitgeist then. In fact, the Skandia project formed part of a joint programme between the Swedish central social partners with these objectives.

The top management were positive to Skandia's participation in the national programme. The head of the western division of Skandia had been active in an internal project trying to support development of more democratic work forms. And in this division, one of the department heads was known for his support of humanistic and democratic ideals. He was willing to take on the challenge of developing a new work organization, and simultaneously merging with another department in Skandia. Together, the two departments had about 100 employees. The union in Skandia was also positive regarding the changes, and the fact that there was no separate union for the supervisors was believed to facilitate the development of democratic work forms, which entailed drastic changes in the roles and numbers of supervisors.

A team of five researchers conducted studies in Skandia on worker participation at the strategic, administrative and operational levels. The research team's frame of reference for the studies was based in the socio-technical systems theory that had been developed and used in the earlier British and Norwegian action research studies. Two people, Docherty and Stjernberg, were primarily responsible for the action research study on the transformation of the operational department. Docherty (1976) wrote a detailed description of the action researchers' roles and activities in the Skandia project, in which he reported roughly 50 major interventions made by the researchers. A project group – with veto rights for both personnel and management representatives – had responsibility for planning and implementing the transformation of the department. Most of our interventions were made as suggestions to this project group – but they seldom took the form of proposed organizational solutions. Instead, we suggested meetings and activities, and we tried to influence both the agenda of the project group and the priority given to the organization development project.

Interventions also took place in staff units and management at higher levels, such as by arranging meetings between the management of the department unit and representatives of staff responsible for, for example, rationalization processes that were thought to interfere with the development processes. Other examples of interventions were to initiate meetings with the department's employees to discuss the development and the new work organization suggested, to initiate a discussion of conflicts between existing salary norms and the new organization, and to argue for also including the low status tasks, such as typing, in the integrated work groups. The impact of the suggestions/interventions varied from not being acted upon to being of importance. The roles of the action researchers and their associated activities are shown in Figure 13.1.

The company had no previous experience of 'researcher-supported participative development projects'. Thus, *selling* entailed the researchers making the norms for this participation and what it would mean for individuals in the department – not least in terms of extra and new tasks – as clear as possible. The 'selling' ended in a secret ballot in the department, where the employees voted to accept the researchers' involvement, and where they appointed six employee representatives that would share the power over the change process with the management team of the department.

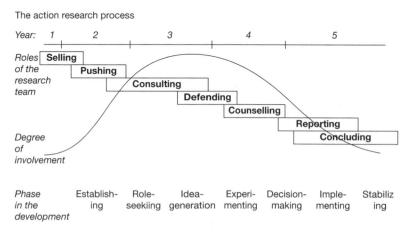

*Figure 13.1* The main phases and activities of the action research team in the Skandia project (based on Docherty 1976: 20).

Thus, the *selling* went much beyond establishing formal written contracts. The selling of the action research project may be described as a series of steps, anchoring and developing the norms about researchers', management's and employee representatives' roles and visions through discussions between the employers' and unions' national confederations, with the top management and union within Skandia, and within the division, and finally within the department. Thus, legitimacy was not achieved through a single decision, but through a series of measures that resulted in establishing positive preconditions for successful change primarily in the department concerned and, to a certain extent, in its broader organizational context.

Though the referendum and election confirmed a basic level of legitimacy, trust for those responsible for the project, the researchers and the project group, had to be developed as they worked through their roles in a series of meetings.

The project group, at first, did not feel any sense of urgency in getting to grips with their assignment to develop a new work organization which would give their colleagues increased participation in and influence over their work. The researchers resolved to communicate their understanding that the project entailed much more than 're-drawing' the boundaries of the responsibilities of the different teams and their members. It entailed establishing a dialogue with their colleagues to influence their attitudes, involvement and commitment, and conducting experiments with different partial solutions to generate experience and stimulate innovativeness. We *pushed* the project group to intensify their work, often in the face of strong pressure from the day-to-day workload. The researchers came to be active participants in the project group, and argued their ideas as intensely as others argued theirs.

This active participation eliminated, probably, the hopes of finding shortcuts through adapting 'scientifically' proven solutions. Thus, the researchers managed to show, by contributing their knowledge, that most of the relevant knowledge for the design process was available within the department and within Skandia. By honestly contributing as much of our knowledge as possible at project meetings, the researchers managed to 'demystify the relevant knowledge sufficiently'. This is a very important lesson – it is *not* by contributing but by holding back one's potential contributions that the academic researchers tend to maintain their power in developments. Thus, our *consulting* did not take on the form of merely giving advice, or carrying out studies on behalf of the project group, but rather by contributing on equal terms.

Any 'local' development process tends to run into conflicts with 'higher-level' developments. In insurance, the production technology is computer-based information technology (IT). In the 1970s, IT was the prime mover of change even more than today: IT systems were developed first, then organizations were adapted to be able to use them. This violates the core of normative socio-technical systems ideals – stating that technical and social developments should take place in a joint optimization process.

The project group was informed that the company was developing new IT systems that would radically affect the department's routines and business. Some of the proposed features of the new systems were seen to clearly interfere with important features of the organizational developments that the project group planned for the department. The researchers became strongly involved as spokespersons, *defending* the interests of the department. It was not customary for operational departments to question or make demands on the work of central corporate development departments. As researchers we were less at risk in broaching such issues, utilizing our academic legitimacy, our socio-technical framework, and our understanding of the commitment, expressed by the CEO at the start of the democratization project, to give room for the local development activities. Our stance at this stage of the project gave rise to immediate and considerable irritation in some parts of management, but understanding and agreement were reached relatively quickly.

The radical ideas about new work roles, and about sharing power in the department between the management team and the employee representatives meant that many issues surfaced, some of which were rather personal. The trustful relationship between the project team, especially the department manager, and the researchers, meant that we became partners, *counselling* in the discussions and deliberations during the implementation of these ideas. The development work lead to semi-autonomous groups, where most tasks were integrated, rather than, as before, handled separately by functional specialists. It also led to the transfer of the department manager's formal rights to take decisions to a joint body, where the power was equally shared between management and employee representatives.

The researchers were involved in the *reporting* both in Skandia, and in the writing of academic texts, and thus took on more traditional research roles towards the end of the project, bringing *conclusions* from the project to the academic world – a process that had been going on all through the research project, but was intensified by our writing towards the end.

It is important to note, however, that although the reporting of the research was more intensive towards the end of the process, this was based on continuous theorizing and documentation throughout the entire project. Every week the research team met for half a day to discuss and try to make sense of the experiences in Skandia, and to analyze the realized and possible interventions. This may be seen as the core of the research part of the action research project – where action and research are parallel processes.

As researchers, we experienced a number of the classical balancing dilemmas in action research that have to do with the researchers' expert role, i.e. the risk of manipulation and/or coercion and problems of value and goal conflicts (White and Wooten 1986). Basically, it concerns balancing our own ambitions for the practitioners with their own ambitions for themselves. Are we pushing them too far? How do we continue action research in the face of opposition? How should the 'advocate role' play out: how does the cost/benefit relationship appear for different parties? Who are winners and losers in the short-, medium- and long-term? Or at the individual, group, departmental, regional office or corporation level? This is not simply a matter of avoiding sub-optimizations. The line between being politically astute and unethical is very fine.

Docherty (1976: 41) commented that the researchers' view of their roles partly conflicted with how the project group leading the change process wanted to see the researchers do their work. An example was the expressed wish of the project group that newsletters to the employees in the department undergoing change should be written by the researchers. The idea of writing newsletters was one of the researchers' interventions. We refused to take on the role of authors, however, because we did not want to shoulder a task that we believed should be the project group's responsibility. In this case, as in several others, the dilemma that the researchers faced was to make interventions without risking taking over the responsibility for the change process. Ownership should stay in the department undergoing change. Åke Philips later formulated a similar point as the 'change dilemma' of the champions in change processes – to balance between being directive, in order to get results, thus removing ownership from those concerned, or being supportive, but with little assurance that the changes will occur (Philips 1988; Stjernberg and Philips 1993).

## Action research as studies of interventions in change processes

One way of conceptualizing action research is to see it as the study of interventions, i.e. actions, in change processes. Such a view of the concept means that there would be grounds for including aspects not only from the 'traditional' action research literature in this knowledge area, but also literature from the organization development (OD) field, as long as the focus is on interventions.[2] This is important in our context, as it forces us to try to understand the effects of different types of interventions and strategies in which these interventions are embedded. The key guiding principle for these interventions in action research, and in the Skandia case, is respect for the need for the practitioners involved to own their own change process, and thus the interventions. One aspect of focusing on interventions is that the complex and shifting character of the researchers' roles and acts is focused, as in the description of the Skandia case.

Coghlan and Brannick (2001) have used the metaphor of a clock to describe the different interventions that may take place in a change process. At one level, symbolized by the hour hand of the clock, interventions concern the change process at large, instigating it and taking part in making it progress. Progressing means many interventions of short duration – the minute hand – such as taking an initiative to a workshop, during which also a series of interventions takes place, symbolized by the second hand. The strength of action research as a research approach is the ability to study how change is progressing through the many interventions taking place at different levels.

Guiding these interventions, on a meta-level, are more general philosophies about research and about the roles of the individual actors in the organizations and societies experiencing these developments. In the later part of the 1970s, Max Elden (1979) summarized the developing experiences of the research interventions in the Norwegian work democracy efforts. He described the changing intervention strategies by using three metaphors: the 'sleeping bag' period, the 'tool kit' period and the 'do-it-yourself workshop' period. According to Elden:

> The first and second generations are variations on a common theme, demonstration and diffusion of a particular organization form, while the third generation attempts to develop and diffuse a participative way of organizing the form-giving process in organizations. The aim in the third generation projects is to develop internal capacities to alter one's organization as needed.
>
> (1979: 230)

All three approaches share, according to Elden, the focus on democratizing work, although the development of these approaches coincides with a widening of the focus from the workplace to the interaction between the workplace and the larger society. The 'sleeping bag' period (with continuous long-term on-site engagement by the researcher as expert) in Elden's analysis took place between 1964 and 1967, the 'tool kit' period (applying previously developed concepts and instruments, with the researcher acting as consultant) took place from 1968/69 to the early 1970s and the 'do-it-yourself workshops' (where the researcher was more of a co-learner and co-producer of learning – rather than a consultant) from the early 1970s. The workshops' purpose, according to Elden, was to 'demystify the relevant knowledge sufficiently, so that anyone with no more than an hour or two of "training" can begin to analyse his own workplace' (1979: 232).

'Ownership' of the change is the crucial difference between the approaches. In Elden's words:

> The most striking difference between the generations is how the change process is organized. *Who* takes initiatives? Who defines *what* the problems are? Who decides *how* data are to be gathered and *which* data are to be gathered? Who decides *what the data means*? *Who* is responsible for planning, management, and evaluation of specific change efforts? In the first generation projects, the answer for the most part was the researcher. For the third generation experiments, the answer for the most part is either employees or some combination of collaboration between employees and researchers.
>
> (1979: 234; italics in original text)

Elden's distinctions cover some major developments in terms of the researchers' strategies about how to achieve sustainable development processes. The early developments were based on the belief that the good example would automatically diffuse within and between companies, whereas the toolkit approach emphasized the need to create a local ownership by using general concepts and 'tools' adapted to and by the particular interests involved in a specific change effort. A parallel may be drawn with the concept of 're-invention' as a special form of 'diffusion' in Rogers' later editions of *Diffusion of Innovations* (1983). The 'tool kits' may be seen as attempts to contribute to local re-inventions.

The 'do-it-yourself' phase as described by Elden developed into a rather sophisticated philosophy of organizational (and societal) reform practice. Björn Gustavsen (2001) questioned the idea that practice may be modelled on theory and focused on the interdependence of theory and practice, mediated in discourse. He became very important in the mid-1980s in Sweden as a 'research entrepreneur' of a methodology for 'democratic dialogue', with origins in Norwegian and Australian 'search conferences', as described by Fred and Merrelyn Emery (1974). These dialogues developed into a format aiming to create a wide participation of all involved employees and, in some cases, of the wider local community. The conferences are arranged as one- or two-day workshops in which all key stakeholders including personnel and their unions, are represented. They have recommended structures, procedures and facilitators, and aim to define change and development issues, their causes, priority and suggested action plans. These dialogues had an ambition and potential to widen the ownership from a small project group of managers and employees (as was the case in Skandia) to a much larger social system within the enterprise or community (cf. Gustavsen 1992; Lindhult 2005; and for their evaluation, Naschold 1992; Hansson 2003). The method as adapted by Gustavsen was seen as a practical application of Habermas' (1984) notion of communicative rationality. The democratic dialogue provided structure and processes for the establishment of discourse. This was used in national programmes in Norway and Sweden. However, its potential often proved to be difficult to realize in practice and the utilization of the method, as an intervention strategy, has declined since the 1990s.

## Action research in the twenty-first century

The major part of academic research is conducted from the viewpoint that the design and conduct of social research must aim to be and be seen to be 'objective' in that the scientists and their work are free from contamination by those studied. In Greenwood's critical words:

> The persistence of positivist social science is mainly a product of its institutional posture as a self-referential, socially passive activity in universities and its conception of the professional social researcher as an 'advisor' to power.
>
> (2002: 118)

Unfortunately, involvement in the intensity and importance of social problems has not played a central role in directing social research. There has also been a marked separation between theory and application and practice. Social engagement has been seen to be methodologically suspect, eroding objectivity with unacceptable risks of introducing prejudice or partisanship.

There are other schools that regard action as essential to social theory and that conduct research under such names as, for example, action research, action science, collaborative inquiry and participatory research (Greenwood and Levin 1998; Reason and Bradbury 2001; Greenwood 2002). Action research is built upon the idea that theory is developed through successive cycles of combined reflection and action in practice. Again, to quote Greenwood:

> Precisely because social science knowledge is not about knowledge of objects, but of co-subjects, the mutual and reciprocal reflections generated in human action must necessarily be at the centre of social science.
>
> (2002: 126)

In action research, researchers and practitioners are sharing their different kinds of knowledge in the process of analyzing the conditions in need of change and designing ways of accomplishing the changes desired. The challenges addressed are usually complex, dynamic and demanding. Action research requires an open and eclectic mindset on the part of those involved. Knowledge, theories, concepts and methods, qualitative and quantitative, from many different social sciences may be relevant and efficacious to the issues that are basically multi-disciplinary.

In order to accomplish changes, these changes need to be seen as legitimate by the actors, especially by those in control of the relevant parts of the organization. This creates a dilemma if the needed changes include shifts in the balance of power.

In the 1960s and 1970s, work democracy was a politically correct concern, much like corporate social responsibility, diversity or sustainability today. Few in power are against these issues – in principle. But specific solutions often threaten specific interests.

Today, as in the 1970s, you also find champions, or as literally translated from Swedish – 'souls-of-fire' that 'burn' for the cause, and sometimes 'burn-out'. You find that the politically correct concerns often play a greater role in the rhetoric than in the actual managerial processes of the organization. Thus, action research is not just about participating and studying change processes, but also involves learning about the political dimension of making the changes, the legitimate causes, and influencing day-to-day decision processes. In this respect, the processes of action research of the 1970s are highly relevant for understanding how to study, participate and learn about change today.

The political dimension in action research is well expressed by Gellerman *et al.* (1990) in their discussion of values and ethics regarding change and development processes: researchers should (a) serve the good of the whole organization or activity system, (b) always treat people as *ends*, never only as *means*; as people and not simply as (researchers') subjects or as (organizational) resources, and (c) act so as to close rather than widen the gap between the more and the less powerful actors in the research setting. Regarding the quality of relationships between researchers and practitioners, action research emphasizes empathy, identification, trust and non-exploitive relationships (Punch 1994). Action research encourages people to question the existing situation and to reflect, and it entails change – all of which may be threatening to existing organizational norms, practice and structure.

### Studying sustainable development

The extent and the character of social science research in industry and commerce has changed since the end of the 1980s, so that action research has become marginalized by collaborative management research. This is primarily due to changes in the economic and political climate that have, in turn, led to new priorities amongst all the research stakeholders, management, unions and researchers. Management sees fit to go its own way and major corporations are much more inclined to make decisions in a global as distinct from a national context, to adopt a management perspective as distinct from a joint social partner perspective and to demand continuous return on investment in the short term – even from cooperation with researchers. Unions have had to rationalize their activities, slimming their organizations and focusing their attention more on conditions of employment as distinct from conditions of work (compare the discussion of unions' strategies in the 1970s by Docherty and Berg, 1975). Scarcity of resources limits the unions' ability to work with researchers.

Table 13.1 shows a comparison between three ways for research to work together with practitioners. We have described action research as an accepted feature of social science in Sweden from the late 1960s to the mid-1980s. Work environment issues in Sweden were not simply an issue of industrial safety and health, but had developed to encompass even social well-being and the development of each individual's personal potential in

*Table 13.1* Three ways for researchers to work together with practitioners

|  | *Action research* | *Collaborative research* | *Sustainable development research* |
|---|---|---|---|
| Social issue | To achieve workable political solutions | To revive business processes and performance | To achieve a continuous process of balancing interests |
| Technology | A constraining factor in practice | Perceived as a liberating market leading factor | Perceived as needing a re-orientated development strategy |
| Key interest groups | The social partners | Managements at company and sector level | Society and the social partners, i.e. all major stakeholders |
| Financial backers | Government | Government and/ or companies | Government and companies |
| Theoretical frameworks | Socio-technical systems | Innovation systems theory, project management | Environmental science and management |
| Balance issue | Management/ personnel | Company/customer | Owners/personnel/ customers/society |

the workplace. The frontline of social political debate was concerned with democracy, where the focus moved from industrial democracy to economic democracy in the private sector.

Collaborative management research replaced action research in the private sector during the 1980s and 1990s. Adler *et al.* (2004) provide an excellent example of the developments of this work in Sweden. The research presented is taken from the FENIX programme on the management of R&D in companies, in which the majority of the doctoral students have been acting managers (see also the chapter by Kolody and Shani in this volume). The main difference from action research is that the personnel and their unions have not been represented in the studies. The research has focused on central development functions and their relations with major customers and other organizations in development alliances. The cases have involved trade unions and operational personnel only in isolated instances. In many respects, the lessons from action research projects of the 1970s and 1980s are valid for collaborative research. The academic legitimacy in both is built on the idea that you need to be close to the change process, and to the interventions that produce the change in order to learn in-depth about the conditions of organizational change.

The key difference between action research and collaborative research is not the fact that change concerns shifts in power and benefits per se, but that such shifts in the collaborative research tradition are given legitimacy within one hierarchical structure, i.e. the managerially dominated structure of the organization. Other interests, such as customers' interests, are to a large extent affecting the changes indirectly, as interpreted by management. The action research of the 1970s and 1980s was also dependent for legitimacy on the employees, and the union structures.

At the core of sustainability is the notion that due weight is given to the legitimate needs and ambitions of all the different stakeholders. In business and working life, the stakeholders are employees, owners, customers and society. Organizational changes towards sustainable development need to be open in the sense that the other stakeholders influence and 'own' the changes. The clearer signs of the emergence of 'sustainable development' in the public sector compared with the private sector may be explained by the palpable presence of society and customers (patients, pensioners and pupils) in the former sector (Tiller 1999; Ekman Phillips 2004; Ekman Phillips *et al.* 2004; Rönnerman, 2004).

Failure to achieve balance can give rise to negative effects for one or more stakeholders. At the individual level, it may result in increased intensity of work, limited creativity, stress and ill health. This can originate in any group and spreads quickly through the organization. For example, managers experiencing a high level of stress exercise leadership, which itself creates bad health. At the organizational level, imbalance may lead to decreased innovative capacity, market share and profitability.

The core concept of sustainable work systems is that the resources deployed are regenerated and developed by the system. Human resources to be fostered include skills, knowledge, cooperation and trust, employability, constructive industrial relations and also broader institutional or societal prerequisites (Docherty *et al.* 2002). From an organizational perspective, the sustainability goals refer to competitiveness, innovativeness, productivity, value creation and organizational learning.

Given the growing complexity of the issues facing companies, the need to include all stakeholders actively in transformation processes makes participation more important as well as realigning it from traditional arenas. The action research tradition is thus highly relevant to strategies for studying change in the twenty-first century, which may be noted by a growing interest in the concept and practice. Still, the complexities of the changes across not only two stakeholders in one organization but across a multitude of organizations and stakeholders create challenges requiring developed forms for conducting action research.

## Discussion and conclusion

Although action research may still be regarded as a counter-stream to mainstream social science practice, it has been around for about 70 years. Different action researchers see different pioneers as playing important roles in establishing the school. Pasmore (2001), a leading American researcher, refers to the philosopher and educationalist Dewey's (1933) work on reflective thinking and his focus on teaching students to think, rather than teaching facts as an important influence on the development of action research. Another is the work of John Collier who, as Commissioner of Indian Affairs in 1933 to 1945, underscored that only a participative approach to research could create the conditions under which authentic improvements in race relations would occur. All are, however, in agreement that Kurt Lewin (see, for example, the collection of articles in Lewin 1963) was a key contributor to the foundation of action research. He was devoted to action research as a democratically based approach to advancing science while dealing with practical social concerns.

The focus of the action research may be seen as studies of interventions. The concept of action research means that the researchers learn about the dynamics of organizational change by being very close to the change processes and, in fact, by being allowed to – and expected to – influence these processes. The focus came to be studies of interventions – both the interventions of the researchers and the interventions of other parties. Thus, although whatever actions the researchers take in the system that is studied, these actions may be seen as some form of intervention in the system.

In several projects conducted in the late 1970s, the researchers saw their role as supporting primarily the weaker party (i.e. the employees) in the developments. The concept 'action research' got a more pronounced political connotation. Not surprisingly, this conceptualization of action research met strong resistance among many managers. Thus 'action research' lost its legitimacy as a form of interactive research in industry. The development of collaborative research today may be seen as a version of action research, focusing on joint learning and on interventions – but with no ambition to shake the distribution of power and influence within the organization. It is a joint process with researchers and *relevant* practitioners – addressing not the work organization issues but issues such as knowledge development, product development and competitive strength. The development may sometimes take place in clusters or innovation systems, which may lead to a focus on issues of influence and power – not on power distribution between management and employees as in the 1970s, but between simultaneously competing and cooperating business partners, where strengthening the regional or national competitive interests may be the core shared value in the developments. As the complexity of the networks of the relevant stakeholders increase, and when the purpose of the changes is more directed to causes 'above' the limited goals of particular interests, and more towards social needs such as sustainable development, the complexity of the change processes increases dramatically. Learning about such changes is difficult without involving oneself in the changes – thus, action research.

## Notes

1　Socio-technical systems theory is shortened to STS, but STS is also associated with a different research tradition, science and technology studies, sometimes also shortened to SST.

2　We feel that the term 'intervention research' is too strongly linked to medicine and social policy to be usable for our purpose. Thus, for example, in 2004, FAS, the Swedish agency for supporting research programmes concerning 'intervention research', exemplifies relevant areas as 'studies of measures to improve public health, to improve conditions of work and prevent work injuries, measures to get sick people back to work, measures to improve people's chances in the labour market, studies in the social sector concerning personal support, addiction, children and youth support, and family support'.

## References

Adler, N., Shani, A.B. and Styhre, A. (eds) (2004) *Collaborative Research in Organizations: Foundations for Learning, Change, and Theoretical Development*, Thousand Oaks, CA: Sage.

Coghlan, D. and Brannick, T. (2001) *Doing Action Research in Your Own Organisation*, London: Sage.

Dewey, J. (1933) *How we Think*, New York: Heath.

Docherty, P. (1976) *Forskarroller i ett aktionsforskningsprojekt (Researcher Roles in an Action Research Project), Delrapport 6 i serien Organisationsutveckling för ökat medinflytande i tjänstemannaföretag*, Stockholm: EFI and PA-rådet.

Docherty, P. and Berg, H. (1975) *Fackliga strategier i en föränderlig situation (Union Strategies in a Changeable Situation), Delrapport 3 i serien Organisations utveckling för ökat medinflytande i tjänstemannaföretag*, Stockholm: EFI and PA-rådet.

Docherty, P., Forslin, J. and Shani, A.B. (eds) (2002) *Creating Sustainable Work Systems: Emerging Perspectives and Practices*, London: Routledge.

Ekman Phillips, M. (2004) 'Action Research and Development Coalitions in Health Care', *Action Research*, 2, 4: 349–370.

Ekman Phillips, M., Maina Ahlberg, B. and Huzzard, T. (2004) 'Planning From Without or Developing From Within? Collaboration Across the Frontiers in Health Care', in W. Fricke and P. Totterdill (eds) *Action Research in Workplace Innovation and Regional Development*, Amsterdam: John Benjamin, 103–126.

Elden, M. (1979) 'Three Generations of Work-democracy Experiments in Norway: Beyond Classical Socio-technical Systems Analysis', in G.L. Cooper and E. Mumford (eds) *The Quality of Working Life in Western Europe*, London: Associated Business Press, 226–257.

Emery, F.E. and Emery, M. (1974) *Participative Design: Work and Community Life*, Canberra: Australian National University.

Gellerman, W., Frankel, M.S. and Ladenson, R.F. (1990) *Values and Ethics in Organization and Human System Development*, San Francisco, CA: Jossey-Bass.

Greenwood, D.J. (2002) 'Action Research: Unfulfilled Promises and Unmet Challenges', *Concepts and Transformation*, 7, 2: 117–139.

Greenwood, D. and Levin, M. (1998) *Introduction to Action Research: Social Research for Social Change*, Thousand Oaks, CA: Sage.

Gustavsen, B. (1992) *Dialogue and Development: Theory of Communication, Action Research and the Restructuring of Working Life*, Assen, NL: Van Gorcum and Swedish Centre for Working Life.

Gustavsen, B. (2001) 'Theory and Practice the Mediating Discourse', in P. Reason and H. Bradbury (eds) *Handbook of Action Research: Participative Inquiry and Practice*, London: Sage 17–26.

Habermas, J. (1984) *The Theory of Communicative Action*, London: Heinemann.

Hansson, A. (2003) *Praktiskt taget. Aktionsforskning om teori och praktik – i spåren efter LOM (Action Research in Theory and Practice*, with summary in English), Göteborg, Sweden: Göteborg Studies in Sociology No. 14.

Lewin, K. (1963) *Field Theory in Social Science – Selected Theoretical Papers*, London: Associated Publishers and Tavistock. (First published in 1951.)

Lindhult, E. (2005) *Management by Freedom: From Machiavellian to Rousseauan Approaches to Innovation and Inquiry*, Stockholm: Royal Institute of Technology.

Naschold, F. (1992) *Evaluation Report Commissioned by the Board of the LOM Programme*, Stockholm: Arbetsmiljöfonden.

Pasmore, W. (2001) 'Action Research in the Workplace: The Socio-technical Perspective', in P. Reason and H. Bradbury (eds) *Handbook of Action Research: Participative Inquiry and Practice*, London: Sage, 38–47.

Philips, Å. (1988) *Eldsjälar*, Stockholm: Handelshögskolan.

Punch, M. (1994) 'Politics and ethics in qualitative research', in N. Denzin and Y. Lincoln (eds) *Handbook of Qualitative Research*, Thousand Oaks, CA: Sage, 83–97.

Reason, P. and Bradbury, H. (2001) (eds) *Action Research: Participative Inquiry and Practice*, London: Sage.

Rogers, E. (1983) *Diffusion of Innovation*, third edition New York: Free Press.

Rönnerman, K. (ed.) (2004) *Aktionsforskning i praktiken – erfarenheter och reflektioner*, Lund: Studentlitteratur.

Stjernberg, T. and Philips, Å. (1993) 'Organizational Innovations in a Long-term Perspective: Legitimacy and Souls-of-Fire as Critical Factors of Change and Viability', *Human Relations*, 46, 10: 1193–1219.

Thorsrud, E. and Emery, F.E. (1969) *Mot en ny bedriftsorganisasjon*, Oslo: Tanum. (Swedish translation 1969: *Medinflytande och engagemang i arbetslivet*, Utvecklingsrådet, SAF, LO, TCO; see also, Emery, F.E. and Thorsrud, E. (1976) *Democracy at Work: The Report of the Norwegian Industrial Democracy Programme*, Leider: Martinus Nijhoff.)

Tiller, T. (1999) *Aktionslärande: Forskande partnerskap i skolan*, Stockholm: Runa.

White, L.P. and Wooten, K.C. (1986) *Professional Ethics and Practice in Organization Development*, New York: Praeger.

# Part V

# Concluding management knowledge

# 14 The power of contrasts
## Comparative research for overcoming ethnocentric myopia

*Bengt Stymne and Jan Löwstedt*

### We all design our little villages

The edifice housing Stockholm School of Economics near the town centre is considered a 'classic-modern' masterpiece by the architect Tengbom. The curved lines of its library tower protrude from the strict rectangular forms to make it the building's most prominent feature. From the beginning of his studies, Bengt Stymne was fascinated by the library and the possibilities it opened. You could go to the long rows of small drawers filled with catalogue cards to look through the topic that interested you to get references to suitable works. You then went to a librarian who would fetch the desired books from the stacks and you could sit down at a desk in the reading room to delve into and enjoy what they had to say. After graduation, Stymne received a stipend to the University of Michigan in Ann Arbor. There also, the library has a central position on campus. He soon learned that, even if the physical layout of the libraries had many similarities, there were important differences in the way they were organized. In Ann Arbor, the stacks were open to the students. You could go to a certain shelf of a section and get an overview of all the works related to the topic that interested you. There were small desks placed among the stacks so you could actually skim through the books without moving to another room. This arrangement speeded up the learning process considerably, something that was further reinforced by the fact that the stacks were always open and not closed in the evening and on weekends as they had been in Stockholm.

In Stockholm, Stymne had learned to know what a university library was and how it operated. Also, he had learned to appreciate it as a good thing. But when he came to Ann Arbor his view was shattered and he realized that libraries in spite of their similarity in appearance can be quite different. Also, there are better or worse ways to organize them.

Three lessons were learned from this experience. First, by comparing phenomena like libraries in different settings we come to understand that the world exhibits more variability than we could initially imagine. Second, what we have assumed to be good and desirable is not to be taken as a universal norm. Third, people in each part of the universe create their own idiosyncratic world and by learning from each other we could widen our understanding about what it is possible to construct.

Ideas, values and preferences of scientists are also influenced by the part of the universe familiar to them. By travelling to hitherto unknown places, Darwin was able to broaden our understanding of the development of the species. In a similar way, Malinowski travelled to little-known territories and provided not only insights that were useful for the imperial administration of foreign countries, but that also gave impetus to the new discipline of anthropology.

## Ethnocentric trappings produce research results

Fayol, Taylor and Weber can be counted among the fathers of modern management theory. The experiences and the thinking on which they based the theories that made them famous are very different. They did have one thing in common, though: Fayol thought that experienced business leaders could sit down and agree on the best principles for management; Taylor thought that there was 'one best way' to produce things; and Weber suggested an 'ideal type' of bureaucracy. A comparative study by Joan Woodward (1958, 1965), however, torpedoed their common idea of an ideal way to organize. By comparing a number of British production establishments, Woodward demonstrated that the way they were organized did not conform to one bureaucratic model but varied according to the production technology of the establishment. In the so-called 'classical administrative school' there had been considerable discussion about the proper number of subordinates that could be managed by a supervisor. Woodward showed that, in practice, that number could vary from just a few workers in the process industry to a dozen or more in mass assembly operations.

Hofstede's *Culture's Consequences* (1980) is one of the most influential examples of the use of a comparative methodology from the last half century. In the book, Hofstede warns about the danger of falling into the trap of ethnocentrism by mistaking regularities found in one country for universally valid laws. Applying Hofstede's thinking, it can be noted that Woodward's observations were made in smaller firms in South Essex, England. In that little universe, technology was found to be correlated with organization structure. The danger of ethnocentrism notwithstanding, 'technology' became, and still is, a condition that management science believes determines the way work will be organized.

But what about national culture? By using an international comparative study, Hofstede did in fact suggest culture as an alternative explanation (to technology) for the way work is organized. He found, for example, that the hierarchical structures are higher in Latin countries like France than in Scandinavia. His explanation is that, while Scandinavian culture prescribes a sharing of power between high and low, French culture takes for granted that bosses should have more power.

## Principles of comparative management research

A number of propositions can now be made concerning how and why a comparative methodology can contribute to knowledge creation in management science:

- In management science, theories and reasoning are mainly based on more or less systematic impressions and observations of how temporal regularities occur in a specific social universe and how this universe develops over time.
- The researcher who bases his or her explanations on experiences generated from only one universe risks becoming trapped by the limited variation that occurs within that single case.
- Each universe exhibits its own idiosyncrasies and regularities. By basing one's conclusions on experiences from more than one universe, the management researcher is able to generate many alternative explanations of the phenomenon he or she is interested in.
- A community of researchers that base their conclusions on experiences from one and the same universe can produce more and more fine-tuned theories about any given phenomenon. Since researchers from other communities tend to do the same, the possibilities for communication and joint development between communities are severely limited. The universe described by each community thus tends to become conceptually hermetically closed.
- Already by basing the reasoning on experiences from two different universes rather than many experiences from one, management scientists are able to suggest theories that have a broader relevance. Glaser and Strauss (1967) made this a cornerstone in their 'grounded theory' approach. Their principle of theoretical saturation suggests that when researchers think they have reached a satisfactory explanation of a certain universe, they should go on to investigate another universe that in some essential characteristic is different from the first.
- Many comparative studies try to maximize the number of different universes investigated. This is a sensible strategy if one thinks that all universes follow the same statistical laws upon which a general model can be constructed. However, the law of large numbers may conceal or

even out differences. If one thinks that each universe has its own regularities, it may be more fruitful to restrict the number of universes investigated to a smaller number (Herbst 1970). Such an approach may be especially useful in the field of management, where a manager is often seen to have the task of choosing between different designs. Enlarging the manager's knowledge about different ways of designing organizations will broaden his or her vision of the range of possibilities and make organizational innovation more likely.

## Comparative studies in management research

Management theory was long rather context-less. It had to do with managing the firm in any context. Starting with Woodward and other contingency theorists, the context of the firm has become more and more relevant. The management of global firms has to cope with many environments with different legislation, cultures, education levels, economic development and customer preferences. The expansion of management theory has to a large extent come from theories that increasingly incorporate the context of the firm. Among other things, this has resulted in theories of strategy and the theory of new institutionalism, which is interested in how organizational forms diffuse.

Another trend in management research seems to centre more on the very micro-processes that have to do with people's perceptions, how the world is experienced, and how people make sense of the world around them. How do we incorporate the world? Also this trend can be seen as management science moving from being context-less to a situation where the 'enacted' and experienced environment plays a leading role (Weick 1969).

Any management theory must explain what context it applies to. Of course, a researcher could say, 'I have based my model on companies from South Essex or from the district of Emiglia Romana, and I cannot claim that it is applicable elsewhere.' There are several reasons why a justification like this is not good enough, though. One very pragmatic one, is that the researcher may be the only one interested in the exact little universe he or she has investigated. Other management researchers, as well as practitioners, are interested in the reports or scholarly findings because they may be applicable in their area of interest.

Another reason why it is not good enough to leave the question of the field of application of one's theories unanswered, is that it does not contribute to the development of the field. By discussing instead the area of application of their findings, the researcher helps management theory to incorporate more and more of the context of the firm.

## Three approaches to international comparative research

There are many ways to design international comparative management research. Below we describe three approaches in which we have ourselves been involved:

- The international comparative large sample study.
- The international comparative case study.
- The international comparative process study.

### *The international comparative large sample study*

Hofstede's (1980) study, with its 100,000 respondents in 40 countries, is an eminent example of a large-scale international comparison. Such studies derive their strength from statistical analyses. To do so, they work with well-defined variables that can be quantified. International comparative large sample studies can be used to investigate whether countries that are similar regarding some attribute that characterizes the country as a whole are similar also regarding other characteristics.

Countries vary in terms of natural endowments, political system, legal and institutional set-up, language and culture, technology, education, and degree of economic development. All these contextual or, as Hofstede calls them, 'ecological' factors are conditions that likely have a profound impact on the problems faced by management. These impacts are, however, difficult or impossible to detect in studies confined to one country.

The importance of the large sample study for transnational management is evident. These studies give descriptions of differences between countries that a manager has to take into account. Findings like Hofstede's, that a characteristic like national culture has a profound impact on structure and other central aspects of organizational behaviour, have consequences for management theory. They provide a good reason to revisit the existing theories of organization design to see if a better one can be formulated.

### *The international comparative case study*

Comparative case study research operates according to quite a different logic than large quantitative studies. Since a comparison is made between two or a few cases, small sample case studies permit the researcher to conceive each case as a whole system with complex relationships. The researcher is thus able to reach a more developed understanding of how each of the cases functions as a system. This makes it possible to suggest mechanisms and processes that can explain observed differences and similarities.

If the comparison is made over national borders, the researcher is able to observe the impact of differences in contextual factors. These factors may well be the same as those included in a large sample study, but the comparative case researcher gets a more detailed understanding of how variables interact. He or she is also in a position to find explanations that involve different constellations of factors. This is not possible in statistical studies since they need to assume that variables are related in the same way at least for the subsets of the population studied.

International comparative case studies have a pedagogical value since they report a direct impression of the differences and similarities between how comparable organizations in various countries can be managed. They have a value also for theory construction. Each system studied can be interpreted as representing a unique combination of characteristics. The management scientist accordingly needs to formulate theories on a higher level that take into account the idiosyncrasies that the cases exhibit. If the international comparative research has not been taken into account, the theory will have a much narrower validity and be more ethnocentric.

### The international comparative process study

The process study is different from the case study in that it does not have the firm as its main focus but is more interested in understanding a certain process. The process study aims at answering questions like: What did the innovation process behind the new product look like? The process study is a bit like a natural experiment. Either the consequences or the antecedents of an identifiable event are observed.

Process studies put a lot of emphasis on how a problem is solved, how change is brought about or how a certain challenge is met. They emphasize the temporal dimension by being longitudinal, historical or retrospective. The basic idea behind process studies is that they make it possible to follow a course of events, which permits an analysis of possible causal relationships.

Comparative process studies describe two or more chains of events from either the same firm or several different organizations. They give the researcher the opportunity to study the effects of different ways to manage that process. If the process comparison is made over international borders, it also permits the researcher to study how, for example, different institutional arrangements impact the outcome of the process.

## Industrial Democracy in Europe: an international comparative large sample study

The *Industrial Democracy in Europe* study, or IDE for short (Industrial Democracy in Europe Research Group 1981), was carried out during the years 1974 to 1980 by a team of researchers from the 12 countries: Belgium, Denmark, Finland, France, Great Britain, Israel, Italy, Netherlands, Norway, Sweden, West Germany and Yugoslavia. Eight thousand questionnaires were filled in by representative samples of employees in 134 firms. In addition, 1000 standardized interviews were held to gather information at the firm level and the nation level.

### A meeting in Dubrovnik

At the height of the discussion about industrial democracy in Europe, a large conference on self management was arranged in the beautiful old Croatian town of Dubrovnik in 1972. Social scientists from all over the world attended. One group among them came to discuss the meaning of the concept of industrial democracy and how provisions for it could be written into European company law.

The discussion became the seed of a large project, the initiative for which was taken by the psychologist, Bernhard Wilpert. The aim of the project was to investigate the range of legal and other formal provisions like agreements between unions and employers. A group of 25 researchers eventually emerged, consisting of two or three researchers from each of the 12 countries. Financing for travel and coordination was obtained from the Thyssen and Ford foundations. The individual country teams had to apply for money locally.

The group as a whole met regularly in different countries, both to plan the project and later to discuss the results. The whole process was organized in a democratic and participative way. All decisions concerning what was to be done and the finalization of research instruments were taken at the project meetings. The chairmanship of the meetings rotated on a daily basis. This process resulted in a very cohesive group prepared to carry out all the hard fieldwork that was involved.

The researchers in the group shared some common values and ideas that became more articulated as the project went on. Basically, we all thought that workers' participation in matters related to their own job was a good thing. We also thought that employees were generally involved too little in such matters. We had all done research on participation and even engaged in practical experimentation. Some had a theoretical affinity with the socio-technical systems school of Tavistock and many were influenced by the thinking of Kurt Lewin and his pupils at the Michigan school of participative management. All were also proud of their own country's approach to industrial democracy.

## Measuring de jure industrial democracy

Even if all of us believed in participation, the group was not sure if partici- pation could be advanced by legal means. Therefore our main research question became: *Does formal participation in the form of legislation and national agreements contribute to de facto participation for the individual employee?* The formally prescribed degree of participation varied from country to country and we had to find a way to compare these national legal systems. We decided to create a Guttman-type scale of 'Formal Industrial Democracy' to measure how much influence a country's laws and agreements prescribed for different actors in different types of matters or decisions:

1   No formal right.
2   The right of information.
3   The right of information beforehand.
4   The right of giving opinions.
5   The right of being consulted.
6   The right of taking part in the decision (co-determination, veto).
7   The right of making the decision.

The actors whose rights were to be described were worker, supervisor, middle management, top management, board, work council, and external bodies (e.g. public authorities). There were 16 different decisions for which the scale, ranging from 'assignment of work tasks' to 'a major capital investment', was to be applied.

We also wanted to see what kind of formal base the rights were based on: legislation, national agreements, local agreements, and industry or company praxis. The description according to the scale of Formal Industrial Democracy of each country's legislation and national agreements was made with the help of legal experts and completed with the help of the company's in-house expert, e.g. the personnel manager.

The procedure for measuring formal participation enabled us to establish the meaning of 'industrial democracy' in each country and made it possible to say which countries had, in a formal sense, more or less industrial democracy. Yugoslavia was the country where the Works Council (or similar institution) was assigned most formal rights of participation, while Great Britain offered the least.

### Degree of de facto participation

The actual degree of participation in each company was estimated by interviewing two to five experts such as the personnel manager and the union leader, who were asked about how much influence different actors had in the 16 decision areas looked at. The measurement instrument used Likert-type items to rank influence from 'no influence' to 'very high influence'.

Correlation analysis showed that there was a reasonable relationship (multiple correlation coefficients around 0.70) between *de jure* participation according to the scale of Formal Industrial Democracy and *de facto* participation according to the influence scale.

### Satisfaction of workers

The influence of workers and their representative bodies had no correlation to worker satisfaction. An interesting finding in this context was that the attitudes of workers were related more to how much influence their representative system was ascribed than to how much influence their representatives actually exercised.

### Results of the IDE study

IDE is arguably the first study that has managed to translate a complex, controversial, legal and institutional system into meaningful scales that can be used for quantitative comparisons between countries. The main result of the IDE study is that it led to a coherent taxonomy for discussing what industrial democracy means as a formal institution. The taxonomy can be used by policy-makers interested in designing a formal system of industrial democracy in their country. The taxonomy provides them with a way of understanding which means can be used, depending on which type of decision they want to regulate for which class of actors. In addition, the taxonomy provides them with a means of comparing their own intended regulation with that of other countries. Also, social scientists interested in the area of industrial democracy have gained a means of systematically comparing countries with each other regarding their institutional system for industrial democracy.

The study has established that formal systems of industrial democracy in Europe are effective in the sense that employees in countries where the system of industrial democracy formally assigns them a high degree of participation also have a high degree of de facto influence. Even if a cross-sectional study like IDE cannot establish a causal relationship, the results of the study at least increase the probability that governments and parties within the labour market will be able to change the influence wielded by different actors by means of industrial democracy legislation or agreements.

The results cast some doubt on the idea that increased influence really makes workers happier. Other factors, like the relationship one has to the boss and to colleagues, are important determinants. We also found that it is not the actual workers' influence that makes them satisfied but rather how much influence that is formally prescribed. The ideological function of industrial democracy, to establish legitimacy for the industrial or, as in the case of Yugoslavia, the political, system, should therefore not be discounted.

### What was learnt from the IDE study

The success of the IDE study depended very much on the cohesion of a sizeable group of researchers from different nations. To obtain this cohesion, a great measure of participative leadership was needed. An essential condition for this to occur was that the researchers could work together as a group for a period of several years. This was made possible by grants that specifically financed management, coordination and the arrangement of frequent meetings of the whole group. Another necessary condition was that the individual national teams got funding from their national bodies. All these conditions have probably become more difficult to obtain nowadays in the social sciences. Funding bodies have become more reluctant to provide money for researchers from other countries and also hesitant to finance projects that go on for more than two to three years.

## Micro-electronics in the service sector (MESS): an international comparative case study

In the spring of 1982, the authors were approached by Professor John Child of Aston University about an international comparative study of the introduction of information technology in the service sector. We had recently completed a study commissioned by a parliamentary committee on the consequences of new technology in the Swedish insurance industry (Löwstedt *et al.* 1981). There, we had found that the consequences from introduction of new technology were more ambiguous than suggested by Braverman (1974). He and other influential voices at that time stated that new technology imperatively led to de-skilling of the workers and lowering of the quality of working life. In contrast, our studies indicated that technological change had been associated with a higher proportion of skilled labour in the firms. This effect was not only due to the elimination of menial jobs, but also to the new types of services to the customers enabled by the new technology (Stymne *et al.* 1986).

We considered the initiative taken by Child as an interesting opportunity to study political, institutional and cultural factors that could contribute to our understanding of the complex relationship between changes in technology and organizational structures and processes. Even if we considered Child's proposal a great opportunity, we were not sure that our participation could be funded. All researchers in our group also had other demanding commitments to honour.

## Another trip to Dubrovnik

In any case, Löwstedt decided to meet the research group that was to be known as the 'MESS' group and recruited his colleague Tomas Brytting to join him. We succeeded in getting a small research grant for a pre-study to cover a low budget trip to Dubrovnik. For two fairly young and inexperienced researchers, this turned out to be the beginning of a long and exciting journey with some of the leading scholars in European organizational research.

The meeting in Dubrovnik went on for three full days. As young and sometimes rather critical participants, we doubted that anything could ever evolve out of the endless discussions amongst these well-known social scientists. The discussions rambled from finding the right word in a definition of 'qualification', to grand analyses of technological development trends in capitalistic versus socialistic economies. We identified a flora of strategies and styles used by different scholars to influence the meeting. Eventually, the meeting managed to agree on a preliminary research agenda and plans for some homework to be done by the national teams before the next international meeting.

After having made a successful application to the Swedish Work Environment Fund for financing, we were also able to recruit two research assistants and get started on the project.

## Research design and checklists as tools of investigation

The MESS project studied the relevance of IT for organization of work, structure of employment, work experience and performance in service organizations. The process of organizing the introduction and application of IT was studied. The three service industries of health care, banking and retailing were selected. Each of these was to be studied in Belgium, Germany (FRG), Hungary, Italy, Sweden and the UK in order to capture the influence of institutional, cultural and other contextual factors. The comparative case study approach was chosen to make it possible to grasp the scope and complexity of the relationship between technological and organizational change. This design permitted us to investigate whether there were consistent national differences and whether such differences were associated with institutional, political or cultural explanations. The depth of the empirical material and how well it articulated the underlying processes were given priority over the choice of the latest technological innovations.

In the discussions at the regular meetings of the research teams, the comparability of cases was of major concern. Great care was taken to choose specific technological applications to make comparisons meaningful. The introduction of the following techniques were chosen: automated blood analyzers, automated teller machines, and electronic point of sales systems (EPOS).

The conceptualization and operationalization of concepts and issues, the recording of the case material and the interpretation of results had to overcome the possible ethnocentric bias of each national team. The different stages of the research process were therefore organized as a continuing iterative process between the research groups and national teams met for two or three days every six months. In order to ensure comparability between cases conducted by the different teams, a detailed checklist listing all the items to be covered by the case studies was constructed. This checklist (Child *et al.* 1990: 66–80) contained the following sections:

- Contextual data at the national, sector and unit levels.
- Decision making about the introduction of new technology.
- Introduction and implementation of the new technology.
- Application of the new technology – organization of work.
- Application – quality of work.
- Application – labour force (division of labour, qualifications, manning, terms of employment, reward systems).
- Application – organizational structure.
- Outcomes of introduction of new technology – productivity, service to the customer, experience of work.

Mostly interviews were used for collecting data. Structured questionnaires were also used to collect data about the personal background of service workers and their work satisfaction. In some cases, diary sheets were used for recording activities of how people worked with the new technology.

### Comparative analysis

The field studies were carried out between 1982 and 1985, with a concentration on the last two years. The complexity and scope of the more than 30 cases made it difficult to penetrate the empirical material in depth during the meetings of the complete international research team. Working groups were instead formed for each of the three service sectors. These sector groups developed the analysis further and examined the validity of the results in terms of how well they did justice to the specifics of each case.

The sector groups encountered certain problems when they went through the details of the case study reports. Despite the previous assumption that fieldwork checklist had delineated precise sub-categories of issues to be pursued and information to be secured, inconsistencies were found in the information reported. Progress on resolving such problems had to be achieved through iterative reformulations of the case study reports. At times, the completion of the task of the work groups was significantly delayed by the necessity to revisit research locations.

Finally, each sector work group produced comparative analyses in a lengthy report. The format and style of these sector reports were standardized by writing them in a sequential order. The international hospital laboratory report was written first by the Swedish team (Brytting, Löwstedt and Stymne) together with one of the German colleagues (Hans Dieter Ganter). The sector reports and various working papers led to several books and publications in international scientific journals during the second half of the 1980s. The most comprehensive presentation of the project and its results was published in *Information Technology in European Services: Towards a Microelectronic Future* (Child *et al.* 1990). The results from the Swedish research project were presented in an edited book (Löwstedt 1989), where the six Swedish cases were contrasted with the other cases in the international study.

One major finding of the MESS study is that the adoption of identical technologies in different countries is associated with very different changes in organizational design. The study refutes the idea that technology determines how work is organized and the quality of working life. Additional contextual and procedural variables have to be taken into account. According to the study, the implementation of new technology in the service sector was very much a learning process, where decisions were taken in the face of uncertainties about the pros and cons of suggested technological changes. These decisions also proved to be modified along the way in the light of experiences situated in the organizational processes of the actual organization. The decision process and the implementation process are therefore both important mediators of the influence of contextual variables on the effects of new technology on the organization. How much room is left for management choice is discussed below in connection with the ORGNOVATION study.

*MESS epilogue*

Until the MESS project began, survey studies were the dominant approach in comparative cross-national research (and maybe still are). The project was developed in a quite critical mood towards such highly structured ways of making inquiries into complex phenomena. The main problems discussed in our critical evaluation of survey approaches were that: (a) the surveys based on questionnaires rely upon the equivalence of meaning expressed by different languages; and (b) many measures and concepts are conceptually ethnocentric, e.g. the meaning of a concept like 'decision' is understood differently in each country depending on its culture and institutions. The MESS researchers shared explicitly the understanding that such challenges were best met by further development of the international comparative case method rather than by refining statistical methods for analyzing large sample data.

Working in an international research project like the MESS project was both rewarding and challenging. It could be frustrating to experience all the time and resources consumed. From the first meeting to the publication of the final book in 1990 took close to ten years. This use of resources could, however, be justified because the impact of factors that explain the relation between technological development and organizational change cannot be meaningfully studied in a more demarcated national study. Nor could they be traced in a more resource-effective survey study.

Another challenge was having to work with colleagues with different backgrounds and traditions. In this case, good and productive relations of work developed. When this happens, the necessity of collaboration turns into a very rewarding experience and contributes to strengthening of the international network needed in modern management research.


## ORGNOVATION: an international comparative process study

A group of researchers from different countries had been meeting for some time to discuss development of new ways to organize work. One outcome of these discussions was an article about how information technology had made it possible for a new organizational paradigm to emerge (Kolodny *et al.* 1996). We also discussed the possibility of creating an 'organizational observatory' with the task of reporting on and analyzing new ways of organizing. When the European Commission issued a call for research on organizational innovations, an enlarged international group of researchers was formed. A bid was submitted and got accepted. The aim of the proposed study was to investigate how organizational innovations come into being and the factors that contribute to their development.

### The process of organization design

Organizational innovation may come about to enable organizations to carry out tasks or offer products that have not existed before. Such innovations are made possible and desirable when conditions in the context of a certain market have changed so much that older models of organizations no longer function well. Similarly, new technology or scientific findings may have made them possible. Just any new way to organize cannot be classified as an innovation. The criterion of success also has to be fulfilled, e.g. that the innovating organization becomes successful or that the innovation diffuses also to other organizations.

Organizational innovations do not always have an identifiable person or group as their originator but may emerge through a rather long process of learning from trial and error. Also, when an originator can be identified, it is of interest to know who and what else contributed to the innovation. Figure 14.1 outlines how we conceived the process of innovation. The model also served as a road-map for the analysis of our empirical material. According to the figure, the process of innovation can be imagined as a funnel. What is put into the funnel is the challenging situation that calls for innovation. These initial conditions are thought of as passing through a number of filters.

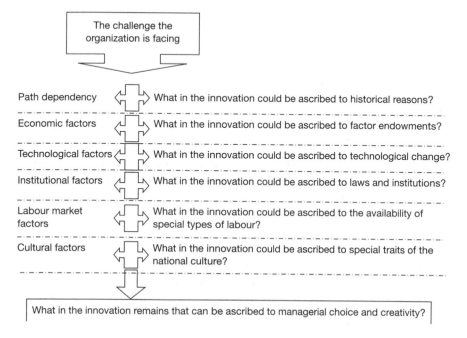

*Figure 14.1* The funnel model of organizational design.

According to the model, the innovation emerges successively from each filter. The first filter is called *path dependency* and consists of restrictions or advantages created by the innovating firm's history and of investments that the innovation needs to adapt to. The second filter consists of *economic factors*, for example whether the innovating system has easy access to some essential inputs or whether it lacks certain types of material considered essential for the task at hand. The third filter is *technology*. The availability of new technology may create an opportunity for organizing in a new way, while the dependency on old technology may constitute a handicap to be circumvented. The fourth filter consists of *institutional factors*, such as laws, agreements and the way a government operates. Sometimes a country's institutions hinder innovation by requiring that activities be organized in a certain way. In other countries, the legislation may be much more permissive regarding what an organization may look like. Investigating organizational innovation was especially interesting since one of the main aims of the EU is to do away with demands that hinder innovations that spur competition. The fifth filter consists of *labour market factors* such as the availability of cheap labour or of labour with certain skills. The sixth filter is national or regional *culture*, which can be more or less conservative.

What remains unexplained after all these filters is the part of the innovation that could be ascribed to managerial choice and original creativity.

The process of designing an innovative organization for the following types of activity was studied:

- *Globalization* of a domestic product.
- *Continuous improvement* of industrial activities.
- *Modernization of public administration.*
- *Technology advice* provided to small and middle-sized companies.

Examples of the process of organizing each of these activities innovatively were taken from all or most of the following eight countries: Canada, France, Germany, Great Britain, Italy, Spain, Sweden and the United States. The main features of the study of designing innovative organizations for globalization are provided below as an illustration (IMIT *et al.* 1996).

### Globalization

The following firms with innovative ways of organizing globally were studied: Benetton, Italy; Chupa Chups, Spain; Glaxo, Great Britain; Joets Jurassiens (a pseudonym), France; SAP, Germany; and Tetra Pak, Sweden.

The description of the process of innovation was created by means of interviews with the people involved and by studying documents such as annual reports, books and articles published about the company. Each innovation process was documented as a narrative. These case studies formed the basis of further analysis.

The first step was to find similarities between the different stories in order to establish a smallest set of requirements that the design of an organization for globalization has to fulfill in order to be successful. The following design requirements resulted from this process:

- Ability to make long-term financial commitments.
- Need for a sustained strategy.
- Need for developing a core competency.
- Ability to exploit synergies with the environment.
- Need for a marketing strategy for attracting and keeping customers.
- Ability to adapt to the needs and peculiarities of the local markets.
- Need for a cost-effective administration of operations.
- Motivating the local staff.

The next step was to investigate how each of the designs had met each of the design requirements. The solutions were compared and an analysis was made to see whether differences between the designs could be explained by one of the filters or whether they had to be ascribed to the exercise of managerial choice.

When it came to the first filter, *path dependency*, none of the organizations investigated seemed constrained by its historical past. Rather, the ability to break with the historical past seemed to be a common characteristic of our cases of innovative ways to organize for globalization.

The *economic filter* seemed to a large extent to have influenced how the innovations were designed. With the exception of Glaxo, the companies investigated had been suffering from a lack of capital. Benetton's innovative solution of outsourcing all its production and use of independent entrepreneurs to build up its extensive retail organization can be explained by its initial lack of capital.

The *technological filter* did not indicate that product technology had any profound influence on the organizational designs investigated. In Glaxo, SAP and Tetra Pak, it was rather the other way around: their organizations were set up in order to be able to develop the technology necessary for the realization of the strategic idea.

The *institutional filter* explained a good deal of the design choices of Glaxo and 'Joets Jurassiens'. Glaxo has adapted its organization to be able to deal effectively with the requirements of the drug administrations in different countries. In order to get access to public financial support, Joets Jurassiens chose to cooperate with a group of other small companies in their first export attempts.

*Labour market*-related factors seem to be a major source of variation in organizational solutions between the companies. The labour market where a company is started determines to a large extent the way it will be organized. Tetra Pak relied on the selective recruitment of gifted Swedish university graduates for the coordination of the global operations. Glaxo's move toward a more focused R&D-based strategy was facilitated by the availability of graduates and researchers in this area in Britain. Eighty per cent of SAP's workforce was made up of university graduates, which the company was able to recruit in Germany. The role of the *cultural filter* could be observed in Tetra Pak's organizational design, with the Tetra Pak organization relying more than the other companies on autonomous country managers for co-coordinating its global activities. This observation may be linked to Hofstede's finding that Swedish culture favours low power distance between superiors and subordinates and that it shows a high tolerance for ambiguity. Benetton's reliance on a network of subcontractors presupposes a high degree of both trust and entrepreneurial spirit, two traits that are said to be characteristic of the province of Treviso.

### Managerial choice

The hand and mind of the organizational designer is visible and has been decisive in the investigated companies. In five of the companies, the main designer was actually the founder of the company. Especially when it came to fulfilling the requirement of basing the international expansion on a sustainable business strategy, it seems that the influence of the designer-owner has been crucial. As an example, the business concept of Tetra Pak existed in the mind of Ruben Rausing long before it became embodied in an organizational set-up. To finance the survival of Tetra Pak, Rausing had to sell his existing company Åkerlund & Rausing. In Glaxo, the management group responded to pressure from below by redirecting company strategy from having been quite diversified to successively increasing its focus on 'ethical' pharmaceuticals.

Many studies of organizational change have found that inertia and path dependencies often determine the shape of an organization. The investigated organizational designs do not conform to that rule. They all represent deviations from their historical past and it makes sense to infer that a good portion of determination and courage on the part of the designers have been necessary to realize that break with the past.

### The results of the ORGNOVATION study

The historical time perspective used in the process analysis of the ORGNOVATION study made it possible to detect the dynamics of the role of each context factor. The contextual factors were found to play an important but not decisive role in developing the organizational innovation.

Different theories about organizing assign a more or less important role to the manager here. At one extreme is population ecology, which sees environmental selection as the designer; at another, are a number of theories about entrepreneurship that assign the entrepreneur and his or her actions the dominating role. The ORGNOVATION study has shown that both the designer and the context are necessary for bringing about the organizational innovation, though also suggests that the role of the designer is the most critical of these two sets of factors.

The theory of new institutionalism emphasizes that imitation and pressure to conform result in organizational solutions that are ill-adapted to their task environment and more geared to the need to exhibit the proper appearance, e.g. to appear 'modern' in order to gain legitimacy (Meyer and Rowan 1977). The ORGNOVATION study has shown that legitimacy can be important, e.g. when it comes to receiving favourable treatment from the government or to treating powerful customers with the appropriate respect. However, the study does not indicate that institutional factors have a general precedence over other contextual factors like the educational level of available labour.

We think that the most interesting aspect of the ORGNOVATION study is that the organizational innovations are to a large extent a product of local conditions in the home country. The peculiarities of the local situation have forced the designer to find solutions that are unique in an international perspective. These unique solutions have then proven themselves to be applicable, viable and able to provide a competitive advantage in the global business environment as well.

The great variability of regional environmental conditions that exists within the EU would appear to serve as a gene pool that makes new variants of organizational innovations possible and desirable. Since economic, technical and market trends in different parts of the world point at least vaguely in the same direction, there is some probability that an innovative organizational design that has proven successful in the local environment may well be viable in the global context as well.

If the above hypothesis is transformed into a policy statement, the EU should facilitate the diffusion of knowledge about local innovative organizational designs. Cases about regional organizational innovations could become a more common topic of discussion in business schools. Such a perspective would break with the prevailing trend in business and government to adhere to models of organizing developed and propagated by American consulting companies. By paying more attention to the organizational innovations created in the regional backyards of Europe, the trend toward organizational 'isomorphism' observed by the New Institutionalists could be broken. Such a change in perspective would lead to more variability and probably also economic growth.

### What has been learnt from the ORGNOVATION study?

The ORGNOVATION study was undertaken by a number of scholars with a profound interest in- and experience of organizational design, and who had also published widely in the area. The process studies performed in each country could therefore be informed by a reasonably common theoretical base, though the direction of the study was more centralized than in the IDE study. The core of ORGNOVATION consisted of a smaller, international group of researchers that had cooperated and written joint papers on organization design before. This centralization aided the development and implementation of the rather complex procedure necessary for gathering and analyzing the process data of the studied innovations.

The study was funded by the EU. Without this funding, it would not have been possible to involve leading scientists in the field. The funding also made it possible to carry out the study without the time delays that would have occurred if the individual participants had been obliged to apply for support from sources in their home countries.

## Conclusion

The three examples given in this chapter illustrate how the power of contrasts can be used to leverage management research through international comparative studies. They have shown that insights can be won and theories created that would not have been possible with research confined to one geographical and cultural area. If organizational theories are based mainly on research done in each such area, they tend to multiply and become non-compatible. A multitude of non-compatible or conflicting theories can inhibit their value for guiding practical action. The plethora of divergent theories may even re-enforce the tendency of practice to imitate or use the models marketed by the large management consulting companies. When management scientists use their cooperation in international comparative studies to hammer out broader theories, those theories may attract more interest from practice. In this way, international comparative research can contribute to bridging the relevance gap between management science and practice.

It should be clear from the examples given that international comparative organization research must be organized as teamwork between researchers from the countries involved. The establishment of such teams presupposes the prior existence of international networks of management scientists. Frequent participation in international gatherings is not enough. Prolonged stays at research centres in other countries are a prerequisite for the creation of the common understanding, shared vocabularies and communication habits upon which future collaboration in international collaborative projects can be built.

To create the preconditions for the emergence of international networks, universities and money-granting bodies should encourage, and perhaps even require, that their doctoral students and academic staff spend prolonged periods at one or preferably several institutions abroad. In order to motivate scientists and doctoral students to do so, periods abroad should be counted as a merit, should be made financially possible, and should not be impossible to combine with family life. It is also necessary that host institutions develop systems and work habits that facilitate a meaningful integration of their foreign guests.

If international collaborative organization research is going to remain possible in the future, funds should be made available by national bodies for projects that both take considerable time and involve many researchers. Substantial funding must in addition be available to finance the management and meetings necessary for the development and leadership of such projects. The EU seems to be in an ideal position to provide this funding. However, to negotiate such financing requires that researchers build their knowledge about how the EU works and form personal relationships with individuals within the EU machinery. Often, some type of joint financing from national sources has to be obtained. National funding bodies should assign priority to levering international funding of comparative projects by co-founding them. Researchers and industry should also be prepared to submit joint offers for comparative projects that benefit them both and offer the opportunity to engage in collaborative research.

# References

Braverman, H. (1974) *Labor and Monopoly Capital*, New York: Monthly Review Press.

Child, J. and Loveridge, R., in collaboration with the Microelectronics in the Service Sector International Research Team (1990) *Information Technology in European Services: Towards a Microelectronic Future*, Oxford: Basil Blackwell.

Glaser, B.G. and Strauss, A.L. (1967) *The Discovery of Grounded Theory: Strategies for Qualitative Research*, New York: Aldine de Gruyter.

Herbst, P.H. (1970) *Behavioral Worlds: The Study of Single Cases*, London: Tavistock.

Hofstede, G. (1980) *Culture's Consequences: International Differences in Work Related Values*, Beverly Hills, CA: Sage.

IMIT and Stymne, B. (main author), with the collaboration of Campanini, L., Carlsson T., Clark, P., Figuera, J.R., Gavetti, G., Hägglund, P., Kolodny, H., Latniak, E., Lillrank, P., Liu, M., Malerba, F., Müller, F., Pekruhl, U., Ramos, R.,

Shani, A.B. and Steward, F. (1996) International Transfer of Organizational Innovation, Research report under contract EIMS 94/106 with Directorate General XIII of the European Commission, Stockholm, June 15.

Industrial Democracy in Europe (IDE) International Research Group (1981) *Industrial Democracy in Europe*, Oxford: Clarendon Press.

Kolodny, H., Liu, M., Stymne, B. and Denis, H. (1996) 'New Technology and the Emerging Organizational Paradigm', *Human Relations*, 49, 12: 1457–1487.

Löwstedt, J. (ed.) (1989) *Organisation och teknikförändring* (Organization and Technological Change), Lund: Studentlitteratur.

Löwstedt, J., Ringh, B. and Stymne, B.A. (1981) *Datoriseringen i försäkringsbranschen – En studie av den tekniska utvecklingens betydelse för informationsörmedlande verksamhet* (Computerization in the Insurance Industry), Stockholm: EFI RP 6221.

Meyer, J. and Rowan, B. (1977) 'Institutionalized Organizations: Formal Structure as Myth and Ceremony', in W. Powell and P. DiMaggio (eds) *The New Institutionalism in Organizational Analysis*, Chicago: University of Chicago Press.

Stymne, B.A., Löwstedt, J. and Fleenor, C.P. (1986) 'A Model for Relating Technology, Organization and Employment Level: A Study of the Impact of Computerization in the Swedish Insurance Industry', *New Technology, Work and Employment*, 1, 6: 113–126.

Weick, K.E. (1969) *The Social Psychology of Organizing*, Reading, MA: Addison-Wesley.

Woodward, J. (1958) *Management of Technology*, London: HMSO.

Woodward, J. (1965) *Industrial Organization: Theory and Practice*, London: Oxford University Press.

# 15 The innovative research enterprise

*Bengt Stymne*

Our view of the world is not primarily constrained by the characteristics of the world but by our ability to make sense out of it and understand it. If we see the world as unchanging, it is not because the world is inherently so but because we are not prepared to change the way we make sense out of it and understand it. An innovation occurs when we conceive of the world, or a part of the world, in a new way. We depart on our 'research enterprise' in order to accomplish such innovations.

In this chapter, I will look upon the organization of the 'enterprise of management research' to see how innovations can be brought about. I have borrowed the frame of reference from Törnebohm, a philosopher of science. Like many of his colleagues, Törnebohm has a background in the natural sciences but I find his ideas enlightening for thinking about and teaching methods of research in management science. I am using the term 'management science' in a broad sense, including attempts to create scientifically valid knowledge in the whole field of management.

I do not intend the chapter as a summing up of the other chapters in the book. Instead, I mean it as a call for researchers to try to organize their own research enterprise so that it becomes innovative. I will place special emphasis on the role of methods and techniques in achieving innovation.

In Figure 15.1, the 'Universe of Management Practice' stands for the world of management and management systems that we want to create knowledge about. The symbols that are placed above the border line of the 'universe', form the 'inquiry system' of the 'research enterprise'. The circles and their segments stand for the sets of all the problems and questions that we would like to know about management (P), the questions and problems that are answerable and solvable (SP), and the present state of scientific knowledge about management (K). The sign $\simeq$ stands for the way we map the universe onto our system of inquiry. For the mapping, we use different methods and techniques (M). Also the perspective (V) on the universe, i.e. the way researchers look upon the field of study, has consequences for what they see.

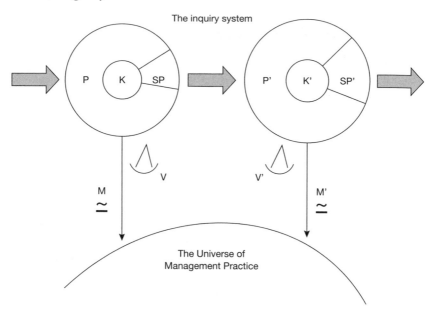

*Figure 15.1* Management research as a system for creating knowledge by sequences of innovations (adapted from Törnebohm 1971).

The set of questions we ask, the set of answers, the set of knowledge and the set of methods are finite at any specific point in time. The Universe of Management Practice, on the other hand, does not have any definite limits. The knowledge we have of it can be regarded as temporary ideas, which will soon change and hopefully also grow.

The system depicted in Figure 15.1 is dynamic and constantly undergoing transformation. The transformations take place as a string of sequences of innovation. The apostrophe (') after the letter symbols on the right of the figure indicates the new state of the inquiry system after an innovative sequence.

The transformation sequence can be triggered by different causes. One cause is new methods that permit the researcher to perceive the universe in new ways. The telescope and the microscope have produced lots of innovations in astronomy and medicine. The computer has had a comparable impact on the social sciences. Methods can of course also be conceptual. Such methods make it possible to manipulate existing knowledge so that new knowledge is created. In the management field, linear programmingwas such a method. Methodological innovations transform questions, which have seemed to be eternal and impossible, so that they become solvable. They may also lead to the posing of new kinds of questions that nobody had dreamt about asking before.

New perspectives can create revolutionary innovations, like the scientific revolution triggered by the change from a geocentric to a heliocentric world view. The change from seeing the company as a profit-maximizing system to conceiving it as a coalition of stakeholders trying to obtain a satisfactory reward, put management science on a whole new track.

## Organization of the research enterprise

Research is a social process and the research enterprise is organized, even if the way it is organized is emergent rather than planned. As is the case with all social organizations, the delimitation of a research enterprise is somewhat arbitrary and can be made pragmatically depending on our aims. An entire science can be regarded as the enterprise. But so can the individual researcher. In between, there are groupings like research teams and schools of thought. In writing this chapter, I have had in mind a rather coherent, not too large a group of researchers such as a research centre or programme in a university department or research institute. The experiences and insights I use as examples are taken from the group of researchers that I have known and worked most closely with.

A number of specific organizational aspects that Törnebohm has suggested as influencing the innovativeness of the research enterprise are discussed below.

## Methods: linking the inquiry system and the universe

Methods are the means researchers use to link their inquiry system to the universe they want to create knowledge about. The methods permit them to get information about the universe they are investigating and to make it reveal its secrets. At the same time, methods are also constraints. They define the limits of the information we can get about the universe and thereby also what we can see. Innovation of methods permits us to gather new information and perceive new phenomena. Such innovations therefore make it possible to create new knowledge by both asking new questions and getting them answered.

Below, I will take a look at various methods that management researchers can use for different phases in the research process: generation of observations from the universe they are investigating; methods for making sense of these observations; methods for theory construction; and writing reports.

## Generating empirical data

### *Gathering of numeric data*

When I started to learn the trade of management research as a graduate student in the beginning of the 1960s, the main methodological problem seemed to be to get data that could be processed using statistical methods. It is understandable that management researchers at that time had become fascinated by quantitative data. Earlier, much of the management literature had been based on insights gained by practitioners. By then, this way of generating observations was becoming looked upon as unscientific. Scholarly writing presented inferences supposedly based on observations but not the observations themselves. Therefore, other researchers had difficulty challenging the theories put forward. This meant that there was no platform to base the research enterprise on.

The quantitative data that now became desirable are available in the accounts of firms or in public sources like census data. The researcher generates data simply by accessing such sources of information. One problem with all data of this type is that the rules for their generation have been defined by someone other than the researcher. The data we use make us see our universe in a particular way. Rules for how firms should report accounting data, for example, are influenced by the State's interest in defining incomes as taxable.

The questionnaire became very popular among social scientists early on as a method for generating observations about their universes. In contrast to other data sources, the rules about how the respondents should answer the questionnaire can be set by the researchers themselves. The problem with a questionnaire survey is that, what can be observed with its help is in a sense predefined by the knowledge of the universe that the researcher already has. Existing knowledge can be refined but the likelihood of surprises that trigger innovations in knowledge is low.

Information technology and standardization of accounting and other ways of generating statistical data have greatly increased the quantitative data available for numerical analysis by researchers. The new discipline of finance is an innovation in the management field that has been enabled by the availability of standardized accounting data and data generated from stock markets.

The Internet is creating many ways to generate numerical data. For example, people's preferences for different types of information and entertainment can be measured in an unobtrusive way by the number of visits being made to various websites. One challenge with observations generated from the Internet is that they are not standardized. The lack of standardization, on the other hand, leaves more room for researchers to develop innovative ways to generate observations from the Net.

There is a deplorable schism between proponents of quantitative methods and proponents of qualitative methods. By negating the usefulness of the other side's method, both sides deprive themselves of useful ways to generate data. They thereby also deprive their research enterprise of an important source of innovation. In addition, the existing schism makes a dialogue between large groups of researchers in the field of management impossible, which of course hinders the development of new knowledge. The schism appears moreover to follow the Atlantic Ocean. Too few synergies are therefore realized from all the resources used for management research in North America and Europe.

## Interviewing

The interview, i.e. the researcher's staging of a dialogue with another person in order to get information about that person and that person's world, is probably the most widely used method to generate observations in the field of management. However, researchers may not be aware of this fact since conversations with others are a taken-for-granted part of life. But nonetheless, most of what researchers know, often tacitly, also stems from such encounters. By interviewing and recording the information gained in a more conscious way, researchers might generate better information from their universe, articulate insights that would otherwise have remained tacit, and also gain more control over the sources of error inherent in internalizing information from others in a non-reflected way.

Freud's psychoanalysis was an innovative method for interviewing that led to a knowledge revolution in the fields of psychiatry and psychology. In this book, Chapter 4 by Jesper Blomberg, Chapter 5 and Chapter 8 are illustrations of different ways to use interviews constructively.

## Observing

In a course on qualitative methods that I have been giving for many years, we let the students go out and make observations in order to learn more about ethnographic methods. They have to choose everyday situations that can be observed without a special permit. I have been pleasantly surprised by how much they are able to see by observing a specific scene for just a few hours and then analyzing it. For example, by observing the behaviour of customers in front of some shelves in a retail store, they have been able to formulate hypotheses about organizational weaknesses that could hardly have been revealed in a large customer satisfaction survey.

Sune Carlsson's (1951) observations of how managers spend their day, later repeated by Mintzberg (1973), led to a completely revised understanding of what executives do. Instead of thinking about the future, which is the picture many management textbooks give, the observations show that the manager's day is fragmented by the necessity of responding to problems that come up and are brought to them. In Chapter 6 of this book, Ulrika Tillberg tells how she has combined observational methods taken from ethnography with other techniques in order to gain a better understanding of how schools are managed.

The researcher is equipped with both ears and eyes. Most of the time we listen with our eyes closed. The accounts that managers give us about what they do, show little resemblance to what we see them doing. It is therefore probable that a better balance between listening and looking would render observations that lead to more innovations in management research. Chapter 5 by Pernilla Bolander exemplifies the use of observation to gather data about decision making. Observational methods are not only developed in anthropology and ethnography but can be borrowed also from social psychology (Bales 1950). As yet little-used new technology can facilitate observations and their treatment. Processes ranging from board meetings to movements of material on a building site can be recorded digitally by video-cameras, which enables the use of a computer to analyze, in detail, process steps of down to tenths of a second.

## Experimenting

No knowledge is really accepted in the natural sciences until proven in an experiment. The experiment is what defines *the* scientific method in the natural sciences. Why is it that the experiment is used so seldom in the social sciences in general and in management science in particular? After all, management is about acting in order to achieve results. Does that not have a ring of the cause and effect reasoning in the natural sciences?

One reason for why experiments are not more common in management research may be that the natural science experiment tries to create variation in the laboratory that cannot easily be observed in nature. Like most other people, managers do not like to be put in a laboratory to be observed. As Werr shows in Chapter 7, it is still possible to design experiments also in management science that managers find worthwhile participating in. In addition, managers like to act. Especially if they collaborate with researchers, they may be able to frame their actions as experiments. The action research approaches described by Torbjörn Stjernberg in Chapter 8 are examples of such framing.

Another reason for experiments not being used in management science is that the natural science experiment tries to control the impact of the result of all factors other than the experimental treatment. A firm is an ongoing activity and there is no way to control everything in it or around it. However, the manager and the researcher can together establish a model of how the manager's world hangs together. The outcome of the action under study can be evaluated against the model, and conclusions can be drawn about both the impact of actions and the appropriateness of the model. In natural science, rats are often used in experimentation but, even if rats are intelligent animals, our means of communicating with them are quite limited. In contrast, conceiving action in firms as quasi-experiments makes it possible to use the managers' intelligence and insights as partial substitutes for laboratory controls. A whole chain of interpretation and translation processes has to take place before the responses from the rat can be used for a drug that can help an ill person. Contrary to rats, managers have the ability to interpret the consequences of their action and incorporate that interpretation in their articulated model of future action.

## *Historical research*

The case study approach has become more common in management research. One of the strengths of this method (see also Chapter 14) is that it permits the researcher to describe developments over time and illustrate complex interactions between chains of events. However, most case studies do not fully utilize the historical perspective but concentrate on the recent situation based on interviews with present-day participants and stakeholders.

Use of historical methodology makes it possible to describe longer periods of development, thereby adding the important dimension of time to the researcher's understanding of the investigated universe. The historical method was applied by Alfred Chandler (1962) in a study of the development of a number of American companies. That study triggered several innovative developments in management. It discovered the importance of the divisionalized structure and explained some of the mechanisms that made it a superior way to design diversified organizations. The divisional form is arguably the most important organizational innovation of the twentieth century. In addition, Chandler drew the conclusion that it is the firm's strategy that leads it to adopt a certain structure. This finding gave impetus to the development of the discipline of management strategy, which in turn has functioned as a core knowledge base for the consulting industry's rapid expansion.

One argument that much can be gained from a more widespread use of the historic method in management science is that organizations are systems with a lot of inertia. They thrive on their initial successes, they make invest-ments that result in path dependency, they develop core competencies, and they become institutionalized in order to stabilize their relations to different stakeholders. Organizations are products of their past, and their actions are influenced by their role in the context of other organizations. Another argument for historical research methods is that stories told by managers are based on limited knowledge about the historic past and lack memory of even more recent events. They also have a tendency to see the develop-ment according to the plans they have made for the organization rather than the events that are actually unfolding. Applying the rules of historical research for critical evaluation and corroboration of sources would increase the quality of case studies. Also, it would permit a problematization of the gap between the organization's historical character and management's conception of it.

## Interpretation of data

Observations and data do not acquire meaning until they are interpreted. For numeric data, multivariate methods like regression analysis and cluster analyses are veritable machines for helping the researchers to see patterns, to find possible causal relationships, and to find clusters of highly correlated characteristics. Most prestigious American journals are dominated by articles using this machinery for analyzing data.

Also, observations of more qualitative character can be treated by methods that permit finding relations and patterns. Content analysis, which is discussed by Anell in Chapter 9, can be used to find patterns in written material such as speeches and advertisements. Such analyses, for example, could create cognitive maps of how people think.

One innovation for analyzing only partially ordered data is derived from so-called 'non-metric' methods. Such analyses are based not on numeric scales but rather on judgements about which of two pairs have the most similar members. A conjoint analysis makes it possible to draw a map show-ing perceived distances between, for example, different cars. This map can also be made to show how the consumers are spread in relation to their 'ideal' car. The conjoint analysis has been an innovative force in market research (Green and Srinivasan 1978).

The introduction of methods influenced by hermeneutics and phenome-nology has had far-reaching consequences for management research. They interpret how people look upon and make sense of their world. The ontology behind these methods is based on the assumption that individuals and collectives construct their world and that they think and act out of these constructions. Such methods of interpretation have contributed to a critical approach to management. This approach can demonstrate, for example, that the firm that people perceive is a construction masking more fundamental features, e.g. the domination of capital over labour, or men over women.

The interpretative methods have triggered also a development of theories that emphasize the processes of how management and workers, management and investors, as well as engineers and business people can join in making sense of the joint endeavour they are engaged in.

## Theory construction

Scientific knowledge is codified in theories and models. Still, only a limited amount of knowledge defined in this way exists in management science. Many research reports in our field make much more limited claims about what they contribute, e.g. 'shed light on', 'explore a little-known phenomenon', 'contribute to the understanding of', 'suggest a taxonomy for', etc. This dearth of scientific knowledge is a sign of the difficulty of formulating theories in the field of management, especially if they are to be generalizable to a reasonably broad spectrum of situations. In the area of theory building, the management field is open for innovations!

Formal models using mathematical language have been held in high regard since the management field began to develop into a science. The idea behind this type of model building is to define a set of plausible assumptions from which deductions can be made. The derived propositions can be used to explain observations made or to suggest actions in a specific situation. Such model building was inspired by mathematical models used for planning military operations during the Second World War. Applied in the management field, they led to many innovations in logistics and the planning of manufacturing. With the exception of the field of finance, such models have not been able to create innovations in knowledge that concern the more strategic aspects of management.

Inductive theories have been suggested as possibly more suited for theory building in management science. Induction in the form of 'grounded theory' (Glaser and Strauss 1967) is discussed by Tomas Brytting in Chapter 10. The grounded approach can use both quantitative and qualitative data and has yielded many theories in management. Usually these theories are not formulated to cover more than a rather local phenomenon. They also have difficulties meeting some of the criteria of relevance accepted by a broad spectrum of researchers.

As Thomas Durand discusses in Chapter 11, the metaphor seems to be a form of theorizing that has led to innovations in management science. Cohen *et al.*'s 'Garbage Can Model of Organizational Choice' (1972) is probably the metaphor in management science that has gained the most attention in the last 50 years. Other influential metaphors are Michels' (1911) *iron law of oligarchy* (see Michels 1998), Weber's (1958), *iron cage*, Crozier's *bureaucratic phenomenon* (1964), Selznick's (1960) *organizational weapon* and Hedberg *et al.*'s (1976) *camping on seesaws*. A good metaphor is useful as a theory because it builds on concepts that already have a meaning for the reader. On the other hand, the metaphor does not aspire to depict the investigated phenomenon in detail, claiming only that there is a similarity. Therefore, metaphor can also be of use in other situations that are in some sense similar to the metaphor.

## Writing

The management researcher writes reports for many reasons, such as to communicate findings or to be published in a respected journal. McCloskey (1987) has pointed out that the impact an article has depends less on the results being reported and more on how well it is written. However, the writing of a report is not only about reporting the results, but is also a method for discovery or, as Sims says in Chapter 3, for 'both knowledge production and self-production'. Writing can be used as a journey of discovery (Richardson 1994). Suddenly, bits and pieces come together filling the researcher with a feeling of accomplishment.

Writing's double function of discovery and communication makes it a method that can help to link the universe being investigated to the system of inquiry. A well-written article or book can contribute to the diffusion of innovative knowledge and also trigger further innovation.

## Organizing the research enterprise

### Exemplary research

In the 1950s, physics became, at least in our school, a role model for management research. This role model inspired a strong emphasis on the generation of hypotheses that preferably should be locked up until the research was over. Much effort was put into operationalizing the concepts into measurement methods. The attempts to mimic physics led to rather mechanical research designs with little possibility of producing innovative results.

Economics is also regarded as an exemplary form of research by some management researchers. Having this model as an ideal inspires an emphasis on mathematical modelling, sometimes at the expense of the empirical grounding of the models. The discipline of finance has been well-served by having economics as its ideal. For other disciplines, economics remains an unattainable ideal, and the pursuit of this ideal may be somewhat discouraging for researchers trying to accomplish innovative management research.

During a stay at the University of Michigan during the 1960s, I was influenced by the keen interest that was paid there to systems theory. I later co-founded a research institute (SIAR or Scandinavian Institute for Administrative Research). Systems theory as developed in biology and medical science became a kind of ideal model for us. This ideal inspired us to develop clinical research as an approach to interact with practice. We also used analogies from biology to develop theories about how organizations could adapt to variations and discontinuities in their environment.

In the years around 2000, the 'actor network approach' developed by the group led by Callon and Latour (1987) at Ecole des Mines in Paris became regarded as a model of 'exemplary research' by many researchers at our school. The actor network research looks retrospectively at how scientific 'facts' have come into being. It shows that this happens when a sufficient set of animate and inanimate actors concur in support of a certain meaning. That model has inspired well-written analyses of complicated processes related to management problems. Such accounts have been innovative by showing that phenomena that have been ascribed to deterministic economic laws of supply and demand can instead be explained as an outcome of indeterminate social processes.

Exemplary research models for the research enterprise can apparently shift as time passes. I think that such shifts spur innovation. New generations can be aided by a new champion in their attempts to make an impact by creating something new. Model shifts also provide the impetus for innovative research.

## Perspective: how we look upon the universe of management practice

The perspective applied to the studied universe has profound effects on the research enterprise. Above, I referred to the revolution in management science triggered by a change from the inside perspective to an outside perspective. The inside perspective saw the management of the manufacturing process and other processes going on inside the firm as the main problems for management. The outside perspective sees the challenge of management as searching, maintaining and changing the role that the firm is performing in a network of exchange with other firms and stakeholders.

Other perspectives are also possible. One research group may use management's perspective. Another group may look at management from below. Still another perspective is to look at the micro-processes in the firm, e.g. how decisions are actually taken, or at the macro-processes, e.g. how the strategy of the firm develops.

## Criteria of relevance

The criteria for what is relevant and acceptable research is not only up to the individual research enterprise to decide. The criteria are developed and defined by the whole international community of researchers, by the faculty of universities, by the supervisory committees of doctoral candidates, by the reviewers of journal articles, by the research foundations, and in the academic seminars where research is discussed.

The research enterprise that chooses criteria other than the dominating ones may be more innovative but runs the risk of having its budget cut and not getting its research results published. To strengthen its position, such a group had better establish contacts and form coalitions and networks with like-minded researchers and sympathetic sponsors.

Parts of the community of management science require that statistically significant differences between cases or sufficiently high correlations between variables should be reported. Such criteria of relevance may rule out certain types of research, for example research that uses the case study methodology.

One main dividing line goes between proponents of practical relevance and proponents of academic relevance as criteria of acceptable research. Many forces in the field of management research tend to make academic relevance the exclusive criterion of relevance. Few if any voices suggest making practical relevance the only criterion. A research enterprise that wants to produce practically relevant knowledge must therefore observe and adhere to both sets of relevance criteria.

## Habits of communication

The members of the research enterprise can communicate more or less intensively, have regular meetings to discuss research, or rely only on informal internal communication. The communication can flow in one direction, from senior members to younger members, or can be two-way. Senior members may form one sub-group that exchange information and junior members another. There may be more or less communication between these two strata. Research on organization of research indicates that communication structures that make some researchers dependent on only one other person are bad for innovation (Pelz and Andrews 1966). Having immediate access to a knowledgeable person when a researcher needs help speeds up learning in the group. The innovativeness and productivity of a research group can be increased by conscious design of the internal communication patterns.

The communication pattern with the outside world also influences the innovativeness of the group. Generally, an external network that is diversified to include both its own and other disciplines, practitioners and international contacts, is advantageous for the ability to innovate. If each member of a research group had contact with all these outside groups, however, it might be a waste of resources. What seems to be important is that each member have at least some outside contacts and that effective mechanisms exist for sharing relevant information from the outside when needed.

## Suppliers of problems

As shown by Michael Earl in Chapter 2, the choice of issues to tackle in the research enterprise is critical for the possibilities for innovative research. Different sources can be chosen or impose themselves as suppliers of problems. As discussed by Kolodny and Shani in Chapter 12 and Docherty, Ljung and Stjernberg in Chapter 13, collaboration with practitioners can result in knowledge innovations by facilitating research relevant to both management science and management practice.

## Hoisting the sails of research enterprise

I believe that the mission of management research is to keep on creating knowledge that will change management practice as it is known at any particular point in time: knowledge that changes people's ideas of what management is about; knowledge that changes what management does; knowledge that changes the consequences of management's actions; knowledge that changes the definition of what good management is; and knowledge that changes the effectiveness of management.

Knowledge innovations are required from management science in order to bring about such change in practice. Of course, knowledge innovations do not necessarily feed directly into change of management practice, but I believe that this ultimate justification of management research should be kept in mind. In this chapter, I have given examples of knowledge innovations in management that really have had an impact, not only on management science itself, but also on the world of practice. To feel that I, as a management researcher, have been out on a voyage of discovery and innovation has provided me with excitement and satisfaction in my professional life. I wish that all 'management research enterprises' could be organized so that their members not only feel the excitement of being out on a voyage of discovery but also are allowed to experience the joy of having made an innovation.

I have emphasized two aspects of organizing the innovative research enterprise. One is recognizing the importance methods have as a link between the 'universe of practice' and the 'inquiry system of researchers'. Innovations in methods constitute perhaps the most important condition for subsequent innovations in knowledge. The second aspect is that an innovative research enterprise must leave its windows and doors open. It has to let in methods developed in other disciplines. It has to welcome cooperation with practitioners and other researchers.

# References

Bales, R. (1950) *Interaction Process Analysis: A Method for the Study of Small Groups*, Reading, MA: Addison-Wesley.

Carlsson, S. (1951) *Executive Behaviour*, Stockholm: Strömbergs.

Chandler, A.D., Jr. (1962) *Strategy and Structure: Chapters in the History of the Industrial Enterprise*, Cambridge, MA: MIT Press.

Cohen, M.D., March, J.G. and Olsen, J.P. (1972) 'A Garbage Can Model of Organizational Choice', *Administrative Science Quarterly*, 17: 1–25.

Crozier, M (1964) *The Bureaucratic Phenomenon*, Chicago: University of Chicago Press.

Glaser, B. and Strauss, A. (1967) *The Discovery of Grounded Theory: Strategies for Qualitative Research*, Chicago, IL: Aldine.

Green, P.E. and Srinivasan, V. (1978) 'Conjoint Analysis in Consumer Research Issues and Outlook', *Journal of Consumer Research*, 5: 103–123.

Hedberg, B.L.T., Nystrom, P.C. and Starbuck, W.H. (1976) 'Camping on Seesaws: Prescriptions for a Self-designing Organization', *Administrative Science Quarterly*, 21: 41–65.

Latour, B. (1987) *Science in Action*, Bristol: Open University Press.

McCloskey, D.N. (1987) *The Writing of Economics*, New York: Macmillan.

Michels, R. (1998) *Political Parties: A Sociological Study of the Oligarchical Tendencies of Modern Democracy*, Glencoe, IL: Free Press. (First published in 1911.)

Mintzberg, H. (1973) *The Nature of Managerial Work*, New York: Harper & Row.

Pelz, D.C. and Andrews, F.M. (1966) *Scientists in Organizations: Productive Climates for Research and Development*, New York: Wiley.

Richardson, L. (1994) 'Writing: A Method of Inquiry', in N.K. Denzin and Y.S. Lincoln, *Handbook of Qualitative Research*, London: Sage, 516–529.

Selznick, P. (1960) *The Organizational Weapon: A Study of Bolshevik Strategy and Tactics*, Glencoe, IL: Free Press.

Törnebohm, H. (1971) 'Forskning som ett innovativt system', *Ekonomiskt Forum*, 54–57.

Weber, M. (1958) *The Protestant Ethics and the Spirit of Capitalism* (translated by T. Parsons), New York: Charles Scribner's Sons.

# Index

academic discourse 13–14
Academy of Management (US) 11
Accenture 106
action learning 206, 212
action research 14, 53, 136, 206, 216, 221–34, 266
action science 229
actionable knowledge 16
actor network approach 271
Adler, N. 200, 214, 232
Adorno, Theodor 150
Agar, M.H. 97
Alchian, A. 149
Alexandersson, M. 55
Allport, G.W. 154
Alvesson, M. 13, 78, 95
analysis of variance 26
analytic bracketing 76–7, 79, 85
analytic surveys 33
Andrews, F.M. 272
Archer, Jeffrey 39
archival data 209
Astra-Zeneca 206
Atkinson, P. 72, 73, 77
attitudes 133–5, 184, 186, 189
authoritarianism 150

Baker, C. 73
Bales, R.F. 150
Barley, S.R. 119
Barnes, J. 185
Benetton 254, 255, 256
Benhasat, I. 33
Bennis, W.G. 44
Berg, H. 231
Berg, P.O. 13
Blomberg, J. 57, 65
body language 152
Booth, S. 55

Bourdieu, P. 63
Brache, A.P. 113
Bradbury, H. 44, 212, 229
Brannick, T. 212, 227
Braverman, H. 248
Brown, A.D. 44
Brown, J.S. 10
Brulin, G. 127
Brunsson, N. 7
Brytting, Tomas 158, 249, 251
Buckley, W. 11
bureaucratic phenomenon 270
business administration 7
business integration model 113, 123

Callon 271
'camping on seesaws' 270
CapGemini 106
Carlsson, S. 7, 266
case data presentation 110–12
case study investigation 32
category formulation 162, 167
cathexis 48
cause-map sub-cluster identification 171
Centre for People and Organization (PMO) 11, 12
Chalmers, A.F. 58, 66
Chandler, Alfred 267
change dilemma 226
change process 227
change theory 119
Cheever, John 42
chief knowledge officer (CKO) study 27–8, 30
Child, John 248, 249, 250, 251
Chupa Chups 254
Clark, B.R. 101
Clark, K.B. 179

classical administrative school 240
Clegg, S. 39
climate, organizational 13
cluster analysis 8, 114, 268
Cochran, T.C. 150
Coghlan, D. 212, 227
cognitive mapping 140, 175, 179,
    268
Cohen, M.D. 269
Colas, H. 192
collaborative approach 199–219, 229,
    232
Collier, John 233
communication patterns 272–3
communicative rationality 229
communities of practice 192
community of inquiry 209
comparative analysis 199–219
comparative management research
    239–59
competence 178
    classifications of 182
    degree of 183
    dynamics of 187
competence leaves 180, 185–93
concurrent verbal reports 108
conflict resolution 138, 139
conjoint analysis 268
content analysis 8, 33, 55, 63, 148–57,
    268
    basis 150–3
    categories and coding 152–3
    history 150
    of verbal protocols 120–1
contingency analysis 155
continuous improvement 201–4
contrasts as puzzles 135, 136
co-occurrence analysis 155
Cooksey, R.W. 107
corporate social responsibility (CSR)
    12
corroboration 81
criteria of research relevance 272
Crozier, M. 11, 270
cultural scripts 73
culture, organizational 13
Cyert, Richard 11, 149

Dall'Alba, G. 55, 58
data capturing 112–13
data generation 264–8
data interpretation 268–9
data reception 187
*de facto* participation 247
*de jeure* participation 247

de la Ville, V. 192
deductive research 174
Demming, W.E. 215
democratic dialogue 228
Denzin, N.K. 75
descriptive surveys 33
detailed description 81
Dewey, John 54, 233
Dickson, G.W. 23
discourse analysis 72–90
discursive psychology 79–80
Docherty, Peter 139, 212, 217, 219,
    222, 226, 231, 233
dogmatism 150
'do-it-yourself workshop' period 227,
    228
Drisse 179, 190
dual technology trees 179
Duguid, P. 10
Durand, T. 178, 179, 181, 182, 186
Durkheim, Emile 63

Earl, M.J. 24, 27, 28, 29, 30
Eco, Umberto 55
e-commerce 28–9
Edley, N. 79, 80
Edwards, D. 81
Edwards, L. 39
Ekman Phillips 232
Elden, Max 227, 228
Emery, Fred 11, 221, 222, 228
Emery, Merrelyn 228
empathy in interviewing 133
empiricism 69
Engwall, L. 6, 11
Engwall, M. 6
epistemological assumptions
    159–61
epistemology 53–4, 55
Ericsson, K.A. 108, 126, 127, 139,
    206
ethics 12
    interviews 133
    of knowledge production process
    14–16
ethnographic approach
    characteristics 96–7
    to school management 93–104
ethnography 8, 14, 95
ethnomethodology 8, 72–90
European Group of Organization
    Studies (EGOS) 11
Evans, P. 28
'exemplary research' model 270–1
experimentation 266–7

face validity 34
fact construction 81
facts and thoughts in interviews 137–8
Fayol 240
FENIX 205–6, 232
field studies 33
Fielding, N.G. 121
Fiol, C.M. 55, 65
Fontana, A. 132
Forssell, A. 101
framework-guided search 169–71
Freud, Sigmund 265
Frey, J.H. 132
funnel model of organizational design
    253–4

Ganter, Hans Dieter 251
Garfinkel, H. 75, 76, 78
Garsten, C. 96, 97
Geertz, Clifford 96, 101
Gellerman, W. 230
General Enquirer, The 150, 154–5
gestalt 144
Gibbons, M. 43
Gilbert, G.N. 79, 80
Gill, J. 33
Gill, R. 81
Glaser, B. 33, 35, 161–2, 163, 167,
    174, 175, 241
Glaxo 254, 255, 256
'glocal' character 10–12
Goffman, E. 38, 185, 188, 191
'going native' 14, 103
Gonard, T. 178
Green, P.E. 268
Greenwood, D.J. 229
grounded theory approach 8, 32,
    35–6, 58, 158–76, 241, 269
group interview 133
Gubrium, J.F. 75, 76, 77, 78, 85
Guerra Viera, S. 181, 182
Gustavsen, Björn 228, 229

Habermas, John 54, 65, 66, 229
Hamel, G. 178
Hansen, M.T. 106
Hansson, A. 228
Hasselgren, B. 55, 58
Hedberg, B.L.T. 270
Hedlund, G. 11
Hegel, F. 65, 66
Hellgren, B. 138
Hepburn, A. 78
Herbst, Philip 11, 17, 135, 221, 242
Heritage, J. 75, 76, 77

Herzberg, F. 135
hierarchical cluster analysis 115, 116
historical research 267–8
Hofstede, G. 240, 256
Holstein, J.A. 75, 76, 77, 78, 85
Holsti, O.R. 151, 152, 156
Husserl, E. 56, 59
hypothetico-deductive approach 33

ideal types 58–61, 69–70
IKEA 97
inductionist approach 58
inductive research 174
industrial democracy 245–8
Industrial Democracy in Europe (IDE)
    study 245–8
influence 97
information acquisition behaviour,
    analysis of 107, 108
information technology 28–9, 224–5
integrity 14
international comparative case study
    243–4
international comparative large sample
    study 243
international comparative process
    study 244
international comparative research
    243–4
interpretative frames 188, 191
interpretative repertoires 78, 79–80
intervention research 234
interviews 8, 131–46, 265
    analysis 142–5
    authenticity in 72–4
    facts and thoughts 137–9
    group 133
    open-ended 74
    as relationship 132–3
    scheduling 133
    semi-structured 140
    unstructured 140
iron cage 270
iron law of oligarchy 270
Ishikawa, K. 215
issue-driven research 23–36

James, N. 108, 112, 126, 127
James, William 54, 59
Johnson, P. 33
Jørgensen, M.W. 78
judgement analysis 107

Kant, Imanuel 59
Kaplan, A. 17, 150, 152

Karlsson, C. 106, 107, 109, 110, 111, 112, 126
Kärreman, D. 78
Khan, B. 29
know-how 183, 186, 189
knowledge as foliage 180
knowledge creation 208, 213–14, 217
knowledge, definition 182, 184, 189
knowledge-in-action 16
knowledge management (KM) 27, 29–31, 191–2, 193
knowledge of reality 160
knowledge production, social systems and 9–10
Köhnke, K.C. 69
Kolodny, H. 199, 252
Komatsu 204
Krippendorff, K. 55
Kroger, R.O. 81
Kuhn, T. 12
Kunda, Gideon 13, 96, 119
Kvale, S. 58, 131

Larçon, J.P. 189
Lasswell, H.D. 150
Latour 271
Laukkanen, M. 175
leadership, definition 95, 103
leadership research 95
Lee, R.M. 121
Legge, K. 87
Levin, M. 229
Lévi-Strauss, Claude 150
Lewin, Kurt 141, 233, 246
Likert scale 141
Lillrank, P. 199, 205, 215, 219
Lindholm, S. 160
Lindhult, E. 228
Liu, M. 201
long-term memory 127
Löwstedt, J. 140, 248, 249, 251
Luo, X. 7

McCarthy, T. 65
McClelland, D.C. 153
McCloskey, D.N. 270
McKinsey & Co. 106
management research 6–8
  networks of practice 10–12
  in time and space 12–14
management science 7
management training programmes 7
March, James G. 11, 149
Marton, F. 12,, F. 55, 58

Mead, G.H. 53
Merton, R.K. 62, 150
metaphor 269–70
  organizational knowledge as 178–94
Meyer, J. 257
Michels, R. 270
micro-electronics in the service sector (MESS) 248–52
Mikaelsson, J. 205, 206
Miller 160
Mintzberg, Henry 7, 184, 266
Mitki, Y. 200
module team concept 207
Morgan, G. 97
motivation needs, theory of 153
Mounoud, Eleonore 179, 192
Mulkay, M. 79, 80
Myrdal, Gunnar 9

Nahapiet, J.E. 30
Naschold, F. 228
neo-Kantianism 56, 66, 69
networks of practice 10–11
New Institutionalism 257
'new paradigm' research 44
Niederman, F. 23
non-metric methods 268
Nordic Academy of Management (NFF) 11
Normann, R. 11
Norusis, M.J. 116
numeric data gathering 264–5

objectified instrumental broker type 65, 66
objective structures 63
objectivist approaches 74
observational methods 265–6
Ochberg, R. 39
Ontario Quality of Work Life Institute 12
ontological assumptions 159–61
open-ended interviews 74
organization theory 119
organizational action 214
organizational change 133–4, 140, 141, 142
organizational climate 13
organizational competence 181
organizational culture theory 13, 95
organizational design 107, 199–219
organizational development (OD) 13, 226
organizational knowledge as metaphor 178–94

organizational stories 101
organizational unit of analysis 208–9
organizational weapon 270
ORGNOVATION 251, 252–8
O'Toole, J. 44
ownership of change 228

Paige, J.M. 154
participatory research 229
Pasmore, W. 233
Patrick, J. 108, 112, 126, 127
pattern generation methods 33
pattern recognition 212
Payne, J.W. 107
Pelz, D.C. 272
Perrow, Charles 6
personality tests 82
personality theories 154
perspectival accounts 74
Pestalozzi, J.H. 179, 185
Pettigrew, A.M. 11
phenomenography 53–69
phenomenological bracketing 75, 76–7
phenomenological epistemology 56, 59
phenomenological variation analysis
    63
phenomenology 12
Philips, Åke 15, 140, 144, 226
Phillips, L. 78
physics envy 39
Piaget, Jean 188, 192
Popper, Karl 160, 175
positivism 67, 69, 159
Potter, J. 75, 78, 79, 80, 81, 85
power relations 97
pragmatism 56, 59, 66
Prahalad, C.K. 178
problem-solving processes 106–27
product of research 16–17
'product of work is people' concept
    17
psychoanalysis 265
Punch, M. 230

quality of life 133–4, 140–2
questionnaires 209

radical constructivism 160
Ramanantsoa, Bernard 179
Ramsden, P. 55
Rapley, T. 73
reality 160
Reason, P. 44, 212, 229
references, use of 11
reflective inquiry 206, 212

reflective practitioner 115, 124
reflective thinking 233
reflexive knowledge production,
    writing as 38–48
regression analysis 268
Reicher, S. 79
re-invention 228
Reitter, R. 189
relativism 160
repetition 81
Research Centre for People and
    Organizations (PMO) (Stockholm
    School of Economics) 11
research, organization 263
retrospective verbal reports 108
RGB methodology 113, 123
Rhenman, E. 11, 106, 107, 109, 110,
    111, 112, 126
rhetorical organization 81
Richards, L. 121
Richards, T.J. 121
Richardson, L. 270
Rokeach, M.R. 150
Rolander, D. 11
Rönnerman, K. 232
Roos, J. 192
Rouleau, L. 192
Rowan, B. 257
Rowan, J. 44
Rummler, G.A. 113

Sacks, H. 76
sagas 101
Salin-Andersson, K. 6
Salzer-Mörling, M. 97
Sandberg, Jörgen 12, 55, 56, 62
SAP 254, 255
Scandinavian Institute of
    Administrative Research (SIAR)
    11, 271
Schein, E.H. 13
Schön, D. 115, 124
Schutz, Alfred. 54, 56, 58, 59, 63, 69,
    75
Schweiger, D.M. 126
Schwenk, C. 185
Scott, I.A. 27, 28, 30
search conferences 228
selection
    as forming a professional judgement
        87
    in organizations 81–9
    as play-acting 87
self-production, writing as 38–48
Selznick, P. 270

semiotic analysis 55–6
Senge 188
Shani, A.B. 199, 200, 212, 214, 217,
    219
Shorko Films 30
short-term memory 127
SIAR (Scandinavian Institute of
    Administrative Research) 11,
    271
Silverman, David 72, 73, 74, 75, 77,
    85
Simon, Herbert A. 7, 11, 108, 126,
    127, 139
Sims, D. 39, 41, 45, 47
simulation
    case presentation 111–12
    case selection 109–11
    data analysis 113–21
    data capturing 112–13
    delimiting 108–9
    designing 108–13, 114–15
    information acquisition 115–18
    recruitment 113
    verbal protocols 118–21
Skandia Insurance Co. 221–26
Skandia International 30
'Sleeping bag' period 227
small firms, theory building
    158–76
Smircich, L. 97
social facts 63
social phenomenology 66
social psychology 53
social representation 179
social responsibility 12
socialized interactional broker type 65,
    66
social-phenomenology 56, 66
sociology 53
socio-technical systems theory (STS)
    222, 234, 245
'souls-of-fire' 15, 230
Spiegelberg, H. 59, 63
spoken word 40
Srinivasan, V. 268
stake inoculation 81
Starkey, K. 43
statistical generalization 135
Stebbins, M. 199, 200
Stjernberg, T. 15, 138, 139, 144, 222,
    226
Stone, P.J. 150, 154
storied lives 39
strategic information systems planning
    (SISP) 24–7

Strauss, A. 33, 35, 161–2, 163, 167,
    174, 175, 241
Stubbart, C. 185
Stymne, B. 178, 201, 248, 251
subaltern storytelling 45
subjectivist approaches 74
surveys 33, 134
sustainable development 230–3
Sveningsson, S. 95
Swedish Centre for Working Life
    12
systems research 271

Tapscott, D. 28
Tavistock 245
Taylor 240
Telia-Sonera 206
ten Have, P. 73
Tetra Pak 254, 255, 256
theoretical generalization 135
theoretical saturation 162, 167
theory construction 269–70
think-aloud exercises 8
Thorsrud, Einar 221, 222
thought processes 139–40
Tiller, T. 232
'tool kit' period 227
Törnebohm, H. 261, 263
total quality management 215
Tranfield, D. 43
triangulation 24, 31–4, 35, 74
    examination 33
    exploration 31–3
    exposition 34
Trist, Eric 11
trust 14, 16

Universe of Management Practice
    261–2

validity 34
van Maanen, John 9
variability, discourse analysis and
    81
'velveteen rabbit' 47–8
verbal protocols 107–8, 118–21,
    139–40
Vivian, P. 27
Volvo Car Corporation (VCC)
    206
von Hippel, E. 179
von Krogh, G. 192, 206, 208, 214

Wallraff, Günter 15, 132
Walton, R.E. 138

Weber, M. 270
Weber, R.P. 53, 55, 58, 69
Weick, K.E. 11, 112, 242
Wernerfelt, B. 178
Werr, A. 113
Wetherell, M. 78, 79, 80, 81, 85
White, L.P. 226
Widdicombe, S. 87
Wilpert, Bernhard 245
Wood, L.A. 81
Woodward, Joan 240, 242
Wooten, K.C. 226

writing 38–48, 270
    for knowledge production 40–1
    for self-production 41–3
    vulnerability to attack 45–8
Wurster, T.S. 28

xABC method 113, 117, 124

Yin, R.K. 32, 135

Zagmani, V. 6
zeitgeist 12–13